Languages and Languaging
in Deaf Education

PROFESSIONAL PERSPECTIVES ON DEAFNESS: EVIDENCE AND APPLICATIONS

Series Editors

Harry Knoors

Marc Marschark

Social Competence of Deaf and Hard-of-Hearing Children

Shirin D. Antia and Kathryn H. Kreimeyer

Mental Health and Deafness

Margaret du Feu and Cathy Chovaz

Auditory (Re)Habilitation for Adolescents with Hearing Loss

Jill Duncan, Ellen A. Rhoades, and Elizabeth Fitzpatrick

Literacy Instruction for Students Who Are Deaf and Hard of Hearing

Susan R. Easterbrooks and Jennifer Beal-Alvarez

Introduction to American Deaf Culture

Thomas K. Holcomb

*Nurturing Language and Learning: Development of Deaf
and Hard-of-Hearing Infants and Toddlers*

Patricia Elizabeth Spencer and Lynne Sanford Koester

Evidence-Based Practice in Educating Deaf and Hard-of-Hearing Students

Patricia Elizabeth Spencer and Marc Marschark

Languages and Languaging in Deaf Education: A Framework for Pedagogy

Ruth Swanwick

Languages and Languaging in Deaf Education

A Framework for Pedagogy

Ruth Swanwick

OXFORD
UNIVERSITY PRESS

Oxford University Press is a department of the University of Oxford. It furthers
the University's objective of excellence in research, scholarship, and education
by publishing worldwide. Oxford is a registered trade mark of Oxford University
Press in the UK and certain other countries.

Published in the United States of America by Oxford University Press
198 Madison Avenue, New York, NY 10016, United States of America.

Library of Congress Cataloging-in-Publication Data
Names: Swanwick, Ruth, 1963– author.
Title: Languages and languaging in deaf education : a framework for pedagogy / Ruth Swanwick.
Description: New York, NY : Oxford University Press, [2017] |
Series: Professional perspectives on deafness: evidence and applications |
Includes bibliographical references and index.
Identifiers: LCCN 2016024254 | ISBN 9780190455712 (pbk. : alk. paper)
Subjects: LCSH: Deaf—Education. | Deaf—Means of communication. |
Language and languages—Study and teaching.
Classification: LCC HV2430 .S95 2017 | DDC 371.91/2—dc23
LC record available at https://lccn.loc.gov/2016024254

9 8 7 6 5 4 3 2 1

Printed by Webcom, Inc., Canada

CONTENTS

1. Languages in, and of, Deaf Education   1

2. Deaf Children's Bimodal Bilingualism and Education   23

3. The Plural Use of Sign and Spoken Languages   39

4. Languaging and Learning in Deaf Education   61

5. Translanguaging   81

6. Multicompetency and Repertoire   101

7. A Pedagogical Framework   121

8. Teaching and Talking with Deaf Children   141

9. Creating an Evidence Base for Practice   163

10. Unlocking Learning   181

References   195

Index   231

Languages and Languaging
in Deaf Education

1 Languages in, and of, Deaf Education

This chapter outlines the intention and structure of the book and sets the research and educational context. The questions about deaf children's language and learning that the book will address are presented and the theoretical perspective through which these questions will be explored is previewed. To ensure that this text is accessible to a wide audience, this chapter explains the provenance of some of the language and terminology used in deaf education and studies, outlining why certain terms have been adopted for use in this book and showing how they do—and do not—align with the wider field of language research and education. Working definitions are given for the key terms used in this book (bilingual, bimodal, multilingual, languaging, translanguaging, repertoire, competency, plurality, and diversity) in preparation for more in-depth discussions of these concepts chapter by chapter.

THE RESEARCH QUESTIONS

This book addresses two main questions about deaf children's language and learning.

The first of these is concerned with how we understand and describe deaf children's language use and experience in terms of current concepts of language plurality and diversity. A number of contextual factors drive this question. First, deaf children's language lives are becoming increasingly plural in terms of their use of sign and spoken languages (Knoors, 2016). Sophisticated hearing technologies have increased the potential for deaf children to learn two (or more) spoken languages, and, as society becomes more linguistically diverse, deaf children are increasingly likely to encounter different spoken languages at home and at school. Although sign language continues to play a part in deaf children's lives, the interplay between sign and spoken language is becoming a more adaptive and flexible aspect of deaf children's communication in social and educational contexts (Archbold, 2015).

With this changing plurality, the language profiles of deaf children have become more diverse as individuals deploy their repertoire of sign and spoken language skills in different ways and for different purposes. The dynamic language situation that pertains to deaf children is seldom explored within the wider context of language and bilingual research. It is the intention within this text to extend current concepts of diversity and plurality to include deaf children's language experience and use and to increase the visibility of this topic within the wider arena of language research and education.

The second question links these language issues with learning by asking how knowledge of and a different perspective on deaf children's language diversity and pluralism can inform pedagogy. The imperative underlying this question is the current need in deaf education for a pedagogical approach that joins up what is known about language with what is known about learning. The bringing together of these two areas of research will establish a theoretical framework for language planning, teaching, and assessment in deaf education.

The framing of this discussion in terms of pedagogy—that is, the theory and practice of education—provides a rational underpinning approach to teaching that is not often visible in the deaf education literature. Chapter by chapter, this text develops an argument for a particular approach to teaching that is based on understandings of how learning takes place in formal and informal contexts and the central role of interaction in this process (Bruner, 1960, 1966). Only with a conceptualization of the learning process can pedagogy be properly discussed.

In deaf education, discussions of pedagogy are often obscured by or conflated with issues of language policy. This happens in two ways: first, approaches to teaching are sometimes discussed only in terms of what language or language modalities should be used in the classroom. Such discussions do not give attention to how deaf children are using language and learning but instead focus on "implementing an approach" (Mayer, 2016, p. 41). From this perspective some general educational principles can be drawn, such as how to make accessible the language of the classroom or how to deliver an area of the curriculum. These issues may be construed as pedagogical but actually do not incorporate a theory of how deaf children learn and how teachers can help them. Second, the outcomes of education and deaf children's learning is often measured according to the type of education program under scrutiny. This could be construed as a measurement of pedagogy, but, actually, such evaluations do not speak of a pedagogical approach but only outline language policy (e.g., Hrastinski & Wilbur, 2016). Language policy in deaf education historically does not necessarily embody a theory of how children learn and is certainly not synonymous with pedagogy.

To seriously address pedagogy in deaf education requires a re-focusing that moves issues of language policy to the background and brings issues of language and learning to the fore. This necessarily involves a reconceptualization of what language is and what language can do. This implies a move away from educational policies that are predicated on a categorical and boundaried view of languages and toward a broader conception of language practices and a more nuanced approach to educational provision. This involves a shift of attention from *mode* to *manner*, where language is conceptualized as a dynamic tool for learning (Swanwick, 2015).

To make this step change involves a re-shaping of thinking and of ideas about deafness, learning, and teaching. Such an outcome cannot be achieved by the establishment of a list of "do's and don'ts" for teaching or a teaching textbook. Instead, what is needed is the establishment of principles for teaching that are informed by research and a structure within which to enact these principles in the educational context. With informed guiding principles, questions of "how to" become more easily approachable and practically answerable in many different ways. There is no need for only one teaching method: more important is openness to the infinite number of ways of teaching that are all grounded in the same principles.

A framework for pedagogy thus provides a theoretical rationale that brings coherence to practice but allows for flexibility and a dynamic response to the teaching context. Such a framework not only guides classroom practice; it also provides directions for teacher development and opens up the research dialogue around issues of deafness, learning, and teaching. Although not visible to deaf pupils, a framework for pedagogy should translate into an educational experience that promotes, supports, and measures learning in a consistent and coherent manner. What this means in terms of practice specifically is discussed fully in the pedagogical Chapters 7 and 8. For developing professionals and training teachers of the deaf, a framework for pedagogy should effectively link theories about education and learning to practice and provide a stable knowledge base for an informed and critical approach to teaching. These professional development issues are discussed fully in Chapter 10.

THEORETICAL PERSPECTIVES

To take understandings of deaf children's diverse and plural language experience and use into a discussion of pedagogy entails the articulation of the relationship between language and learning. The development of these ideas is grounded in a sociocultural perspective.

This perspective examines how deaf children's language learning and use takes place within a social context and how language practices and repertoires evolve because of the interactions among individual, social, and contextual influences (Lantolf & Thorne, 2006; Vygotsky, 1986). This perspective recognizes language experience and use as cultural and social as well as linguistic and that these phenomena are dynamic and intensely context-related. Within this theoretical framework, deaf children's language experience and use will be explored in various social and communicative contexts, recognizing the diverse individual factors in play as well as the proximal influences of home and school relationships and the wider linguistic and cultural context (Hornberger & Link, 2012). This approach seeks to understand the full language ecology of a child's life in order to properly describe repertoire and plan interventions and support for learning; that is, to "translate the possibilities of human communication into educational practice" (Padden, 2008, p. xii).

The exposition of these ideas is underpinned by the notion of language as a set of practices and resources. Language use is conceptualized as the dynamic and adaptive deployment of these resources that often leads to new forms of language and thus to a change in the language resources themselves (García, 2009). This dynamic systems approach is increasingly prevalent in the context of language use and learning. This thesis conceptualizes language as a set of components that we "manipulate and manoeuvre according to the situation, and moment-by-moment" (Larsen-Freeman & Cameron, 2008, p. 155).

To describe one's languages in terms of resources or repertoire represents a development in ways of thinking about bilingualism and multilingualism in deaf education and studies research. Discussions about bilingualism in the context of deaf education often work from the premise that there are two (or more) separate language systems in operation that interact to a greater or lesser extent (e.g., Mayer, 2009). Instead of conceptualizing bilingualism as two language systems with one common underlying proficiency, an integrated view suggests that all the language and skills within a person's repertoire are an interconnected whole, "an eco-system of mutual independence" (García,

2009, p. 21). This perspective connects issues of language and learning by focusing on how learners "soft assemble" their language resources to make meaning (Garcia & Li Wei, 2014, p. 5). This "asset-focused" approach eschews the deconstruction of separate language abilities and explores instead ways in which deaf children take advantage of their language resources to make meaning, communicate, learn, and express identity and affiliation (Antia, 2015).

DEAF CHILDREN AND HEARING CHILDREN

It is anticipated that this book will not only develop research and practice in deaf education, but also bring new dimensions to the wider field of languages research and education. Throughout the text, theoretical and practical synergies between the two areas are explored, never forgetting that deaf children differ from hearing children, not only in respect of their hearing abilities. "Deaf children are not hearing students who just cannot hear" is an often-used phrase in deaf education classrooms and research (Knoors & Marschark, 2015, p. 2). In fact, it is fair to say that individual differences between deaf children have increased rather than diminished over the past twenty years (Archbold, 2015; De Raeve, 2015). Deafness can have a profound impact on the life, language, and learning experiences of children, and, for any discussion of plurality and diversity to be relevant, it is important to recognize what this means for language and learning.

Because deafness can compromise early access to language and communication, the development of language fluency (in a sign or a spoken language) is complex. For some deaf children, the development of a fluent sign or spoken language may be more is usually more delayed than for normally hearing children. These different early language experiences have significant implications for deaf children's access to the language of instruction and of the curriculum in schools and for literacy development. Indeed, deaf children's reading and writing development is the most researched area of deaf education because of the complex challenges that deafness presents for the reading process (Kyle & Harris, 2010, 2011). Deaf children's underachievement in literacy hampers overall progress in school and influences life and work choices (Garberoglio, Cawthon, & Bond, 2014; Toscano, McKee, & Lepoutre, 2002).

The factors that influence early language experience and the subsequent impact on literacy development are myriad. As with all children, learning success is in part explained by individual characteristics, motivation, ability, and life experience. For deaf children, the variable nature of hearing increases this heterogeneity. In the United Kingdom, hearing loss is categorized in terms of mild, moderate, severe, or profound depending on the different thresholds at which sound is perceived in a test situation (British Society of Audiology, 1988). The loudness at which sound is detected for normal hearing is considered to be anything between 0 and 20 dB (decibels). For a mild hearing loss, this range increases to 20–40 dB. For a moderate hearing loss, the range is 41–70 dB. For a severe hearing loss this is 71–95 dB, and for a profound hearing loss, the threshold for hearing is in excess of 95 dB.

Although these audiological descriptors give an indication of loudness thresholds, it is impossible to define categorically what each level of hearing loss means for individual language access, experience, and development (Maltby & Knight, 2000). There are many other influencing factors to be considered, such as type of hearing loss, age of identification, and technologies in use. A hearing loss even in the "mild" category can be "disabling" (World Health Organization, 2015) and can impact on spoken language and literacy development and the overall experience of education. Hearing technologies and the age at which they are made available also change the nature of early language experience and enhance deaf children's potential for developing spoken language and literacy skills. Such technologies have, in some ways, mitigated the impact of deafness but not in others. Cochlear implants, available to profoundly deaf children, have revolutionized the potential for spoken language for children with the most disabling levels of deafness. Around 7% of children in the United Kingdom have at least one cochlear implant (Consortium for Research in Deaf Education, 2015). Although this technology has improved children's access to education, implants have not changed deaf children into hearing children (Archbold & Mayer, 2012; Marschark, Sarchet, Rhoten, & Zupan, 2010; Wheeler, Archbold, Gregory, & Skipp, 2007). The audiological aspects of deafness and the potential of different hearing technologies are described extensively elsewhere (e.g., Maltby, 2007). For the purposes of this text, it is sufficient to acknowledge the diverse nature of deafness and to stress that even the most sophisticated hearing technologies do not replace the experience of normal hearing (Castellanos, Pisoni, Kronenberger, & Beer, 2016).

The language(s) of the home will also present different opportunities, whether this is a sign language, one or more spoken languages, or, more likely, a combination of these. Deaf children who arrive in school with a fluent sign or spoken language tend to be more successful in school and develop literacy skills commensurate with their hearing peers (Hrastinski & Wilbur, 2016). Most deaf children are born into hearing families (Karchmer & Mitchell, 2005). 95% of deaf children have parents who are not deaf. Many hearing parents do learn sign language and use a combination of sign and spoken languages at home, but this is not the same as being surrounded by a fully accessible, fluent language from birth (Chamberlain & Mayberry, 2000; Mayberry, 2007; Rathmann, Mann, & Morgan, 2007).

These are fundamental issues for the discussion of linguistic plurality and diversity, but the differences between deaf and hearing learners extend beyond the domain of early language and literacy. A growing body of research suggests that the learning styles and profiles of deaf children differ from those of hearing children. This has been explored in terms of cognitive and metacognitive processes and, in particular, visual perception, attention, and working memory (Marschark & Hauser 2008; Marschark & Knoors, 2012). Understanding that the experience of deafness can change how children approach learning has implications for thinking about language diversity in the educational context. Added to this, there is increasing evidence of differences between deaf and hearing children in terms of social-emotional development and functioning (Hintermair, 2015; Morgan, 2015; Wolters & Isarin, 2015).

THE RESEARCH CONTEXT

This text focuses primarily on the UK context (England, Northern Ireland, Scotland, and Wales) but draws on relevant research about language plurality and diversity in deaf children's lives around the world. According to the available national data from the Consortium for Research into Deaf Education survey (CRIDE, 2015), there are around 48,000 school-aged children (0–19) in the United Kingdom. In England, this figure is around 41,000. In the 2015 data, it is reported that at least 13% of deaf children in England use a spoken language at home other than English. The survey also reports that 10% of children use sign language "in some form" either on its own or alongside another language. The data from this survey are reported with a caveat that many services were unable to identify the languages used by all of the deaf children in their area. Furthermore, around 8,000 deaf children are unaccounted for in the figures. This information is, therefore, only a starting point. In reality, however, the number of deaf children with English as an additional language (EAL) is likely to be nearer the national figure of 15% because Bangladeshi and Pakistani heritage children constitute the most prevalent and identifiable group of deaf children (Cline & Mahon 2010; Mahon et al. 2011). In addition, increasing numbers of deaf children with Eastern European and Roma backgrounds are also being identified on school and service caseloads (personal communication).

This book draws on materials from a two-year period of research with teachers, pupils, and parents in deaf education. One aspect of this research was the collaborative development of a Language Planning document for deaf education schools and services (Swanwick, Simpson, & Salter, 2014). The production of this document involved the development of a protocol for collecting local authority language demographics (language landscapes) and individual language profiles of deaf children. The resulting "Toolkit" provides guidelines for developing an ecological approach to language planning in schools and services.

The second aspect of this research, funded by the British Academy, constituted the development and implementation of the language planning tools to collect national language demographics across four research sites in Northern England and to build in-depth language case studies of individual deaf children within these sites. This project work was done in collaboration with practitioners and parents, with the intention of collecting broad and relevant information about settings and individuals as well as to build professional understanding and skills. The project is reported in full elsewhere, but the theoretical discussion that unfolds throughout this book is sometimes illustrated by examples of deaf children's language experience from these case studies (Swanwick, Wright, & Salter, 2016).

LANGUAGE AND TERMINOLOGY

To come to a text on deaf children's language and learning with no previous experience of the field of deaf education and studies can be, at the very least, bewildering. It is certainly an intriguing area of research from a linguistic, psychological, and educational perspective but sometimes less than accessible to those outside of the immediate field. The main reason for this is the language and terminology used and the way in which it is deployed across different disciplines for different purposes. Furthermore, the various historical, social, cultural, and political nuances of discourses in deaf education and studies can be confounding and sometimes obscure the relevance of the research and development work for a wider readership. To pre-empt these difficulties, this chapter navigates the main language and terminology hot spots and sets out the terms to be used in this book, aligning this as far as possible with the wider field of language research and education.

Talking About Being Deaf

A significant contested issue for this field is how to write about deafness, deaf people, being deaf, and who has the authority to undertake such writing. A novice reader of material from this field may wonder what the distinction is between the terms *deaf* (with or without an uppercase D), *hearing impaired*, and *partially hearing, partially deaf, hard-of-hearing*, and *deafened* and what constitutes the currently appropriate terminology.

The main debate here is the distinction between descriptions of deafness in audiological and pathological terms (carried in words such as impairment, partially, or loss) and the contrasting use of the term "deaf" that recognizes the linguistic and cultural aspects of being deaf, such as using sign language and identification with Deaf culture and community (Senghas & Monaghan, 2002). Notwithstanding these political issues, there are also, of course, personal preferences. There is no one term that is preferred by all deaf children/young people and adults or parents of deaf children. All of these terms are thus found in the research literature as well as in educational policy description and legislative documentation. The search for a neutral term is therefore fraught.

The current and most preferred term in use internationally is *"deaf and hard-of-hearing"* (shortened to DHH). The use of this term seeks to avoid the pathological connotations of loss or impairment and is inclusive of diverse cultural perspectives and audiological experience. This term usefully reminds that there is a broad spectrum of hearing loss from profound to mild and so provides an inclusive stance. In the United Kingdom, the term "deaf" is preferred and used in the same way to include any level of hearing loss significant enough to impact on language development. This is the term that national organizations predominantly use, such as the National Deaf Children's Society (NDCS) and the British Deaf Association (BDA). This term is also widely used in the UK educational context and endorsed by the British Association for Teachers of the Deaf (BATOD). The term "deaf" will therefore be used throughout this book to refer to children, young people, and adults. Audiological terms will used where they are contextually appropriate, such as to describe individual hearing profiles. The use of uppercase "D" will be used where specific reference is made to Deaf culture and community (Woll & Adam, 2012).

A related issue is the question of whether being deaf is a prerequisite for writing about deafness, language, and learning. This is currently an impossible aspiration. Apart from a small number of exceptions, much of the world's academic literature in this field is written by hearing scholars, albeit many in collaboration with deaf colleagues. This is not a desirable state of affairs, and it is slowly changing but it is a fact that there are far fewer deaf than hearing academics leading research and publications in this field. Wherever possible in this book, the research and perspective of deaf scholars will be brought to the fore. It is thus acknowledged that the author brings a hearing perspective to this topic but that the priority is the rigor of the writing in terms of academic evidence and support.

Talking About Languages

The second obstacle for a newcomer to the topic of deafness, language, and learning is likely to be the terms used to describe the languages involved. This should be straightforward since the languages concerned can be referred to by name, as in the case of English and British Sign Language (BSL) or American Sign Language (ASL), French and Langues de Sign Français (LSF), Dutch and Nederlandse Gebarentaal (NGT), and so on. These labels are not problematic in themselves; the confusion begins when more general terms are used, such as "spoken language" and "sign (or sometimes 'signed') language." These more general terms always require further qualification. The use of the general term "sign language" usually refers to a natural sign language, such as one of those just mentioned. Sometimes the general terms such as "sign" or "signing" include reference to the use of signs alongside spoken language. This can confuse the distinction between a form of communication and a language. Spoken language may or may not imply the written form. Some spoken languages do not have written forms, and so it is usually better to specify. This is sometimes qualified in the use of the term "oral language," and, as a result, the term "oral deaf children" has become an accepted way to describe deaf children who use spoken language (predominantly) in their daily lives. This way of categorizing children is not considered a useful or meaningful label for the purposes of the discussion in this text.

Throughout this text, the names of specific languages will be used wherever possible. These will be predominantly English, BSL, and ASL. The generic terms "sign" or "sign language" are used to refer to one of these, or other, natural sign languages. Spoken languages will also be referred to, wherever possible, by name, and the convention of spoken/written language will be used to emphasize consideration of the written form where this exists. Individuals will not be categorized as "oral" or "signing"; rather, the focus will be on the sign and spoken/written language repertoires of individuals.

Talking About Being Bilingual

A further terminology issue to establish for this book is how to describe the use of sign and spoken/written language since the term "bilingual" does not adequately convey plurality of modality as well as language. One of the terms in current use in the deaf education and studies literature to describe bilingualism in the context of deaf people is "sign bilingual" (Swanwick, 2010). This term can mislead because it suggests the use of one or more sign languages. In the US literature, the term "bilingual-bicultural" is more frequently used to describe sign and spoken language bilingualism (Marschark & Lee, 2014). This has different connotations to sign bilingual but is still problematic because of the underlying assumptions made here about the cultural identity and affinity of people who use sign language. The relationship between the use of sign language and an association with Deaf culture is not a categorical one and is contingent on context, experience, and individual differences (Monaghan, Schmaling, Nakamura, & Turner, 2003).

To manage these ambiguities, the term "bimodal bilingual" has evolved in the research literature to refer to deaf and hearing people who use sign and spoken/written languages (De Quadros, Lillo-Martin, & Chen Pichler, 2016; Ormel & Giezen, 2014). This option signals the fact that more than one modality is involved and avoids assumptions about culture and affinity. Although the two main modalities in question here are sign and speech, it is recognized that in most cases the use of a spoken language also implies an interaction with the written form of the language.

To talk about bimodal bilingual language use involves reference to the ways in which individuals use sign and spoken language in different contexts for different purposes. For any bilingual person, this is likely to entail the separate and mixed use of languages that is recognized as a natural part of bilingual language repertoires (Creese & Blackledge, 2010; García,

2009; Hornberger & Link, 2012). Because bimodal bilingualism affords two different types of language mixing, it is important to be very precise about the terms used (Plaza-Pust & Morales-Lopez, 2008a). In this text, "language mixing" will be used as the over-arching term to encompass all of the different ways in which features of sign and spoken languages can be combined, either simultaneously or sequentially. The term "language switching" will be used to refer to ways in which individuals switch from one language to another, between sentences, or mid-sentence. The use of this term is synonymous with "code switching," which, in the context of deaf and hearing communication involves stopping signing and starting speaking (Hauser, 2000; Napier, 2006).

The term "language blending" will be used to refer to ways in which features of two different languages are used simultaneously. This is synonymous with "code blending" (Emmorey, Borinstein, Thompson, & Gollan, 2008). Although it is not possible to use a sign and spoken language at the same time, certain features of sign language (more usually verbs and nouns) can be used alongside spoken, mouthed, or finger-spelled words (De Quadros, Lillo-Martin, & Pichler, 2016). This type of language synthesis or blending, sometimes referred to as Sign-Supported Speech (SSS) or Sign-Supported English (SSE) in the UK, is a natural and spontaneous feature of contact among deaf and hearing children and adults (Pfau, Steinbach, & Woll, 2012; Sutton-Spence & Woll, 1999).

As well as being a natural result of language contact, versions of SSS and/or SSE are also used to purposely support the comprehension of speech for pedagogical purposes. This usually involves the use of signs from BSL or ASL in English word order with the intention that the linguistic integrity of the spoken English (i.e., the dominant aspect of the utterance) is retained. Discussions of language blending in this book thus encompass the interaction between the two language systems that is a natural result of language contact and the more contrived, or pedagogical use of SSS/SSE in the classroom to support learning.

What is known about deaf children's bimodal bilingualism and the interaction between sign and spoken languages is explored in Chapter 2. Insights are provided into the bimodal bilingual language practices of deaf children and ways in which children use sign and spoken languages in various contexts, including the alternate and blended use of sign, spoken, and written language. This chapter reflects on what has been learned from research in this area and highlights the gaps in knowledge about the extent of deaf children's bimodal bilingual and multilingual language use. Based on this review, the chapter presents an argument for conceptualizing bimodal bilingualism in terms of language plurality and diversity.

Language Plurality and Diversity

The use of the terms "plurality" and "diversity" in this text is intended to widen attention from two languages and two modalities to many languages and many different ways of using those languages to make meaning. This reconceptualization entails recognition of the extent to which diversity reflects individual differences, language ability, and the language and cultural milieu, as well as social orientation and identity. This represents altogether a different approach to thinking about language and deafness, one in which there is a shift of emphasis from language as a structure and a set of skills located within individuals to language as a practice or an activity located in context (Pennycook, 2010).

Chapter 3 explores such concepts of plurilingualism and diversity in the context of deaf children, focusing on linguistic repertory and communicative competence in its broadest sense (García, 2009). This chapter considers a global perspective on deaf children's plurilingual language practices at home and at school in different cultural milieux. It provides a review of knowledge regarding the demographics of deaf children's cultures, signed, and spoken language, outlining the ethnographic work that has begun in some contexts but recognizing that knowledge is incomplete. The chapter illustrates that this growing demographic understanding is motivating the development of assessment tools and approaches that accurately describe individual spoken, sign language repertoires, thus providing examples and pointing to areas for development. Drawing on studies of deaf children's multilingual language development, this chapter suggests issues for language and learning and proposes new research agendas.

Languaging and Translanguaging

The term "languaging" is introduced in this book to articulate a perspective on language as always situated or bound to the context in which it is used (Bakhtin, 1981). The use of this term captures what we do with language and, how, through our language use, we express who we are and our relationship to others in the world, recognizing that language use always has intention, perspective, and position attached (Swain, Lapkin, Knouzi, Suzuki, & Brooks, 2009). The notion of languaging broadens attention from what we know about language to what we "do" with language and how we "become" through language (Becker, 1995). Language in this context is thus conceptualized as an activity rather than a structure (Pennycook, 2010).

Some scholars have extended the term "languaging" to "translanguaging" to talk about the language practices of individuals who use one or more languages in their daily lives. Translanguaging refers to ways in which bilingual and multilingual learners integrate their language skills and practices in creative and critical ways for cognitive and social purposes (Garcia & Li Wei, 2014, p. 82). Translanguaging describes ways in which individuals "pool" their language knowledge to construct something new in order to make meaning.

Translanguaging involves combining and alternating different linguistic structures and systems, including modalities, as a way of "meaning-making, shaping experiences, gaining understanding, and knowledge through the use of two languages" (C. Baker, 2011, p. 288). These behaviors incorporate, but are not synonymous with, language switching and blending. Translanguaging is more than the movement across and between two or more separate language systems. It is, instead, the "deployment of a speaker's full linguistic repertoire" that is unconstrained by the boundaries of different language systems (Otheguy, García, & Reid, 2015, p. 281).

Discussions of languaging and translanguaging are increasingly prevalent in research into language classrooms (Garcia & Li Wei, 2014; Swain, 2006) and studies of language and cultural diversity (Blackledge & Creese, 2010; García, 2009). These concepts have not been extensively explored in the deaf education literature. They are embraced in this text as a means of re-focusing attention on how children and adults use language, through dialogue, to make and share meaning. This conceptual shift re-envisions deaf children's bimodal bilingual, plural, and diverse language experience and abilities as one integrated set of resources rather than separate and compartmentalized skill sets. From this perspective, connections can be made between language and learning that support the development of a pedagogical framework for deaf education.

Chapter 4 explores the concept of languaging and its relevance to deaf children's learning and the wider context of deaf education. The role of languaging in mediating learning is discussed, focusing particularly on classroom learning and on the dialogic nature of languaging. This reveals ways in which deaf children bring their language repertoires into being for meaning-making and learning and the learning challenges they experience. Languaging as a means of positioning and an expression of social identity is also explored with reference to the deaf education context. Examples are given of languaging in deaf education policy and the impact of this on the development of practice. It is proposed that a focus on languaging provides a theoretical framework for examining deaf children's classroom learning and developing pedagogical approaches in deaf education. The chapter concludes by suggesting that the development of the construct of languaging to encompass translanguaging provides a further conceptual tool for understanding and describing plurilingual practices in deaf education.

Chapter 5 extends the concept of languaging to translanguaging. The provenance of translanguaging theory is reviewed and the relevance of translanguaging theory to deaf children's language experience and use is tested. Examples are given of bilingual children's translanguaging practices in home and school contexts that illustrate the extent to which deaf children translanguage in their everyday lives. It is proposed that this concept provides a relevant framework for describing and analyzing deaf children's use of sign, spoken, and written language and their dynamic and flexible use of these languages for meaning-making. In conclusion, it is argued that this perspective offers rich insights into the diversity of deaf children's language experience, enhances current approaches to the description and assessment of bimodal bilingualism, and provides directions for pedagogy.

Repertoire and Competency

Throughout this text, the concepts of "repertoire" and "competency" are developed to talk about individual language abilities and the ways in which deaf children use all of their language resources to make meaning. The concept of repertoire captures the constellation of linguist and cultural resources that deaf children bring to communicative acts. Competency refers to the diverse ways in which these resources are deployed in meaning-making (Blackledge & Creese, 2010; Blommaert & Backus, 2012). Deaf children's language repertoires will differently constitute sign, spoken, and written languages but repertoire is more than the sum of the languages that one knows (Li Wei, 2011). Repertoire comprises language skills but also life experiences and an understanding of the behaviors and expectations of others (Blommaert & Rampton, 2011).

Having a language repertoire is one thing, but using this repertoire requires a level of competency over and above discrete abilities in any one particular language. It entails the "critical and creative" use of language and the ability to deploy communicative sensitivity, cultural awareness, and metalinguistic awareness to manipulate the communicative context (Garcia & Li Wei, 2014, p. 10).

Chapter 6 discusses deaf children's language abilities in terms of multicompetency and the diverse and flexible use of language resources in terms of repertoire. Illustrative case study examples are given to support this theoretical perspective and explore the relevance and applicability of these concepts to the bimodal bilingual context. It is argued that the constructs of multicompetency and repertoire imply methodological and pedagogical directions that extend current discourses of and approaches to research and practice in deaf education. The chapter completes the trilogy of chapters on languaging, translanguaging, repertoire and competency that provide the theoretical framework for discussions of pedagogy.

PEDAGOGY IN DEAF EDUCATION

The language of individual languaging in deaf education is already complex. Institutional languaging can be equally inaccessible to those outside the field of deaf education. There are two reasons for this. One is that the terminology deployed in deaf education policy is often esoteric and emotionally charged (Tevenal & Villanueva, 2009). The second reason is that institutional approaches to deafness, language, and learning are sometime conflated with individual language experience (Knoors, 2007). What is written in a language policy does not necessarily reflect, nor does it determine, how children use language. As educators of teachers of the deaf, we often remind training teachers that deaf children do not read our language policies; rather, they get on with using language to make meaning in all the ways that they can. Debate about the best methods for teaching deaf children has given rise to plethora of terms to describe different approaches that make no sense beyond the deaf education context. Three main approaches are usually described in the literature.

The *auditory-oral approach* is an umbrella heading for pedagogies in deaf education that have the specific aim of enhancing deaf children's access to and use of spoken language. These approaches prioritize the use of spoken language in deaf children's education with the support of appropriate technology. Sign language is not part of the teaching repertoire in these approaches. Instead, there is an emphasis on the development of deaf children's listening, speech reading, and spoken language development (Moores, 2010).

The second overarching heading is *Total Communication* (TC), which is really a philosophy and not an approach or a communication method. The principles of TC are that language should be made accessible to deaf children in whatever way possible and that this should include the use of sign and spoken language as appropriate for the individual (Mayer, 2016). Because this approach often includes the blended use of sign and spoken language, the term TC is sometimes also used to mean *simultaneous communication* (also known as SimCom). This is a corruption of the original meaning of the term but nonetheless very much in use in schools in the United Kingdom and the United States to describe communication rather than a communication philosophy (Ormel & Giezen, 2014).

The third key term in the discussion of educational approaches in deaf education is "sign bilingual" or "bilingual bicultural" in US contexts (Marschark & Lee, 2014). Philosophically, *bilingual education* embodies the goals of social inclusion and diversity. A central principle of this approach is that deaf children are given the opportunity to learn sign language and spoken/written languages and to have access to the curriculum in whichever language is most accessible to them in an environment that values deafness, sign language, and Deaf culture (Swanwick, 2010).

The philosophy, policy, and practices associated with these different approaches have been described in full elsewhere (see, e.g., Moores, 2010). It is not the remit of this book to describe, critique, or evaluate one approach or another, and this categorization of approaches has in many ways outlived its usefulness. Deaf children's language and communication needs vary and change, and there is no one right way to support this individual development in the learning context. Deaf children cannot be described within communication categories. Practitioners have to make responsive and pragmatic decisions about language use that traverse these approaches. However, these terms will arise sometimes as part of the contextual information regarding individual experience. In these cases, it is important to recognize the distinction between descriptors of language policy and of individual language use and experience.

The discussion about pedagogy in this book does not enter into what Knoors and Marschark describe as "the war of methods" in deaf education (2015, p.1). Instead, the focus is on the deaf children's increasing linguistic diversity and how educators might respond to this in the classroom. Chapter 7 suggests a pedagogical framework for deaf education that builds on a sociocultural perspective and the role of interaction in learning. Pedagogical principles are proposed that recognize the dialogic nature of learning and teaching and the role of language as "the tool of all tools" to facilitate this process. Building on established work on classroom talk in deaf education, the issues of dialogue in deaf education are extended to consider deaf children's current learning contexts and contemporary understandings of children's diverse and plural use of sign and spoken languages. Within this broad language context, the languaging and translanguaging practices of learners and teachers are explained as central aspects of the learning and teaching process that can be developed and as pillars of a planned pedagogical approach.

Chapter 8 explores how such a framework works in practice and the extent to which this approach is responsive to the diverse learning needs and contexts of deaf children. The ways in which a dialogic approach has thus far been explored in deaf education are taken forward to explore how such practices can be developed and how translanguaging can enhance this approach. Building on the fundamental principles of a dialogic approach, practical teaching strategies are suggested that draw on successful approaches in the wider field of language learning but also take account of the particular learning experience and contexts of deaf children. This practice-orientated chapter demonstrates the broad, inclusive, and responsive nature of the pedagogical framework that brings together the best of practice in deaf education and eschews a "one-size-fits-all" mentality.

DEVELOPING AN EVIDENCE BASE

It is recognized that the ideas explored in this text are in their infancy in terms of their visibility in the literature and the limited work going on in this area. The thesis and pedagogical framework that this book proposes is nonetheless a starting point for establishing research agendas, gathering more evidence, and developing practice. Chapter 9 discusses the issues of creating an evidence base for research and practice about deaf children's language plurality and diversity. This begins with consideration of what we mean by evidence—what we need to know about deaf children's language experience and use and why. Approaches to building this knowledge base in the field of deaf education, the strides that we have made thus far, and the outstanding questions are reviewed. Drawing on methodological approaches from the wider field of language research, ways to extend our breadth and depth of knowledge in this area are discussed. The importance of transactions between research and practice are underlined as central to the successful gathering of new knowledge and developing of evidence-based practice.

FROM LANGUAGE TO LANGUAGING IN DEAF EDUCATION

The intention of this text is to situate deafness and language learning within a contemporary plurilingual context, open up new ways of thinking about language and learning in deaf education, and offer creative approaches to pedagogy. Approaches to bilingualism, multilingualism, and learning are explored that integrate issues of language and learning and that reflect the dynamic language experiences of deaf children. Deaf children are often set apart from hearing bilingual and multilingual learners. Throughout this text, the potential transaction between these two areas of research and practice is highlighted, never forgetting the particulars of the deaf bilingual context.

The conclusion of the book brings together the theoretical and pedagogical issues that the study of deaf children's language plurality and diversity exposes. The relevance of a theoretical framework that conceptualizes language as a set of resources in practice and not as separate entities is discussed. What this shift in perspective means for deaf education schools and classroom as sites of multilingual language practices is explored in terms of research and practice implications. It is a tall order to establish a pedagogy that does not rigidly categorize the roles of sign and spoken languages and that takes account of state-of-the-art hearing technologies in an increasingly linguistically diverse world. The premise and practices of such pedagogy are open to critique and development. Judgment rests on the extent to which the pedagogical framework is responsive to dynamic language use and development and to the shifting language competencies of all deaf children.

2 Deaf Children's Bimodal Bilingualism and Education

    The established research on deaf children's bimodal bilingualism and education provides the starting point for exploring the broader concepts of plurality and diversity in deaf education. This research has advanced knowledge about bimodal bilingual language learning and begun to help us understand the language practices of deaf children. This includes the ways in which children use sign and spoken languages in various contexts, including the alternate and blended use of sign and spoken/written language. Some links have been established between bimodal bilingual linguistic enquiry and pedagogical research. These connections need to be strengthened if we hope to galvanize deaf children's bimodal bilingual resources to enhance their learning. In particular, we need a greater understanding of deaf children's multilingual and plural language experience and use and the implications of this diversity for the development of pedagogies in deaf education. The theoretical underpinnings for such pedagogies can be usefully drawn from the wider field of language learning, as long as the issues that are unique to bimodal bilingualism are recognized.

THE BIMODAL BILINGUAL LANGUAGE LEARNING CONTEXT

Bimodal bilingualism refers to the use of a sign and a spoken language. Use of this term does not necessarily imply the use of only two languages (one sign and one spoken), but, in the deaf education and studies literature hitherto, this has normally been the case (Swanwick, 2016). The use of this term makes clear the differences between bilingualism that involves two or more spoken languages and bilingualism that involves a sign language as well as a spoken language. The term "bimodal" communicates the fact that the reception and production of sign language and spoken language takes place through different channels: sign language deploys primarily the use of vision and gesture, whereas spoken language relies on audition and voice. The two languages are thus articulated and received through (two) different modes, as distinct from unimodal bilingualism, where there is a shared modality (De Quadros, Lillo-Martin, & Chen Pichler, 2016).

This unique experience of bilingualism has given rise to questions in the research about how bimodal bilingual skills develop and how the two languages interact (Ormel & Giezen, 2014; Plaza-Pust, 2014). Fundamental to this research has been the establishment of equivalence between sign and spoken languages in terms of their properties and functions (Stokoe, 1960).

Linguistic research has demonstrated that, notwithstanding the modality differences, sign languages fulfil the same linguistic, social, and cognitive functions as spoken languages (Emmorey, 2002). Furthermore, sign languages are organized and processed in the same left-lateralized network of the brain as spoken languages (Hickok, Love-Geffen, & Klima, 2002). In linguistic terms, the difference in modality does not therefore constrain the potential for bimodal bilingual language development. However, for deaf children, the development of bimodal bilingual language skills depends on a mix of other factors. This includes early language experience; the nature, extent, and age of diagnoses of individual hearing loss; and the timing and experience of intervention and access to hearing technologies.

Deaf children's experience of spoken language development will depend on the nature and the extent of individual hearing loss and how this affects the experience of early interaction and access to the ambient language and conversation in the home (Knoors, 2007; Knoors & Marschark, 2012). Exposure to spoken language is also contingent on age of onset and type and degree of deafness, as well as access to and use of technology (Archbold, 2015). Over recent years, however, deaf children's potential to develop fluent spoken language at an early age has been greatly enhanced by the advances in hearing technology and screening protocols. Cochlear implants (CIs) in particular have revolutionized the audiological management for children with a profound hearing loss (Walker & Tomblin, 2014). At the same time, the development of digital technologies has transformed hearing aids, and the range of auditory implants (middle ear implants, bone-anchored hearing aids, and brainstem implants) have greatly improved access to audition for different levels and types of hearing loss. In addition, the development of screening and diagnostic techniques has resulted in the introduction of newborn hearing screening programs that allow congenitally deaf babies to be identified very shortly after birth. Further developments in the field have enabled audiologists to successfully fit hearing aids and CIs to very young children thus enabling them access to audition during the first year of life (Archbold, 2010). Such technologies are now giving profoundly deaf children increased opportunities and potential for the development of spoken language(s) and changing their language profiles (De Raeve, 2015). With these technologies, and timely intervention and support, deaf children now have much more opportunity to develop spoken language skills commensurate with their hearing peers (Marschark, Machmer & Convertion, 2016).

In ideal language learning conditions, there is comparability between sign and spoken language development in terms of developmental stages and process. Deaf children who develop early fluency in sign language have been shown to achieve age-appropriate word- and sentence-level milestones and pragmatic skills (Lillo-Martin, De Quadros, Pichler, & Fieldsteel, 2014; Morgan & Woll, 2002; Most, 2003; Petitto et al., 2001; Rinaldi & Caselli, 2009). However, the development of fluency is contingent on the early experience and use of sign language in the home. The amount and nature of exposure to sign language will depend on parents' language, and whether they are deaf or have contact with other deaf signers. Early access to fluent users of sign language is not obtainable for most deaf children because most deaf children are born to hearing parents who have no prior experience of deafness or sign language (Woll & Sutton-Spence, 2011). Many hearing parents do learn to sign but struggle to achieve sufficient fluency to straightaway enable everyday conversation and routine interactions that can normally be taken for granted where there is a shared home language. In consequence, many deaf children do not achieve age-expected levels of British Sign Language (Herman & Roy, 2006).

Families do often develop their own "homesign"; that is, a gestural system made up by the family. The use of homesign commonly arises in contexts where none of the family members knows a conventional sign language (Botha, 2007; Richie, Yang, & Coppola, 2014). However, these communication strategies do not fulfil the experience of early access to a fluent language from birth (Woll & Adam, 2012). The families' experience of deafness and sign language and the language(s) used in the home are thus a major influencing factor for bimodal bilingual language development. This is very different from the experiences of most hearing bilingual children who normally have full access to the spoken language of the home. For this reason, the use of terms such as "first" and "second" language with reference to children's sign and spoken languages are not meaningful, and it is more helpful to think in terms of language practices and repertoires.

Alongside the issues of early language experience, a number of other factors make bimodal bilingualism an exceptional language-learning situation. One of these is the fact that sign language does not usually have a territorial association or geographical location. There are some examples of small communities that are more densely populated with sign language users, such as communities around deaf education centers or in remote language communities (Kusters, 2010; Woll & Sutton-Spence, 2011; Woll, Sutton-Spence, & Elton, 2001). However, these examples do not constitute what we would normally consider to be a "nation" with an identity, language community, and geographical boundaries normally associated with this (albeit contested) concept (Makoni & Pennycook, 2006). The existence of bimodal bilingual communities is further inhibited because sign language does not tend to travel down a family line in the way that spoken languages usually do. It is unusual to find two generations of deafness in a family, and so deaf children are rarely born into a sign language environment (Woll & Adam, 2012). As well as contributing to the uniqueness of the bimodal bilingual experience, this is also one of the reasons that there are so few longitudinal studies of bimodal bilingual language development.

BIMODAL BILINGUAL LANGUAGE USE

The context for bimodal bilingual language development has been explored in full in the deaf education and studies literature. In this literature, there is extensive exploration of the constraints of this language-learning situation and implications for developing educational approaches and early intervention (see, e.g., Knoors & Marschark, 2012). Aside from the focus on educational policy, substantial linguistic research has also developed over the past twenty years into the linguistics and development of sign language (Pfau, Steinbach, & Woll, 2012). Studies that have focused on the development and use of both languages are few and far between. However, the research available provides some insights into the interaction between sign and spoken languages in terms of children's repertoires and language practices (for a full review, see Swanwick, 2016).

For bimodal bilingual deaf children, the potential for exposure to different ways in which languages are produced and used together reaches beyond what is normally available in unimodal bilingual contexts. For a beginning, there are potentially at least two languages and three modalities in play (sign, spoken, and written) that differently deploy vision, gesture, hearing, and speech for through the air and written communication.

A second issue is that for one of these modalities—sign language—input needs to be face-to-face (Meier, Cormier, & Quintos-Pozos, 2003). This difference between sign and spoken languages has major implications for language learning and for the role of sign language in mediating learning incidental and formal situations (Marschark, Machmer, & Convertino, 2016). Finally, as outlined in Chapter 1, a number of forms of communication also exist that mix and blend sign and spoken language in different ways (Mayer, 2016).

Because of these modality issues, it can be argued that this is a unique language-learning situation that cannot be equated with theories of and educational approaches to unimodal bilingualism. Such a perspective has sometimes inhibited the exploration of the language potential of bimodal bilingual children and the growth of appropriate pedagogies. Although the exceptional nature of this bilingual language-learning situation does need to be acknowledged, it is proposed here that a focus on bimodal bilingual deaf children's language practices can develop this understanding and identify the commonalities with other bilingual learners.

BIMODAL BILINGUAL LANGUAGE INTERACTION

Research into bimodal bilingualism is beginning to reveal the different (cognitive and social) dimensions of language interaction in terms of deaf children's organization and deployment of their "separate but interconnected" language systems (Plaza-Pust, 2014, p. 45). Although the focus of this book is the visible ways in which sign and spoken/written language interact in terms of deaf children's language practices, research into the internal (nonvisible) bilingual language processing affords some insights into the interaction between the linguistic systems underpinning these "readily observable" language practices (García, 2009, p. 44).

A major line of enquiry in the bimodal bilingual language interaction research has centered on the processing of sign language and written language. The research questions in this domain have focused on the extent to which sign language knowledge (phonological or semantic) is activated during reading (Hermans, Ormel, & Knoors, 2010; Morford, Wilkinson,

Villwock, Piñar, & Kroll, 2011; Ormel & Giezen, 2014; Ormel, Hermans, Knoors, & Verhoeven, 2012; Tang, Lam, & Yiu, 2014). One aim of this research has been to demonstrate the positive relationship between two languages with different modalities and structures. This body of work provides evidence of the cross-modal transfer of some linguistic knowledge but does not enlighten us in terms of children's language practices. However, evidence of crossover between sign and written language makes an important contribution to the much debated concept of the language transfer in bimodal bilingualism.

Discussions of language transfer in the deaf education and deaf studies have examined the extent to which Cummins' linguistic interdependence theory (1991) applies to the language learning contexts of deaf children. The Cummins model itself has been largely unquestioned and has been used throughout the literature as the main reference point for debating a theoretical model of deafness and bilingualism (see Knoors, Tang, & Marschark, 2014). This debate has centered on the extent to which skills in sign language can support deaf children's literacy development and, specifically, whether or not skills and abilities in sign language can be transferred to the learning and use of the written language (Mayer & Akamatsu, 2000; Mayer & Wells, 1996). The central question is whether linguist transfer can take place between two dissimilar languages. The uncritical use of Cummins's transfer theory is problematic here, but it has nonetheless driven research to explore the extent to which knowledge of a language that is received and expressed through the visual and gestural modality can be transferred to the learning of the written form of a spoken language (Holzinger & Fellinger, 2014).

The debate on this issue has matured over twenty years and has expanded beyond initial conceptions of language transfer at a phonological level to consider the potential of language transfer at conceptual, metalinguistic, and linguistic levels (Cummins, 2006). For example, it has been argued that the enhanced use of evaluative devices seen in the writing of good sign language users is also evidence of language transfer (van Beijsterveldt & van Hell, 2010, 2012). This thesis suggests that the integral communication of evaluative information about objects or people (emotion states) in sign language carries over into the writing process. The most convincing reported evidence of transfer is between sign and written vocabulary (Hermans, Knoors, Ormel, & Verhoeven, 2008; Hermans et al., 2010; Holzinger & Fellinger, 2014). However, indubitable claims cannot be made about this other than to recognize the positive influence of sign language development on the development of written language and the potential of transfer to be taught or at least "cultivated" (Hermans et al., 2010, p. 194). This opening up of the concept of transfer signals an understanding that phonemic awareness may not be the only pathway to literacy development for some learners. There is evidence in the literature that this may indeed be the case where deaf learners' errors in their writing relate more to orthographic and syntactic structures than to sound–letter correspondences (Plaza-Pust, 2014). The research into bimodal bilingual language transfer, although exercised by the modalities issue, thus provides some insights into the interaction between sign and spoken language with regard to the writing process and extends our understanding of transfer between dissimilar languages (Tang et al., 2014). These questions challenge interpretations of the concept of language transfer and signal the need for a more nuanced interpretation of linguistic interdependence (Pennycook, 2010).

One of the problems in this research is that the distinction between correlations between sign language proficiency and literacy skills and actual evidence of linguistic transfer are sometimes blurred. Correlations are frequently reported between sign language proficiency and reading development (Hermans et al., 2010; Menéndez, 2010; Niederberger, 2008; Wolbers, Bowers, Dostal, & Graham, 2014). Although these reports reflect a positive interaction between sign and spoken/written language, they are not necessarily evidence of transfer. Nonetheless, in this research, we can begin to see how the transaction of knowledge, skills, and experience across sign and spoken/written languages is played out in the bimodal bilingual written language practices of deaf children. As such, the research on language transfer provides a helpful step between the nonvisible and visible forms of language interaction straddling the psycholinguist and sociolinguistic perspectives on bimodal bilingualism.

In terms of language use, the concept of language interaction refers to ways in which children mix their use of sign and spoken/written language in their daily lives. Language mixing is used here as an overarching term to refer to the range of ways in which languages or features of languages can be used together (Napier, 2006). This includes the alternate use of two languages (language switching) and the simultaneous use of features of two languages (language blending).

The research into bimodal bilingual language mixing to date has tended to focus more on adults, but studies of children's bimodal bilingual interaction are emerging. These show that the alternate and blended use of sign and spoken language is a normal and spontaneous part of interaction and a natural aspect of contact between and among deaf and hearing people (Donati & Branchini, 2013; Fung & Tang, 2013; Tang, Yiu, & Lam, 2015). De Quadros et al. (2016) suggest that the various ways in which code blending is used to construct a single message from content in two modalities can be explained through a theoretical model that they describe as "language synthesis" (p. 187). This seems to bring together concepts of cross-linguistic transfer and translanguaging that are discussed in detail later.

Sign and spoken languages exist alongside each other in the world. In addition, as with other spoken languages, this creates language contact situations and behaviors that reflect competency, awareness, and choice not confusion (Hauser, 2000; Lucas & Valli, 1992; Plaza-Pust & Morales-Lopez, 2008b). Bimodal bilingual children are able to switch flexibly between languages and modes. Indeed, in some studies, the most advanced use of language in terms of lexical richness and syntactic complexity is observed when sign and speech are used together (Klatter-Folmer, van Hout, Kolen, & Verhoeven, 2006; Krausneker, 2008; Lindahl, 2015; Rinaldi & Caselli, 2009; Tang et al., 2015).

The description and assessment of deaf children's bimodal bilingual skills is problematic and yet practitioners need this information for individual language planning and support (Swanwick, Simpson, et al., 2014). A small number of sign language assessments, and many spoken language assessments, have been developed for deaf children, but practitioners currently lack tools and protocols to document deaf children's mixed use of sign and spoken languages. Customized measures that have been developed for different language contexts go some way to reveal the linguistic complexity and communicative richness of deaf children's mixed utterances (see, e.g., Klatter-Folmer et al. 2006; Lichtig et al. 2011). These studies suggest that the separate assessment of languages does not demonstrate the linguistic complexity of which deaf children are capable. These findings have prompted questions about the status of language mixing and whether it is a stage in developing competence in both languages or a creative use of new language structures. This theoretical question challenges a fractional view of bilingualism that focuses on separate proficiencies in separate languages and suggests instead a more flexible view of bilingualism as an integrated set of language resources (Grosjean, 1992). This theoretical perspective is fully explored in Chapters 4, 5, and 6.

BIMODAL BILINGUAL EDUCATION

The practice of educating deaf children bilingually with sign language alongside written and spoken language initially developed during the 1980s in Scandanavia, the United States, and the United Kingdom. This approach developed as a response to concerns about deaf children's attainments within traditional spoken language approaches (see, e.g., Conrad, 1979). The development of this approach was encouraged by research demonstrating sign languages to be naturally evolving, rule-governed languages (see Woll & Sutton- Spence, 2011, for an overview of phonology, morphology, syntax, pragmatics, and discourse). The development of a bimodal bilingual approach became the focus of much debate and critique in professional and research forums because this innovation challenged traditional methods that hitherto had focused solely on deaf children's spoken language development.

There is no one globally agreed-upon definition for the bilingual education of deaf children. Policies and practices vary markedly across different national contexts, particularly regarding the role and use of spoken and written language (Marschark, Knoors & Tang, 2014; Swanwick, 2010; Svartholm, 2010; Swanwick, Dammeyer, et al., 2014). However, there is a common philosophy and an underlying set of principles that do traverse countries and cultures. Philosophically, bilingual education strives toward the humanitarian and democratic goals of social inclusion and diversity. It is an approach to education that recognizes the unique and distinctive features of deaf language and culture, validates the linguistic and cultural choices of deaf people, and celebrates this diversity.

This approach is referred to as "sign bilingual" in some contexts and "bilingual bicultural" in others (Marschark & Lee, 2014). The focus on language policy in bimodal bilingual deaf education has to some extent obscured the development of a coherent pedagogy. The controversy associated with this approach in deaf education fueled the need for extensive articulation and debate of language policy, and, for some years, the dialectic about bilingual education for deaf children was more prevalent in the educational literature than pedagogical discussion (Marschark et al., 2014; Swanwick, 2010). The controversial issues, at one level, centered on anxiety about the use of sign language in deaf education and concerns about compromising what was seen as one of the main goals of deaf education at that time: the development of deaf children's spoken language (Ahlgren, 1994). At a philosophical level, this became a polemic struggle between a traditional pathological view of deafness and a habilitative approach to education, and a perspective recognizing the value of linguistic and cultural diversity and the role of sign language in deaf children's lives (Anderson, 1994; Barnum, 1984; Lane, 1992; Parasnis, 1997).

Bimodal bilingual education has continued to develop and to be debated. The philosophical position of the bilingual approach as an expression of the humanitarian and democratic goals of social inclusion and diversity is no longer questioned. It is recognized as an approach that validates the unique and distinctive features of deaf language and culture and celebrates this diversity (Grosjean, 2010). It is now the implementation, effectiveness, and sustainability of this approach that are argued, and attention to pedagogy is still very much overlooked (Knoors & Marschark, 2012). The big questions for sign bilingual policy are how to facilitate early sign language fluency and improve deaf children's literacy skills and academic outcomes. There is no shortage of writing on these issues for bimodal bilingual education, but the learning and teaching at the heart of this educational approach has yet to be fully considered.

BIMODAL BILINGUAL PEDAGOGIES

Despite the extensive attention to bimodal bilingual language policy in the deaf education literature, there is no apparent pedagogical model and surprisingly little research into teaching methodologies. The main theme in the existing literature on teaching and learning centers on the role of sign language in supporting deaf children's literacy development. The correlation between sign language and literary skills is explored extensively, and there is evidence of a positive relationship between the two (Dubuisson, Parisot, & Vercaingne-Ménard, 2008; Hoffmeister, 2000; Niederberger, 2008; Prinz & Strong, 1998). However, the reasons that good signers are often good readers are more to do with children's early language experience and having deaf parents than pedagogy (Marschark & Lee, 2014; Plaza-Pust & Morales-Lopez, 2008a). Nonetheless, there is consensus that the use of sign language in the teaching context can facilitate literacy development as the medium through which children can develop their world knowledge and metalinguistic skills and be taught about word meanings, sentences, and discourse structure (Wilbur, 2000).

The detailed attention to classroom practice in the literature tends to be on the use of sign and spoken language for text-based activities. Such studies have attempted to explore the role of sign language as a "bridge" to facilitate deaf children's understanding and use of written language and the specific role of English-based signing in the learning process (Akamatsu, Stewart, & Becker, 2000; Andrews & Rusher, 2010; DeLana, Gentry, & Andrews, 2007; Mayer & Akamatsu, 2000; Power, Hyde, & Leigh, 2008). Because literacy development is a central concern in deaf education, it is not surprising that the focus of most pedagogical studies is on ways of making connections between sign language and written language (Humphries & MacDougall, 2000).

However, there is no agreement in the literature about how sign and spoken and written language can be effectively deployed in the teaching process, and no consensus about dual language methodologies. Some approaches advocate the separation of sign and spoken language in the classroom (R. E. Johnson, Liddell, & Erting, 1989). The underlying rationale for this is to ensure that learners are exposed to fluent models of sign language rather than only the selective use of signs alongside spoken English, such as for Sign-Supported English or SimCom. In these cases, sign language is usually described as the main language of instruction, and exposure to English is facilitated primarily through the written form. In this context, teachers aim to avoid the blended use of sign and spoken language (Andrews & Rusher 2010; DeLana et al., 2007). Other studies specifically explore ways that sign and spoken language can be used together in English-based signing to support deaf children's literacy development (Mayer & Akamatsu, 2000; Power et al., 2008). It is argued that that the blended use of signs alongside spoken language helps deaf children to develop an internal representation of English and also provides lexical, semantic, and conceptual support for learners who may not be fluent signers or speakers.

A coherent pedagogy does not emerge from this body of research. Although a number of different bimodal and bilingual instructional practices are documented in these studies, few conclusions can be drawn about the relative effectiveness of one approach or another. At best, we can conclude that the dual language approaches described do not impede deaf children's learning (Mayer & Akamatsu, 2000). Furthermore, the preoccupation in this literature is language modality; that is, what language or form of communication to use and when.

This eclipses any attention on how to use language in the learning and teaching process. The few studies that do begin to look beneath the issues of modality raise important issues for classroom practice and for the development of a pedagogical model for bimodal bilingual deaf children. One of these is the quality of interaction and dialogue around learning that deaf children experience (Kelman & Branco, 2009; Molander, Halldén, & Lindahl, 2010). This includes interactions between children as well as teacher talk to the whole class, a group, or an individual. How deaf children engage in learning through dialogue, and how this is facilitated by the teacher or other adults in the classroom, can only be partly understood by focusing on mode of delivery. The nature of talk itself, the quality of interaction and negotiation of meanings, needs to be examined hand in hand with the issues of modality.

A second issue is the need for criticality and flexibility in terms of language use in the classroom. Decisions about which language or language variety to use are often driven by the educational policy of the learning context (Tevenal & Villanueva, 2009). Uncritical allegiance to any particular approach is problematic because it can inhibit attention and sensitivity to the actual learning needs of the individual. Bimodal bilingual delivery in the classroom, even from skilled sign language users, does not in itself guarantee learning (Marschark et al., 2008). The language choices of the teacher instead need to be attuned to individual communication and learning styles as part of an adaptive and dynamic process (Hermans, Wauters, De Klerk, & Knoors, 2014; Knoors & Renting, 2000).

Much work remains to be done on classroom interaction in the context of deaf children to develop the level of knowledge about engagement and learning that has been achieved with regard to hearing children (e.g., Alexander, 2003; Mercer, 1995; Wells, 1986). This endeavor also needs to branch out to the wider school curriculum to encompass the range of subject discourses and teaching styles across the arts, sciences, and humanities. This does not mean that we stop looking at language as the central issue, but rather that we change the perspective to explore language as a tool through which learning is mediated, as well as being a learning outcome in itself. The increasing knowledge base about the cognitive and social dynamics of interaction between sign and spoken languages needs to be joined up to these learning issues. This synthesis will create a pedagogical framework for examining how teachers teach and children learn in different curricular contexts where two (or more) languages and modalities are in play. It is not possible to understand how mixed and blended language use in the classroom can scaffold and support learning if we do not interrogate how language is being used. Attention to manner as well as mode is an important step toward answering emerging questions about the "quality" of bimodal bilingual education (Knoors & Renting, 2000).

BIMODAL BILINGUALISM AND MULTILINGUALISM

The research into bimodal bilingualism demonstrates that bimodal bilingualism affords opportunities for language interaction that reach beyond the examples that we have seen so far in language research because of the potential to combine and alternate different linguistic structures, systems, and modalities. We have only thus far talked about deaf children who use sign and spoken language without reference to the use of multiple sign or spoken languages. This is a growing area of research and practice that is neglected both in terms of demographic data and insights into individual language milieu (Cline & Mahon, 2010; G. Leigh & Crowe, 2015; Mayer & Leigh, 2010; Willoughby, 2012). Migrant and multilingual families make up at least 20% of the population, for example, in Australia, the United States, Germany, Slovakia, and the United Kingdom, and, in these multilingual contexts, many deaf children and their families use more than one spoken language at home. In addition, the increased availability and use of CIs means that it is increasingly possible for deaf children to learn two spoken languages as well as a sign language. The next chapter will therefore expand the discussion of bimodal bilingualism to consider multilingualism and the associated issues of maintenance of community and heritage languages, support for language minorities, and professional training and development. It is intended that this will create a fuller picture of deaf children's language use and development that takes account the dynamic and shifting language competencies of bimodal bilingual deaf children in multilingual societies.

3 The Plural Use of Sign and Spoken Languages

The contexts of deaf children's sign and spoken language learning have changed significantly since sign bilingual education was first established and published research into bimodal bilingualism began to emerge in the 1980s. The increased mobility of people across the world and the ease and speed of travel and communication facilitated by new technologies has increased contact between languages, cultures, and communities. Out of both necessity and choice, the world is on the move. As a result, new and diverse multilingual language communities are constantly emerging within already diverse sites, and there is increased fluidity of movement within and across language and cultural borders. Within this global context, technologies for deaf children have also changed to the extent that bimodal bilingualism is now likely to entail the use of more than one spoken/written language and increasingly diverse individual sign and spoken/written language repertoires. Bimodal bilingualism thus entails a more dynamic experience of sign and spoken languages than we in the field of deaf education have hitherto experienced and appreciated.

For educational policy and pedagogy to reflect this, a greater understanding is needed of deaf children's plural language practices at home and at school and in different cultural milieu.

CONCEPTS OF MULTILINGUALISM AND PLURILINGUALISM

A distinction is made in this discussion between multilingualism and plurilingualism in order to sharpen the focus on the contextual and individual issues. Both terms describe the knowledge and use of multiple languages. However, *multilingualism* tends to refer to the language practices of groups and societies and in particular the coexistence of several languages in a given space independently of those who use them (Council of Europe, 2007). Multilingualism can thus be obtained where diverse languages exist within a community, school, or society or culture even though the individuals themselves may not know or use more than one language.

Plurilingual focuses much more on the individual, recognizing the multiplicities of language and cultural experience that are interwoven in a life and at any one time for individuals. Plurilingualism is also concerned with communicative competence in its broadest sense, in that it encompasses diverse ways in which individuals draw on their knowledge of language and culture to communicate with others:

"[M]ultilingualism" refers to the presence in a geographical area, large or small, of more than one "variety of language" i.e. the mode of speaking of a social group whether it is formally recognised as a language or not; in such an area individuals may be monolingual speaking only their own variety.

"Plurilingualism" refers to languages not as objects but from the point of view of those who speak them. It refers to the repertoire of varieties of language which many individuals use, and is therefore the opposite of monolingualism; it includes the language variety referred to as "mother tongue" or "first language" and any number of other languages or varieties. Thus in some multilingual areas some individuals may be monolingual and some may be plurilingual. (Council of Europe, 2007, p. 8)

This conceptualization of plurilingualism emphasizes a focus on the whole repertoire of language skills that an individual can draw on to make meaning. *Repertoire* may include knowledge of different forms of a language, dialect, or a related language; cultural and contextual knowledge; the ability to shift between languages and dialects; and the ability to adjust language registers or complexity for different audiences or even paralinguistic cues. The important distinction here is that individual language and cultural knowledge is seen as one integrated and dynamic resource rather than a compartmentalized set of skills. This distinction has profound implications for the description, assessment, and support of children's language skills and for the goals of language education:

> It is no longer seen as simply to achieve "mastery" of one or two, or even three languages, each taken in isolation, with the "ideal native speaker" as the ultimate model. Instead, the aim is to develop a linguistic repertory, in which all linguistic abilities have a place. (Council of Europe, 2001, p. 5)

Conceptually, this is a move away from seeing languages as separate entities and recognizing the permeable and flexible properties that enable responsiveness to the communicative context and the audience. We might describe this as a dynamic and ecological relationship among individuals, languages, and contexts as speakers adjust their language use to fit with the environment, thus changing the environment and their own repertoire (Mühlhäusler, 2000).

The use of both "multilingual" and "plurilingual" encompass the different modalities that may be in play without making assumptions about the language of the environment or attaching any one particular set of competencies or language profile to an individual. It is important to investigate the bimodal aspects of individual plurilingualism where they exist but equally important to look beyond this to acknowledge the other modes through which individuals create meaning. This includes our collective and individual social and cultural, and other semiotic resources such as gesture, gaze, image, text, speech action, and artifacts (Bezemer & Kress, 2008; Kress & van Leeuwen, 2001). Multilingualism, as concerned with the whole language environment and context, encompasses plurilingualism, as concerned with individual repertoire. The term "multilingualism" is thus used as the overarching expression when thinking about the many languages in deaf children's lives.

THE U.K. CONTEXT

The United Kingdom is becoming an increasingly linguistically diverse and multilingual society where, on average, 15% of school children use a language other than spoken English at home (this is 45% in London) and where the proportion and relative commonness of languages continues to change in response to increasing superdiversity and migration patterns (British Academy, 2013). Of particular importance to deaf education is the fact that the British Asian population is growing, and there is a heightened incidence (2:1) of hearing impairment for Bangladeshi and Pakistani heritage pupils (Cline & Mahon, 2010). Deaf children from these populations are increasingly using more than one spoken or sign language at home, and yet we currently know little about their language experience and repertoires. This makes it difficult for professionals to provide support and intervention plans for these children and for the families to access appropriate support services and or networks (Atkin, Ahmad, & Jones, 2002; Steinberg, Bain, Li, Delgado, & Ruperto, 2003; Zaidman-Zait, 2007).

Alongside the emergence of increasingly linguistic diverse communities and society, technology is also evolving. Advanced hearing technologies now provide deaf children with greater opportunities to successfully develop one or more spoken languages. There is growing evidence of the potential of cochlear implants (CIs) to enable deaf children to more successfully access the ambient language of the environment and perceive the phonological nuances of different spoken languages (McConkey Robbins,

Waltzman, & Green, 2004). Prior to the development of CIs, the development of fluent spoken language for profoundly deaf children was challenging in the extreme. Even the most sophisticated hearing aids are not able to provide full access to the complex phonology of the spoken language or to facilitate exposure to the natural and spontaneous use of spoken language of others in the environment. Furthermore, the "overhearing" of communication, and the incidental learning that this enables for normally hearing children, is difficult to obtain with conventional hearing aids.

The situation in the United Kingdom is therefore that more deaf children than ever before grow up in multilingual language contexts and have the potential for learning more than one spoken language. These phenomena are not unique to the United Kingdom. Cochlear implantation is established and increasingly available in all developed countries, and the expansion of multilingual societies is an inevitable consequence of increasingly global mobility and the development of enhanced communication technologies. Wherever in the world, the concept of multilingualism in the context of deaf children presents an exceptional language situation that tests the paradigms and terminologies normally associated with the plural use of spoken languages. The first of these is the additional modality factors involved in the use of multiple sign and/or spoken languages. The concept of plural language use in the context of deaf children may entail the use of more than one spoken language and more than one sign language, as well as various means of switching between, and blending, sign and spoken language.

In addition to this, deaf children's plural language use is influenced by factors associated with deafness and the impact of hearing loss on early experience of language. These factors include the cause, type, and degree of hearing loss and the age of diagnosis, as well as the amplification support and language intervention provided. The other unique factor that can vary for deaf children is the type of communication mode use in the home and the extent to which they are exposed to a sign and/or spoken languages. These are issues that do not pertain for hearing children and need to be considered alongside variables known to influence multilingual language experience and development (e.g., individual cognitive skills, language experience and language status, and parents' education).

Research into deaf children's plural use of languages is only just emerging, and there is much that we need to know and develop in order to understand language ability, progress, and trajectories. However, the issues of language assessment are complex. In the first place, it is often difficult to obtain fundamental information about children's second, minority, or heritage languages (L2), and we do not have systematized approaches to collecting this information (Mahon et al., 2011). Second, even though there is a general increase in contexts, practitioners lack skills and tools to assess linguistically diverse deaf children and provide support for families (Guiberson & Atkins, 2012; Williams & McLeod, 2012).

In terms of the national data on deaf children's language exposure and use, the picture is as yet incomplete. The UK-wide survey (Consortium for Research in Deaf Education, 2015) collects some information about deaf children's language experience, but these data are very sketchy and only provide limited insights into language use at home. This survey collects information on the educational contexts and management of deaf children in specialist educational services in all four countries of the United Kingdom. The data are collected from Heads of Schools and Services, and the response rate is high (greater than 98%). The broad demographical picture from this survey is that there are more than 48,000 deaf children between the ages of 0 and 19 across England, Northern Ireland, Scotland, and Wales and at least 41,000 of this number are in England. The report for England includes some information about deaf children's use of other languages. It identifies that 13% of the overall number of deaf children have a language other than English as an additional spoken language at home. However, a number of services were unable to identify the languages of all deaf children in their area, and more than 8,000 deaf children are unaccounted for in the figures. The survey results should therefore be treated with caution, and it is likely that the percentage of deaf children with an additional spoken language at home is likely to be higher than reported.

THE GLOBAL CONTEXT

Published research into deaf children's multilingualism is scare and rarely reaches beyond English-speaking populations even though there must be many examples of deafness and multilingualism in the world considering the prevalence of deafness worldwide. Globally, the incidence of "disabling hearing loss" is reported to be 360 million people (5.3% of the world's population), and 32 million of these are children (World Health Organization, 2015). The World Health Organization (WHO) categorizes a disabling hearing loss as "greater than 40 dB in the better hearing ear in adults (15 years or older) and greater than 30 dB in the better hearing ear in children (0 to 14 years)" (2015, p. 1). The prevalence of disabling hearing loss in children is greatest in low- and middle-income countries. For example, 2–3 out of 1,000 live births are reported with hearing impairment in high-income countries, but this can be as high as 6 in 1,000 live births in regions of South Asia, Asia Pacific, and Sub-Saharan Africa. The focus on English speaking populations (and research only published in English) is therefore not likely to be exposing the full extent of multilingualism in the context of deaf children.

SPOKEN LANGUAGE MULTILINGUALISM

A systematic review of the literature by Crowe, McLeod, McKinnon, and Ching (2014) unearthed only eight studies, published in English, which specifically described deaf children who were multilingual or who lived in multilingual environments. Of the six studies that looked at language outcomes, two of these only considered the children's performance in the dominant community language; that is, the main language used in that geographical context. The other four studies described outcomes in the children's home languages. A prevalent theme across these studies is the potential of CIs to facilitate deaf children's access to and learning of more than one spoken language.

McConkey Robbins et al. (2004), for example, investigate the spoken language bilingual skills of a group of deaf children with CIs. The first

and second (spoken) language skills of 12 children were evaluated at
2-year intervals after implantation. All of the children spoke English
and were also exposed to an L2 in the home and, in some cases, the
school and the social community. The languages other than English
included Hebrew, French, Spanish, Arabic, Yiddish, and German. The
results showed the children's skills in spoken English to be comfortably
in the range of their hearing peers. Their skills in the L2 showed steady
improvement, most notably where they had extended use of a CI and
where they had access to fluent users of the L2 at home and in other settings. Furthermore, it appeared that the children's L2 learning followed
similar patterns of development to that of hearing children in terms of
the grammatical and phonological errors, as reported by the parents.
This is a small study but important for thinking about the support of
children's heritage language use, especially for caregivers who, in the
first instance, where advised to only use English at home even this was
not in all cases their first language. Furthermore, this study provides evidence of the potential of CIs to make accessible different phonological
codes and for deaf children to be able to make use of these to become
multiple–spoken language users.

Further evidence of successful spoken language bilingualism of children with CIs is provided by Waltzmann, Robbins, Green, and Cohen
(2003). This study examined the extent to which deaf children with CIs
can develop spoken fluency in an L2 alongside age-appropriate expressive and receptive spoken language skills in the primary language. On
standard speech perception and receptive and expressive language measures, the participants demonstrated competency in a second spoken language and age-appropriate receptive and expressive language abilities in
their primary language.

Thomas, El-Kashlan, and Zwolan (2008) provide similar evidence of
deaf children with CIs learning multiple spoken languages without compromising the development of English as the primary language. In this
study, no significant differences were found between the language outcomes of children who used a minority language at home when compared with those from monolingual homes. As with the other studies,
the research questions center on the potential of CIs to make multiple

languages accessible to deaf children. In each case, the language data collected do not provide in-depth information on the children's skills in their additional languages. This was not the main driver for the research and, the researchers did not have the multilingual language skills or assessment tools to achieve this. Instead, the results focus primarily on spoken English outcomes with only some information provided about the children's relative proficiency in their additional language via rating inventories completed by parents (MacArthur-Bates Communicative Development Inventory and the Student Oral Language Observation Matrix).

Although these studies provide useful information about the potential of CIs with regard to multilingual language development, the stance of the research limits what we can learn about being deaf and multilingual. These projects tend to seek evidence of the extent to which being multilingual affects children's spoken language development of the majority language. The study by Boons et al. (2012), for example, shows that multilingualism in children with CIs has a negative impact on their Dutch language skills. The study by Teschendorf, Janeschik, Bagus, Lang, and Arweiler-Harbeck (2011) provides a further example of this orientation: in this study of 93 profoundly hearing-impaired children with CI, 52 of the participants were from bilingual homes in Germany. Some basic information was collected about the children's additional language skills via a questionnaire. However, the main focus of the study was the evaluation of the children's spoken German skills after cochlear implantation using standard speech perception and receptive and expressive language measures. This study explores the extent to which growing up in a bilingual home does, or does not, affect children's performances on speech tests in the majority language (in this case German). Within this paradigm, success is seen in terms of the achievement of high levels of skill in spoken German. Furthermore, the importance of the German language skills of the parents, the social integration of the family, and their compliance with the CI support program are considered to be key factors for this success. This perspective gives confidence in the potential of CI but does not explore the wider language expertise that deaf children bring to the learning context and the value of cultural and linguistic affiliation and inheritance.

A small number of studies have looked more specifically at heritage language and culture. The work by Crowe, McLeod, and Ching (2012) achieves this through a population-based investigation of the cultural and linguistic experience of 3-year-old children prior to starting school. Demographic characteristics for 406 children and their caregivers were analyzed from a longitudinal study of the audiological, speech, language, academic, and psychosocial outcomes of deaf children in three states of Australia (Ching et al., 2010). Information was collected from caregivers and educators about children's sign and spoken language use through a questionnaire. In this population, 28 spoken languages other than English were reported to be used by children and their caregivers, as well as Australian Sign Language (Auslan) and mixed sign and spoken language communication. Despite this evident language diversity among this population, the majority of the 406 children used spoken English at home and generally used fewer spoken languages than their caregivers. The authors raise concerns about the children's less frequent use of multiple spoken languages (at home and at school) compared to their caregivers and the implications in terms of heritage language attrition.

This study, and the follow-up work by Crowe, Fordham, McLeod, and Ching (2014), represents a scarce line of inquiry in deaf education and studies that looks beyond questions of sign and spoken modality to ascertain deaf children's experience of other (signed and spoken) languages in their lives. As such, this body of work provides an in-depth insight into one multilingual context to reveal which spoken and sign languages deaf children have experience of and what influences language use at home and at school. These findings suggest priorities for language intervention and support.

On a smaller scale, the study by Willoughby (2012) of seven migrant families with deaf children in Victoria, Australia, provides further insight into deafness and multilingualism in the context of heritage languages. Through the use of seven case studies, this work provides further examples of the opportunities that increasingly sophisticated hearing technologies afford for facilitating the development of two spoken languages. The study specifically explores the ways in which families support their children to use their heritage language. In this work, Willoughby illustrates the value placed on sharing the heritage language among these families and how parents' motivations and strategies for maintaining the home language vary according to individual spoken language potential. As with the work by Crowe and colleagues, this study further underlines the need to support the multilingual practices of children and their families within the clinical and educational context.

SIGN LANGUAGE MULTILINGUALISM

The use of multiple sign languages in deaf children's lives is even more scarcely reported in the literature, even though an increasing number of sign languages are recorded around the world every year (the last entry in 13th edition of Ethnologue lists 136) and there are increased opportunities for interaction and meeting across sign language communities (Woll, Sutton-Spence, & Elton, 2001). Some research is emerging that looks at the language outcomes for deaf adults acquiring skills in an additional sign language (Chen Pichler & Koulidobrova, 2015; Hickok, Love-Geffen, & Klima, 2002; Quinto-Pozos, 2011). This growing literature suggests that adult learners can very successfully acquire a sign language as an L2 (where the first language is also a sign language), even when they are exposed to it beyond the suggested critical period for fluent language development (Chen Pichler & Koulidobrova, 2015). One explanation for this is the positive transfer between sign languages in terms of their shared and common linguistic features, such as the use of space and iconicity. Work on the interaction between an individual's two sign languages also suggests patterns of code switching that are equivalent to spoken language multilingual contexts (Quinto-Pozos, 2008). This research is very much in its infancy because of the scarcity of examples of plural sign language contexts and individual repertoires.

Hiddinga and Crasborn (2011) suggest that the reason for this phenomena is that sign languages do not tend to become connected with one another via multilingual speakers in the same way that spoken languages do. In their critique of Swaan's (2001) theory of a global language system,

Hiddinga and Crasborn argue that the transnational communication that facilitates spoken language multilingualism is not applicable to sign language multilingualism. They suggest that Swaan's hierarchical model of how languages of the world interconnect is flawed with reference to sign languages. This model privileges English as the central language through which most other languages connect because of its global economic and cultural value. Hiddinga and Crasborn argue that no one central sign language can be recognized as the equivalent medium for international exchange. Certainly, there is evidence of the strong influence of some sign languages on others, particularly through education, such as ASL, French Sign Language, and Swedish Sign Language (Woll et al., 2001). However, there is no one sign language that acts as a lingua franca across geographical and community borders. International sign language, although used at international gatherings alongside the sign language of the host country, is highly variable, and meanings are often negotiated. International sign language has not become a lingua franca through which other sign languages connect. Furthermore, its use precludes the need to attend to different sign languages in a multilingual context. Given these circumstances, it is not surprising that few deaf people have the opportunity to become multilingual signers.

METHODOLOGICAL ISSUES

The research available into deafness and multilingualism thus far reveals the extent of multilingualism in the lives of many deaf children and the potential for individuals to develop plural sign and spoken language skills. The research is, however, problematic. There are many gaps in our knowledge in terms of the language demographics of populations, countries, and communities and in our knowledge of individual linguistic plurality. A number of methodological issues explain this scarcity of knowledge.

The first of these is that it is often difficult to obtain information about children's second, minority, or heritage languages (Mahon et al., 2011). Practitioners lack skills and tools to assess linguistically diverse deaf children and thus to provide support for families (Guiberson

& Atkins, 2012; Williams & McLeod, 2012). Standardized or norm-referenced measures do not exist in many languages, and, even where they do exist, native speakers able to administer these are not always involved in the research or available in the educational context. As a result, language skills are often assessed by report, usually from educators, researchers, and/or parents. Typically used measures include the Language Proficiency Profile (Bebko, Calderon, & Treder, 2003). This is a multiple-choice rating scale that can be completed by educators and/or parents. The scale rates children's expressive language and communication skills. Because it is not language specific, it can be used to capture the pragmatic skills in both spoken and sign languages. Other types of inventories frequently reported in the research include the MacArthur-Bates Communicative Development Inventories (Feldman et al., 2000) and the Student Oral Language Observation Matrix (McConkey Robbins et al., 2004). Although these provide useful profile information, the limitations of collecting information through report rather than assessment are acknowledged.

Information about children's multilingual language skills is therefore often incomplete, making it difficult to draw conclusions about what factors affect language acquisition in multilingual deaf children and what support is needed in the educational context. The challenge is to be able to identify and measure the full range of skills across the spoken—and possibly sign language—that they use. Assessing this repertoire necessarily includes attention to the ways in which children switch between and blend features of different languages as part of their overall repertoire of language skills.

Another issue is the extent to which the research is limited by the questions that are being asked. It may be, for the methodological reasons posed earlier, that questions are not asked about the multilinguality of deaf children because the tools and skills to explore this issue are not available. There are possibly also ideological issues in play here, embedded within the discourses and values in deaf education research, where the importance of children's development of the majority language is prioritized in research and practice. Few studies look beyond this agenda to include issues of cultural and linguistic diversity.

To broaden this research discourse and extend the scope of research in this area would involve looking beyond individual language expertise (in the majority language) to the wider issues of affiliation and inheritance as proposed by Rampton (1991, 1995). Knowledge about language expertise only provides a fractional view of multilingual contexts and individual experience. The notion of affiliation provides a useful way to think about deaf and hearing language identities and deaf children's different friendship groups in school and in the wider community. A focus on heritage ensures that we consider the language tradition of the home, close family, and community. These are details that hitherto have not been thoroughly considered concerning deaf children's language experiences, repertoires, and implications for support.

Finally, the dissemination of knowledge about multilingualism is constrained by the lingua franca of academia. There are likely to be more studies in existence, but not published in English. The development of an international overview of research into deafness and multilingualism is thus ironically limited by the discourse of research and the language skills of the scholars. To investigate these methods and outcomes, researchers have to work multilingually and find ways to share research questions, methods, and outcomes across language boundaries.

AN APPROACH TO GATHERING LANGUAGE INFORMATION

Recognizing the need to build our knowledge in this area in the United Kingdom, Leeds University established a collaborative Language Planning project with schools and services for deaf children. The main impetus for this project was the identified need for information about deaf children's exposure to and use of multiple languages as a basis for the development of individual language plans. The work was led by Leeds University and developed in collaboration with practitioners and managers from schools and services in England. The published resources provided for practitioners by this project were commissioned using funding provided by the Department for Education under contract with the National Sensory Impairment Partnership (NatSIP). These are now widely used in schools to collect language demographic information and develop language profiles of deaf children, and they have been developed as a methodological approach for collecting contextual and individual language data (Swanwick, 2016; Swanwick, Simpson et al., 2014; Swanwick, Wright, & Salter, 2016).

This project adopted an ecological approach to the collection of information about deaf children's exposure to and use of different languages in their daily lives and the influencing factors on the development of their language repertoires. This approach was based on Bronfenbrenner's ecological model (Bronfenbrenner, 1979, 1992, 2005). This model provided a framework to encompass the breadth of information about language exposure and experience and use in the different contexts of deaf children's lives. An ecological way of looking takes into account the individual, proximal, and distal factors that influence deaf children's language repertoires, such as hearing loss, hearing technologies in use, languages spoken at home and school, the social environment, and the educational and societal ideologies and values embedded in this environment. As such, this approach allows information to be gathered that recognizes language philosophies and ideologies as influencing factors but is not boundaried by them as a way of categorizing individual skills and experiences. An ecological approach to language planning encourages consideration of how the following range of factors might influence individual language exposure and use:

- Individual characteristics and the interactions that individuals have with those closest to them, such as family and peers
- The relationship between the individual's different environments (such as home and school), how they interact, and how this impacts on the individual
- External and contextual factors, such as how sign and spoken languages are used and distributed within the networks and communities beyond home
- The wider cultural constructs surrounding the individual, such as educational and cultural values and ideologies
- Individual development, growth, and advances or change in society, knowledge, and the environment

Using this conceptual framework, two protocols were developed for collecting information about deaf children's contexts for language learning and individual language repertoires; these are referred to as *language landscapes* and *language profiles*, respectively.

The protocol for creating the language landscapes involved the extraction and analysis of data from the UK 2011 National Census (Office for National Statistics, 2011). This provided general demographic information for the local authority population in terms of size, nationalities, ethnicities, and languages in use. More specific information about the caseload

Table 3.1 The Language Landscape Protocol

Source of Data	Information Collected
Government census information	Size of population
	Comparison to other local authorities
	Breakdown of population by gender and age groups and any significant differences between gender or age groups
	Nationalities within a population, including number of people who were born outside the UK
	Ethnicities within a population
	Dominant languages used by residents
	Household languages used within a population and how proficient residents are at using English
Local authority deaf education service caseload population	Numbers of children (0–19) on the caseload
	Age ranges (as numbers and a percentage)
	Level of deafness (as numbers and a percentage)
	Numbers of children with cochlear implants
	Number of children in resourced provisions and/or schools for the deaf
	Ethnicity and nationality within the caseload (not all services record nationality)
	Languages used within the caseload, including sign languages (often these data are incomplete, and, for some families, no dominant or preferred language is recorded)

Table 3.2 The Case Studies Protocol

Source of Data	Information Collected
Teacher reports on individual pupils	Educational background and management: experience of preschool support and school placement
	Individual language resources: repertoire of expressive and receptive sign and spoken language skills
	Contexts of language use: language exposure and use at home, school and other settings
	Language assessment information: measures, tools, and protocols used to assess children's language development
	Individual language assessment data and reports
	Language learning trajectory: target areas for receptive and expressive language development
Teacher interview	Languages that children and adults use in school
	Languages that the child is exposed to in school in different contexts
	Languages that the child uses in school in different contexts
	Examples of child language use in different contexts
Parent and child interview	Languages that the family use at home
	Contexts for different language use (who and when)
	Languages that the child uses at home
	Examples of child language use in different contexts
Observation	Examples of children interacting in different learning scenarios in the school context (small-group; shared reading; mainstream curriculum group work; lunchtime)
Video analysis of individual children in conversation with parent	Examples of sign and spoken language; the role of language switching and blending; influence on language choice

deaf children in different settings was taken from the national annual CRIDE survey (CRIDE, 2015). This was supplemented by information specific to each setting regarding numbers of children on the caseload, age ranges, levels of deafness, children with CIs, ethnicities, nationalities, and languages in use. This information was not always complete, but the three-tiered approach provided comprehensive set of questions about each setting (Table 3.1).

The protocol for the case studies involved the use of teacher reports and language assessment information; interviews with teachers, parents, and children; observations of children in school; and analysis of short video clips of children and their parents in conversation. Using this range of strategies enabled the development of rich case studies that described individual backgrounds, deafness, and technologies and educational experience; language exposure and use at home and at school; and language abilities (Table 3.2).

Each protocol consisted of a series of headings and prompts to facilitate the collection of detailed individual and contextual language information from teachers, parents, and, where possible, the children themselves.

CASE STUDY EXAMPLES

The initial case studies that emerged from this approach provide a number of multilingual scenarios and examples of individual exposure to and use of multiple languages as well as their cultural experiences, affiliations, and heritages. The four "mini portraits" here give some illustration of this:

CASE STUDY: SHAZIA

Shazia lives with her mother, father, and two brothers. One brother is hearing; the other brother is profoundly deaf. She also has a deaf cousin. Her parents are hearing. Her mother has British Sign Language (BSL) level 2. Father's BSL is more limited. The spoken languages and forms of communication used at home include English and Urdu, BSL, and Sign-Supported English (SSE).

CASE STUDY: ZAK

Zak lives with his hearing mother, younger sister, aunt, uncle, and cousin. The spoken language used at home is mainly Wolof, and the family have competent spoken and written English skills. Zak's mother is currently studying level 2 BSL, and his younger sister uses some elementary signs. The extended family members do not use any BSL. Zak attends mosque school every Saturday, where the instruction is given by deaf adults in BSL, and he is learning to read Arabic. Zak has a very strong network of friends and families in this community, including other families with deaf children.

CASE STUDY: TANYA

Tanya is from a family whose origins are in Slovakia. Her parents came to Britain in 2005 when she was 1 year old. Tanya has a younger brother who is also profoundly deaf and an older hearing brother. Tanya's mother and father are both Slovakian speakers. Father's English is described as "quite good," and her mother has learned English since she arrived. The extended family live locally, including the father's sister, who is moderately deaf and uses spoken language. In Slovakia, Tanya's mother has a cousin who is severely deaf and uses sign language. At home, the family uses Slovakian, English, and some BSL.

CASE STUDY: NOREEN

Noreen is one of three children. Her younger brother is deaf, and her older brother is hearing. Noreen's mother is hearing and uses mainly Urdu and some Punjabi with other extended family members. She has learned some English but tends not to use it with her children. Noreen's father is deaf and uses what she describes as a "homesign language," which he developed in Pakistan. Over time, he has learned more BSL signs from his children. He does not use any spoken or written English. The family all converse with him using homesign Noreen's father has two sisters; both are deaf and use sign language, and he converses easily with them. All other extended family members are hearing and use mainly Urdu and sometimes Punjabi at home. Noreen goes to mosque and can read and recite Arabic from the Qu'ran.

From these short extracts of individual profile data from this project, the complexity in terms of language exposure and use and the potential language repertoires of these deaf children are evident. Collecting more descriptive data of this kind and establishing ways to collect, describe, and analyze this information is a priority to inform language work in schools. The development of these and other case studies provides the first steps toward a closer analysis of deaf children's exposure to and use of different sign and spoken languages at home and at school. Gathering this information and understanding the different contexts for language experience will also enable us to see what children are doing with their languages, how they are using their repertoires, and what competencies they are developing (see Swanwick et al., 2016, for a fuller exploration of this protocol).

PLURALITY, DIVERSITY, AND LEARNING

Taking a multilingual perspective enables some examination of the plurilingual practices of deaf children and their families. This brings something new to current discourses in deaf education that, although increasingly encompassing bimodal bilingualism, less often recognize the multilingual lives of many deaf children. The discourses in deaf education—that is, the "conduct, talk and text" (Roberts, 2011, p. 82) around language use—have tended to be argumentative: questions of what languages should be used in education have dominated over rich description and analysis of what languages deaf children actually use in their daily lives. Furthermore, the discussion of language has focused on the impact of deafness on literacy, learning, and achievement, and so the concentration of research has been gathered around how deaf children can learn the majority language, clearly valuing or privileging these languages among others (Bourdieu, 2000). A multilingual perspective brings other languages and language experience to the fore and prompts new questions about deafness, language, and learning.

To develop this understanding, we need to know more about the continuous interaction between sign and spoken languages in deaf children's lives and to extend this knowledge as far as possible to include non–English-speaking populations. The emerging work in this area reveals some language demographic studies, as well as small population and individual case studies. However, our knowledge is far from complete, and what we have learned raises questions about the development of assessment tools and approaches that accurately describe individual spoken and sign language repertoires.

As we look more closely at multilingualism in the context of deaf children's lives and at individual language repertoires, it becomes increasingly clear that we are looking at a fluid and dynamic set of linguistic resources that combine and interact according to context and audience. This perspective challenges a view of languages as separate and discrete phenomena and recognizes that languages "leak" into one another and are not stored as sealed entities (Makoni & Pennycook, 2006). A plurilingual individual therefore gathers a repertoire of linguistic skills that he or she is able to deploy flexibly to make meaning. Fluency in any one language is only one aspect of this repertoire that needs to be seen alongside the ability to draw on the right language resources for different contexts and audience.

This concept of fluidity and dynamism pertains also to notions of identity, which changes all the time according to how it is socially constructed through language practices in different contexts (Blackledge & Creese, 2009). What we do with language is always situated in a context and is integral to our communicative stance and our view of ourselves.

Having considered deaf children's bimodal, bilingual, and plurilingual language experience, with a particular perspective on language use, the challenge is to take this forward to think about what the plural use of sign and spoken languages means for deaf children's learning. The following chapters extend the concept of language use as a way of acting on the world. This perspective prepares the ground for an educational approach that situates what we do with language at the heart of pedagogy. The concept of languaging is introduced as a way of thinking about this and as a basis for understanding the role of translanguaging in deaf children's lives.

4 Languaging and Learning in Deaf Education

The concept of languaging is introduced in this chapter to consider how the plural and diverse language experiences of deaf children can support their learning and, in particular, how language mediates learning. Thinking about languaging in the context of individuals provides a vehicle for analyzing ways in which deaf children bring their language repertoires into being for meaning-making and learning and what learning challenges they experience. The concept of languaging as a means of positioning and as an expression of social identity is also a useful lens through which to explore approaches to language in deaf education and the impact of deaf education language policy on practice. Languaging theory thus provides a theoretical framework for examining deaf children's classroom learning and developing pedagogical approaches in deaf education that are responsive to multilingual contexts and the plurilingual practices of deaf children.

LANGUAGING

Over recent years, the concept of languaging has emerged in the literature as a way of talking about what we do with our language resources in particular contexts and how our language actions shape and are shaped by our experience and knowledge (C. Baker, 2011; Blommaert & Rampton, 2011; García, 2009; Linell, 2009). The development of the concept of languaging comes from a move in language research to deconstruct language as a concept in order to "understand its power and potential as a discursive tool" (García, 2009, p. 40). The use of this term reflects a poststructuralist view of language as "social practices and actions by speakers that are embedded in a web of social and cognitive relations" (García & Li Wei, 2014, p. 9).

Within this paradigm, the structural view of language or "langue" as an abstract system with rules and conventions intersects with "parole" as our performance in that language (Bakhtin, 1981; Saussure, 2006) to underline what we do with language. In other words, languaging is the interaction among our language knowledge, experience, and our actions and, as such, "how we interact with the world lingually" (García & Li Wei, 2014, p. 8). This is always a dynamic interaction because something happens or, we become something, through what we do with language. Languaging is therefore transformative in that it brings about "a new way of being in the world" (Becker, 1995, p. 227).

Languaging is more than language use in that it is not solely about performance in a language but is instead about how we do something or become something *through* our language practices or language actions. This theoretical perspective conceptualizes language as integral to the internal context of individuals, their experience, and intentions as well as to the external context of the interaction (Bakhtin, 1981). Just as we cannot separate what we do in the world from who we are, neither can we divorce our language experience and knowledge from our language actions. Languaging is a dialogic process in the sense that any language action is part of a "to and fro" or exchange of ideas and meanings, either internally or with those around us (Bakhtin, 1981). Any language action exists only in connection with what has gone before and influences what will come next. Languaging is thus a dynamic dialogue in which our language actions create new meanings from moment to moment (García & Li Wei, 2014).

Languaging and Learning

The concept of languaging places an emphasis on the process of constructing meaning, through dialogue, with others in our social practices and activities. It is consistent with a sociocultural theory of mind that construes language as a cognitive tool for mediating learning and the development of new understandings "to make and shape meaning" (Vygotsky, 1986, p. 107). We use language internally and socially to develop our understanding of new concepts as we construct meaning from our everyday experiences and generalize these newly emerging concepts to more systematic understandings. Vygotsky theorized this process of internalized understanding to rely on an interaction between the spontaneous experience of new concepts and effective instruction, to allow for the transformation that is learning. In this dynamic model, direct instruction of concepts has to be linked to experience, or spontaneous experience has to be mediated by instruction for learning to take place. Languaging creates the learning dynamic by providing an interaction between knowing and doing that fosters conceptual learning. Languaging in the learning context is often considered to mean collaborative dialogue, but it may also constitute private or self-directed speech and, as such, the internal dialogue that mediates our language use (Lantolf & Thorne, 2006).

Languaging and Language Learning

In the language learning classroom, languaging is conceptualized as the way in which learners mediate concepts in the classroom through interaction or dialogue. In this context, agency and action are implicit to the notion of languaging (Swain, 2006). Over recent years, this perspective has become more visible in second language (L2) learning research, where language is at once the subject of learning and the mediating tool. A number of studies reported by Swain and colleagues have explored the role of languaging as a cognitive tool for learning (Swain, Lapkin, Knouzi,

Suzuki, & Brooks, 2009). As part of this body of work, Brooks, Swain, Lapkin, and Knouzi (2010) provide a specific example of this in action, where languaging in the students' first language (L1; English) mediates the use and understandings of grammatical concepts in their L2 (French). Mediation in these contexts refers to the way in which the meaning of the grammatical concept in the L2 is at first noticed and understood in relation to its meaning in the L1. That is to say, new learning is mediated cognitively by what is already known. This is a dynamic process because one language is seen through the lens of the other, and vice versa, thus creating new understandings. Brooks et al. (2010) discuss this in Vygotskian terms as a development from intuitive or "spontaneous" knowledge of a language form (something known already in L1) to a deeper conceptual understanding of its meaning and use in both L1 and L2 (Vygotsky, 1986, p. 161).

The languaging that is described in this context consists of layered activities that constitute a process of developing on-task talk about the target concept—in this case, the use of voice in French. The "languaging sequence" moves from identification of the grammatical form and discussion in L2 through to identification, explanation of the grammatical form in L1, and, finally, its use in L2 (writing). Diagrams and language cards are used as part of this languaging sequence (p. 94). The nature of the students' talk through this process becomes increasingly sophisticated as they move from discussing what they already know to seeing and identifying new language forms and then articulating their own hypothesis about their use (Swain et al., 2009). Learning thus progresses from intuitive knowledge to conceptual and conscious understanding as languaging enables "true acts of thinking" (Vygotsky, 1986, p. 169).

It can be argued that languaging in this context creates the cognitive scaffolding for learners to move from intuitive spontaneous knowledge to a deeper conceptual understanding. To some extent, this is borne out by the Brooks et al. study (2010). During the interactive sequence that they analyze, only minimal prompt-like interventions are provided by the researcher. The authors suggest that increased dialogic mediation by the teacher or among the peer group would have enhanced the learning. They concede that although languaging creates "teachable moments" that are full of opportunity for learning, it is dialogic intervention that transforms these moments into meaningful learning (p. 107).

Implications for planning and assessment are also concluded from this study. The authors found that assessment of the students' use of the French voice in their writing provided an indication of their learning progress but did not reveal how they were learning or expose their deeper conceptual understanding in the way that oral recall did. They found that the assessment addressed the achievement of the teaching objective but did not help to plan for the next learning step. In their words, the written outcome documented "yesterday's development" it did not capture "tomorrow's instruction" (p. 106).

The work on languaging by Swain and colleagues focuses largely on oral L2 development. However, research into languaging as part of the process of L2 literacy development is also a growing area of research (Ishikawa, 2013*a*; Mirzaei & Eslami, 2015; Suzuki, 2012). The focus on L2 writing also accents the dialogic potential of languaging through talk with peers and/ or adults to move the learner from what he "is" to what "he could be" (Mirzaei & Eslami, 2015, p. 6). Through collaborative writing, learners engage in languaging in shared planning, review, analysis, and discussion to solve linguistic problems and mediate their L2 learning.

Mirzaei and Eslami (2015) argue that languaging creates what they refer to as a "dialogically activated Zone of Proximal Development (ZPD)" (p. 6). They demonstrate this in a study of Iranian students learning English as a foreign language. In this study, the students are engaged in problem-solving activities with differently capable peers to create a collaborative written output. During the ZPD-activated writing activities, they observed students to co-construct language knowledge, negotiate meaning, and, at the same time, establish their positions and goals as learners (p. 20). They argue that languaging thus changes what one can do with language and at once influences and provides expression of how one sees and positions oneself as a linguistic subject.

Suzuki takes the concept of languaging as part of L2 writing further in his construction of "written languaging" (2012, p. 1112). In this study of Japanese leaners of English, Suzuki conceptualizes written

languaging as an internal cognitive process of externalizing the inner
dialogue that takes place during writing. Written languaging is the way
in which individuals make the transition between the inner and outer
meaning. Dialogue in this context is with oneself and not with others,
as in the earlier examples. Simply put, writing is like talking to ourselves. The product (the written text) is a complete expression of self
rather than a mediated co-construction through dialogic activity with
others. Although this research is speculative in some ways, it situates
the concept of languaging more firmly in the written domain and provides a theoretical construct that distinguishes between the collaborative and internal dialogue. Both of these constitute different forms of
languaging.

One of the issues for this research is how to make visible the languaging of the learners; that is, how to perceive the internal dialogue during
the writing process. Various studies have tried to do this using "think
aloud" techniques (Qi & Lapkin, 2001), and retrospective reports from
students (Suzuki & Itagaki, 2009). The methodological challenge is to
capture the language used by learners as they reflect on their own language use during a language task and to observe ways in which learners express their grammatical thinking in different modalities (Rättyä,
2013). This type of talk around a writing activity is sometimes referred to
as *metatalk* and has also been described as *metanotes* (Ishikawa, 2013b).
Metanotes are written notes made by students as they complete a language task, such as translation, aimed at capturing their reflections on
their language use and choices and their "noticing" of linguistic problem
and solutions (2013, p. 12). It is not yet clear to what extent this type of
written languaging complements oral languaging in terms of enhancing
L2 learning. Nonetheless, it extends concepts and understandings of languaging in the context of the act of writing.

Languaging as Being

Languaging extends concepts of language knowledge and use to include
self-perception and expression of self and the embodiment of who we
are (Jensen, 2014). Because languaging is concerned with not only what

is said but also with how it is said, it is perhaps better understood as a behavior or an activity that involves our full selves as human beings (Thibault, 2011).

This aspect of languaging has been explored in research studies that have examined the way in which languaging marks social identity and positioning (Dahlberg & Bagga-Gupta, 2013, 2014). Focusing on the language classroom as the social context for learning, Bagga-Gupta and Gynne (2013) suggest that young people's languaging makes visible their identity and social positions in terms of their orientation toward the learning activity, their sense of self, and their role within the learning peer group. As evidence of this, they present examples of dialogue among bilingual learners and their teachers in Swedish schools and of their internal dialogue in their learning diaries.

In the dialogue among the peer group, all with varied repertoires of Finnish, Swedish, and English, the learners collaboratively make links between all three spoken languages and the written English on the white board by translating, repeating, paraphrasing, and clarifying where needed. The learners use dialogue to show equivalence between the languages in terms of meaning. Each contribution is contingent on individual repertoire and the learning needs of others in their group. Through this collaborative dialogue, the learners position themselves differently in the group as helpful, supportive, knowledgeable, and so forth. Bagga-Gupta and Gynne (2013) propose that, in the written diaries, where learners similarly link together the different languages, they reveal their participation in and orientation toward the learning context and their view of themselves. They argue that this type of languaging reveals different "ways of being" part of the learning community and makes visible the fluid and multiple identities in play (supportive peer, reluctant learner, successful learner) from moment to moment (p. 494).

Languaging as positioning, or taking stance, has also been explored in the way in which beliefs, values, and emotions are enacted through our language behaviors and activities. Core beliefs, Aragão (2011) argues, are expressed but can also be challenged through languaging. Jensen (2014) proposes that languaging is a "whole body activity" that encompasses our emotions (p. 2). He envisages affect and emotion as "intertwined with our language behaviour" and expressed through not only words but also gaze, gesture, facial expression, and voice (p. 12). Capturing and describing this aspect of languaging presents further methodological challenge because it requires approaches that adequately record and analyze the verbal and nonverbal dynamics and interaffectivity of face-to-face interaction (Böhme, Boll, Schmitt, & Müller, 2014).

LANGUAGING AND DEAF CHILDREN'S LEARNING

This multifaceted concept of language provides a useful framework for thinking about deaf children's language and learning that encompass different contexts of language use (monolingual, bilingual, multilingual). First, a focus on languaging provides a fresh perspective on deaf children's learning as concerned with how meanings are created through internal or collaborative dialogue within or between languages. This focus has the potential to enrich the established literature on deaf children's language development and use by bringing to the fore ways in which children use their language repertoires for meaning-making and learning. This perspective also emphasizes the essentially dialogic nature of meaning-making and the mediating role of language in the learning process (Blackledge & Creese, 2009).

Second, languaging as the embodiment of stance and orientation to others is also a useful way to think about the educational context of deaf children's learning, particularly in terms of institutional languaging (Lemke, 2002). There are multiple examples of languaging in discourses around deaf education policy, practice, and research that embody positions, ideologies, beliefs, and values about language. This type of languaging has created a boundaried educational context that has sometimes inhibited the development of practice. The concept of languaging thus offers a means to analyze language use in deaf education policy and practice and to provide a framework for pedagogy that connects language with learning.

Deaf Children's Languaging

Examples of deaf children's communication at home and at school illustrate the potential of languaging as a dialogic process to facilitate meaning-making. Because deaf children may be exposed to and use a number of different languages and forms of communication across two modalities, there are diverse ways in which languaging may occur. However, a perspective on languaging is not necessarily only relevant to bimodal and bilingual/multilingual situations. Languaging is a way of drawing on the whole of ones' language resources to make meaning, recognizing that we all do this in different ways and for different purposes, in different contexts. When we look at deaf children's languaging, we are therefore interested in how individuals make meaning through their language use rather than how they perform in any one language in particular.

Languaging as Social Variation

Languaging can occur within one language. This is equivalent to the social variation that we see when speakers or signers adapt their language use (register, complexity, accent, etc.) to a given social situation or with particular communication partners. This happens in both sign and spoken language use where, for example, regional variations, social affiliations, and/or the communicative context influence choices about language use.

There are regional varieties of sign language, or dialects, even though deaf people do not tend to live in identifiable geographical communities, apart from some very specific cases (e.g. Groce, 1985; Schmaling, 2000; Senghas, Senghas, & Pyers, 2014). Nonetheless, regional dialects in British Sign Language (BSL) and other sign languages are identifiable and in some cases can be traced back to schools for the deaf or major university centers. In these communities, language is adapted, changed, and passed on through generations (Woll & Adam, 2012). As part of these communities, deaf children and young people are not only using sign language but are also actively creating and evolving language. Languaging in this context is an active process of "being and doing" with language by a community.

Aside from regional dialects, there are other variants of sign language use that illustrate ways in which languaging, as a cultural tool, constantly adapts to dynamic exchange with others and enables the expansion of language repertoires (Martin-Beltrán, 2014). Sutton-Spence and Woll (1999) give a number of examples of the different influences that explain social variation such as age, home language, ethnicity, formal/causal contexts of use, and differing audiences. Many of these influences on sign languages pertain also for spoken language variants, but there are some factors that are unique to sign language context (Lucas, 2001). One such factor is that most deaf children are not exposed to fluent sign language from birth. Not surprisingly, therefore, the variant of BSL used by deaf signers from deaf families differs from the variant used by deaf children from hearing families (Sutton-Spence & Woll, 1999).

Advances in hearing technologies, early identification of deafness, and the increasing educational placement of deaf children in mainstream schools mean that spoken English is increasingly prominent and accessible to deaf children. As a result, children's sign language use may be heavily influenced by English and, in many contexts of use (with hearing peers and adults), becomes a variety of signing with substantial mixing and blending of English.

Languaging as social variation is influenced by not only biology, biography, and context; it also constitutes an enactment of who we are. The case study extracts presented herein provide some examples of this. Each extract differently illustrates ways in which deaf children language by moving between different forms and styles of communication in order to make meaning and "be" in different ways with others. These examples also point to certain influences on deaf children's languaging and the dynamic and adaptive nature of languaging as a way of mediating social activity at home and at school.

CASE STUDY EXAMPLES

CASE STUDY: TANYA

Tanya uses mainly sign language (BSL) in school, but with hearing friends she increases her use of facial expression, lip patterns and gesture, to get her meaning across.

CASE STUDY: MOHAMMED

Mohammed communicates in English most of the time at school (in class and socially) and with his parents at home. He also communicates easily with his grandparents and some of his friends, who are Punjabi speakers.

CASE STUDY: JACK

Jack communicates predominantly in spoken English. He uses his cochlear implant successfully for listening and he can converse naturally with his hearing peers. He depends on communication partners to help him follow conversation in groups of more than two or three people and has developed effective strategies for ensuring that he is included in these conversations.

CASE STUDY: LUCY

Lucy uses Sign-Supported English (SSE) at home and at school in order to include deaf and hearing family and friends. She also code-switches between spoken English with hearing peers, friends, and adults and BSL with deaf peers, adults, friends. She likes other people to use SSE with her and will request clarification and repetition if she does not understand or misses something.

Languaging as Being in the World

Languaging as a cognitive tool for mediating learning and social activity is also enactment of self in the world. It is what we do with language, but it is also what we are. Languaging for some deaf children involves creating a system for communication. In exceptional circumstances, deaf children whose profound hearing losses constrain access to spoken language and who have no exposure to sign language over a sustained period of time have been observed to invent their own gesture systems to communicate (Singleton & Newport, 2004; Van Deusen-Phillips, Goldin-Meadow, & Miller, 2001). This research has examined the languaging of young children who are exposed to gestural systems developed within a home or small community where no one knows a sign language. These invented systems are sometimes referred to as "homesign." They constitute a contextually bound means of sharing and making meaning "among deaf children and their families in the absence of a linguistic model" (Woll & Adam, 2012, p. 104). In these circumstances, deaf children have been observed to develop communication systems that are systematically structured in language-like ways without access to input from a conventional language. A "homesigner" is thus a producer of a system that he has not received from others (Hunsicker & Goldin-Meadow, 2013). Homesign is not emergent sign language, nor does it not support sign language acquisition (Morford & Hänel-Faulhaber, 2011). It is, however, an example of languaging as a process of meaning-making and meaning-sharing in exceptional circumstances.

Languaging in the Classroom

Examination of the different types of languaging that take place in the deaf education classroom affords an awareness of the complexities of the learning experience for deaf children. The different types of learning environments are important to mention here because languaging opportunities vary between them.

In the United Kingdom, most deaf children (78%) are educated in their local mainstream school with some support from an itinerant teacher of the deaf (CRIDE, 2015). Pupils who are individually included in this way are likely to have sufficient spoken language skills to participate, for the most part, in the social and academic aspects of school with some specialist language, literacy, and technology support. The level of support varies from individual to individual. Children in this context are not likely to be learning through sign language and may or may not use sign language socially or at home. Occasionally, children are individually included with full-time sign language support but this is not currently the trend for inclusive provision.

Deaf children who do need more than "visiting" language support for learning are likely to be educated either in a school for the deaf or in a mainstream school that is fully resourced for deaf pupils. A resourced mainstream school is a "center" within a school that provides a peer-group environment for deaf learners with specialist staff (teachers of the deaf, communication support workers, deaf instructors) to support the language and learning needs of deaf children and enable their inclusion within the mainstream setting. There are various models of resourced provision, sometimes referred to as the *co-enrolment* or *twin school models* (Antia & Metz, 2014; Hermans, De Klerk, Wauters, & Knoors, 2014; Yiu & Tang, 2014). All of these models are set up with the intention of providing specialist support within a mainstream setting. Language policies vary across these provisions with regard to the pedagogical use of sign language and sign-based systems. In the United Kingdom, approximately 8% of deaf children are educated within resourced provision (CRIDE, 2015).

These different learning contexts present different types of languaging situations for deaf children where they have to use their language resources in different ways to mediate learning and social activity in school. As for all children, some learning activities will be very teacher-led in the form of "from the front" explanation, demonstration, questions and answer, or whole-class discussion. Other, more collaborative learning activities, such group or pair work, may involve working with deaf or hearing peers or mixed groups. Deaf children who need some level of language support in the classroom may have learning support and/or interpretation from a sign language interpreter, communication support worker, teacher of the deaf, or teaching assistant. Spoken language input in class may thus be mediated by further explanation and clarification in spoken language, sign language, or with written language. In different ways, these are all examples of the dialogic nature of languaging that involves interaction with others around learning as well as the internal dialogue involved in mediating one's own learning; this illustrates the diversity of deaf children's languaging across a range of learning contexts where there are different languages and forms of communication in play.

Languaging Challenges for Deaf Learners

Some of these languaging experiences present particular challenges for deaf learners in terms of participation and learning outcomes. These challenges sometimes relate to the language of the learning activity itself or to the context of the learning activity. The dialogic nature of a learning activity may sometimes therefore be obscured by the difficulties that deaf children can experience in the classroom in terms of full participation in learning activities and social interaction with peers.

For children who are accessing the curriculum through spoken English, difficulties may be quite practical and related to the acoustics of the learning context and the quality of the listening experience in terms of noise, reverberation, directionality, and distance (Rosenberg, 2010). Although school classrooms can be acoustically improved and listening technologies can give children good access to spoken language, these technologies do not replace hearing (Nicholas & Geers, 2013). The availability of cochlear implants in particular has increased the placement of profoundly deaf children in mainstream schools (Fitzpatrick & Olds, 2015). It is often assumed that a child with a cochlear implant will be able to fully access the classroom environments and participate as a hearing child. This assumption is problematic when teachers are not made fully aware of the listening and participation challenges (Wheeler, Archbold, Gregory, & Skipp, 2007; Wheeler, Gregory, & Archbold, 2004). Even though a deaf child may have a good command of spoken language and not "sound" deaf to peers and adults, he or she is likely to experience difficulties in initiating or following and maintaining a group conversation even with acceptable background noise (Boothroyd, 2002; Ching, Van Wanrooy, Hill, & Incerti, 2006). Group and pair work that provides a dialogic learning experience can therefore be particularly demanding for deaf children. When visual and auditory distractions become too much, learners are likely to withdraw from participation (Dye, Hauser, & Bavalier, 2008) and communication breakdowns are common (Martin, Bat-Chava, Lalwani, & Waltzman, 2011). Even when there are fewer speakers and background noise is reduced, following spoken language delivery over long periods is challenging and tiring (Hicks & Tharpe, 2002; Hornsby, Werfel, Camarata, & Bess, 2014; Wheeler et al., 2004).

The difficulties of group and pair work are confounded where deaf children lack the curriculum vocabulary that they need to participate fully. For group and pair work to be a joint productive activity, conceptual vocabulary needs to be shared. Deaf children's vocabulary is often not as well-developed as their hearing peers in terms of the depth, breadth, and semantic organization of their vocabulary knowledge and repertoire of specialist curriculum terminology (Luckner & Cooke, 2010; Marschark & Wauters, 2011; Percy-Smith et al., 2013). This can affect the fluency with which deaf children can participate in group discussion and the speed at which they can mentally organize their contribution. Without a mutual understanding of essential curriculum terminology, shared meaning-making between deaf and hearing peers can be compromised (Molander, Haldén, & Lindahl, 2010).

Language difficulties are not the only challenge for learning activities in the classroom; social issues sometimes also play a part in hampering group and peer interaction. Attitudes of acceptance by hearing learners toward deaf peers can be variable. Even where hearing students are generally positive, there is an awareness of differences in terms of understanding and pace of learning (Bowen, 2008; Cambra, 1997). Deaf learners may find it more difficult to be accepted and included as part of friendship groups and learning activities because of their hearing peers' uncertainty about the most appropriate ways to communicate. This is evident even in play situations where hearing children are reluctant to initiate interactions with deaf children, irrespective of their language skills, and are more likely to ignore their attempts to initiate interaction (DeLuzio & Girolametto, 2011). Deaf learners may also lack the social confidence to initiate and maintain interactions in challenging learning situations (Schmidt & Čagran, 2008). These issues pertain to communication in spoken language, but interactions across language modalities, even in informal situations, may also cause communication breakdowns. Keating and Mirus (2003) argue that the different sociolinguistic practices and participation frameworks can present communication barriers between deaf and hearing students communicating across visual and auditory communicative channels.

These issues can arise in languaging contexts between deaf and hearing peers where there is direct, usually face-to-face, dialogue between learners within or across modalities. Languaging may also be a mediated experience for deaf learners. This will occur where a deaf or hearing adult supports deaf learners in a mainstream classroom; this could be a teaching assistant, communication support worker, or teacher of the deaf. In these circumstances, interaction between the deaf learner and the mainstream teacher or their peers may be interpreted and presented in sign language or reframed and explained in spoken language. The languaging experience can thus become more fragmented as dialogue is negotiated through a third party, either simultaneously or in relay. This can be quite disruptive of the group work or peer work dynamic and the dialogic experience of shared meaning. Deaf learners may become less actively involved in languaging and become more cut off from group interaction.

It is also much harder for deaf learners to participate in languaging in the classroom when the experience is being delivered through an interpreter or communication support worker. This can be the case for any learning situation, including group/pair work or from-the-front teaching, as well as in question-and-answer sequences or whole-class problem-solving. The visual demands of watching an interpreter while also attending to other visual stimuli, such as whiteboards, practical experiments, or textbooks, impose conflicting agendas (Christensen, 2010). Although educational interpreters generally fulfil a more comprehensive learning support role in terms of clarification, explanation, and tutoring (Antia & Kreimayer, 2001), the presence of an interpreter in the classroom does not automatically solve all the learning challenges for deaf students (Marschark, Sapere, Convertino, & Seewagen, 2009). In fact, the presence of an interpreter sometimes creates a qualitatively different languaging experience for deaf learners in comparison with their hearing peers. However skilful the language support provided, the presence of an intermediary can still hinder access to the classroom experience and social interaction (Schick, Williams, & Kupermintz, 2006).

Direct interaction with the teacher should be, but is not always, the panacea for these issues because adult discourse is not always helpful in terms of constructing meaning. In a seminal study of teaching and talking with deaf children by Wood, Wood, Griffiths, and Howarth (1986), teacher communication with deaf learners was analyzed in terms of the four categories of power, repair, pace, and linguistic complexity. This study found adults' style of conversation with deaf children to be more authoritative and controlling than facilitative and to exhibit limited complex grammatical features. The controlling discourse was characterized by repair strategies, such as asking for repetitions and asking closed or yes/no questions. These communication behaviors were observed to be used more frequently than were strategies offering open responses (such as phatic comments) that indicate interest and encourage loquacity and engagement.

Languaging in the deaf education classroom has not often been studied in depth, and pedagogical discussions in the literature have tended to concentrate more on mode than on manner of communication. The actual discursive practices of deaf learners and teachers have only more recently come into focus, with increased attention paid to what makes for successful dialogue in the learning context, quality of interaction, and sound teaching practices (Akamatsu, Stewart, & Mayer, 2002; Hermans, Wauters, et al., 2014; Kelman & Branco, 2009).

These issues around deaf children's languaging as a cognitive tool to facilitate learning have centered on dialogue with hearing peers and/or adults at school, and they will be taken forward in the development of a pedagogical framework in Chapters 7 and 8. The development of such a framework needs to take account of how languaging is enacted through the internal, as well as the social, dialogue that is taking place to mediate learning. This has been explored to some extent in studies of deaf students' awareness of their own comprehension and monitoring of their own learning. This research suggests that deaf learners are generally less accurate in their metacognitive judgments than are hearing learners, particularly concerning their self-monitoring of comprehension in literacy activities (Borgna, Convertino, Marschark, Morrison, & Rizzolo, 2011). In particular, students tend to misjudge their own comprehension, overestimate what they have understood, and underestimate what they should understand (Knoors & Marschark, 2014; Marschark, Sapere, Convertino, Seewagen, & Maltzen, 2004). This suggests that internal dialogue is not as helpful to deaf student's learning as it could be. The development of a pedagogical framework needs to explore ways to enhance deaf learners' internal languaging so that it better supports their learning.

LANGUAGING IN DEAF EDUCATION

In deaf education at an institutional level, teachers, researchers, managers, and policy-makers are always trying to share and make meaning through dialogue. As with any other area of language and education, there is an ongoing dialogue (through language) about language and how to talk about language. Languaging in deaf education thus comprises the discourses and dialectics around deafness, language, and learning.

At one level, languaging in these contexts is manifested in the way that deaf and hearing people create languages and forms of communication to enable shared discourse and meaning-making. A strong example of this is the use of International Sign that has been invented for the purpose of meaning-making across languages and cultures (Allsop, Woll, & Brauti, 1994). In addition, languaging that involves blending features of sign and spoken language enables mutual dialogue between and among deaf and hearing people and allows them to share professional interests, expertise, and concerns.

Languaging in the discourses around deafness and education sometimes serves as a means of positioning and can be quite political at an institutional level. This type of languaging in the field of deaf education and studies is evident in the use of various esoteric terms or labels that denote constructs only applicable to this field and that communicate a particular stance or perspective. The distinction made between "deaf" and "Deaf," for example, has been an important means of signaling membership, affiliation, and a sociocultural position. Other terms that have come into the literature, such as "deafhood," (Ladd, 2003) "deafgain," (Bauman & Murray, 2009) and "deaf space" (Valentine & Skelton, 2008) are examples of languaging as a tool to mediate understandings of deafness and develop new shared constructs of deaf culture.

The languaging that has grown up around policy and practice has also given rise to specific terminologies as policy-makers and researchers have sought to deconstruct and reconstruct language policy and approach. Terms such as "sign bilingual," "total communication," and "auditory-oral" have all been developed through languaging in efforts to negotiate and share meaning and communicate stance and perspective.

Discourse practices in deaf education, although harder to pin down than terminology, also construct meanings and ways of thinking about deafness, language, and learning, and they convey position and stance. Polemics are frequently constructed through languaging in this field, and positioning is often imposed through these discourse practices. Sometimes this type of languaging is less than helpful and stifles critical thinking. For example, the sociocultural view of deafness is often presented as oppositional to a medical perspective. This can lead to monolithic models of identity, culture, and affiliation that may not be sufficiently nuanced to express the overlap of the sensory and linguistic characteristics of deafness (Woll & Adam, 2012).

In terms of language pedagogies, sign language and spoken language have often been positioned as adversary. Debates about "sign versus speech" and sign bilingual versus auditory-oral approaches have assumed these two approaches to be mutually exclusive. These polemics are not authentic, neither do they reflect the day-to-day language and cultural practices, behaviors, or affiliations of deaf children. The growth of bilingual education for deaf children has evoked languaging about educational policy, research, and practice that has been particularly emotively charged. The emphasis in the discourse on the judgment of bilingual education, as though being "weighed in the balance" has skewed the discourse. Descriptions of bilingual education as an "experiment" rather than a response to deaf children's language experience and potential have been particularly influential (Knoors, Tang, & Marschark, 2014). The methods debate has been unfortunately counterproductive and wasteful of discussion time and space in the literature. However, understanding such institutional languaging is important, even though it needs to be approached judiciously. Noticing it is enough to help professionals to be critically aware of the context of deaf children's learning and to navigate these discourses in developing an appropriate pedagogical framework.

LANGUAGING AND PEDAGOGY

In this chapter, languaging is defined as a cognitive and cultural tool that combines what we bring to language acts in terms of individual biology and biography with our enactment of self in the world. It is proposed that this is a helpful construct in terms of developing understandings of deaf children's learning and of providing ways of exploring perspectives in deaf education and studies. This perspective opens up the hitherto boundaried discussion of language use and policy in deaf education and affords opportunities to "re-image language as language practices" (García, 2009, p. 40).

The theoretical perspective of languaging provides a framework for exploring pedagogy in deaf education that centers on what children do with language, how they negotiate and construct meaning, and the dialogic nature of deaf children's learning experiences. In the following chapter, the concept of languaging is extended to encompass "translanguaging." The introduction of this term affords a more close-up focus on the languaging of deaf children across languages and modalities and the dynamic ways in which learners use sign and spoken/written languages to make meaning.

5 Translanguaging

The establishment of ways in which the concept of languaging can be applied to deaf children's learning provides the foundation for exploring the relevance of translanguaging theory to this context. To achieve this, it is important to understand the provenance of translanguaging theory and what this means in terms of bilingual children's language practices in the home and school contexts. In this chapter, it is argued that the concept of translanguaging provides a useful and relevant framework for describing and analyzing deaf children's use of sign, spoken, and written languages that reflects their dynamic and flexible use for meaning-making. This is explored using examples of translanguaging from the context of deaf education. It is suggested that this perspective offers rich insights into the diversity of deaf children's language experience that enhance current approaches to the description and assessment of deaf children's language repertoires and provides directions for pedagogy.

FROM LANGUAGING TO TRANSLANGUAGING

In the previous chapter, the concept of languaging was introduced as a way of conceptualizing ways in which deaf children use language, through shared or internal dialogue, to mediate new concepts; make meaning in the learning context; and establish and signal shared affiliations and positions. The use of the term "languaging" establishes a focus on "what is done" with language and marks a step away from the treatment of separate and autonomous languages and toward a focus on the dynamic language practices of individuals that adapt for and re-emerge through meaning-making.

The term "languaging" is considered sufficient by some authors to capture diverse meaning-making within and across languages (Makoni & Pennycook, 2006). Others have taken this further to argue that the term "translanguaging" is more suggestive of the layered language practices of multilingual speakers (Garcia & Li Wei, 2014). The concept of languaging as meaning-making develops in complexity when prefixed by "trans," which signals language fluidity, exchange, and interaction. These layers of complexity are very much present in the context of deaf learners who are exposed to and use sign, written, and spoken languages, as well as different ways of switching between and blending sign and spoken languages. The term "translanguaging" captures and analyzes the ways in which sign and spoken/written modalities and systems are bought into play in different learning and social contexts.

TRANSLANGUAGING THEORY

Translanguaging theory builds on the concept of languaging as focusing on achieving or doing something with language and the active and purposeful use of language for learning. From this theoretical perspective, language is transformed from a noun to a verb, stressing process and action and the practices of the language user. Translanguaging shares with languaging a focus on the discourse practices of people and the ways in which they use their languages within a social context. However, the "trans" prefix emphasizes the communicative practices within and across language, such as code switching and code blending, that are a normal part of making meaning in multilingual communities (Garcia & Sylvan, 2011).

The term "translanguaging" originally came into being as a way to describe a pedagogical approach to the use of two languages alongside one another in the classroom. The ideological roots of this term are located in the shift to a more positive view of bilingualism and bilingual language use in education and an emancipatory approach to using two languages together in the teaching and learning context. Lewis, Jones, and Baker (2012, p. 3) describe this as a move away from "solitudes" toward "synergies." This theoretical shift changes the treatment of language as an outcome of bilingual education to part of the process of bilingual education, where the use of two (or more) languages interact for thinking, doing, engaging, and learning:

> Translanguaging is the process of making meaning, shaping experiences, gaining understanding and knowledge through the use of two languages. (Baker, 2011, p. 288)

Although originally used to conceptualize bilingual pedagogy, the concept of translanguaging recognizes that bilingual children flexibly use all of their language resources to maximize their communication and understanding. It can be argued that bilingual and multilingual children translanguage all the time to learn through language and to learn language, as well as to act socially. The use of language mixing and particularly code switching and translation is thus accepted as a warranted and essential aspect of bilingual pedagogy in the wider field of (spoken language) bilingual education.

Since its original use in the Welsh bilingual context, the term "translanguaging" has been widely adopted in the bilingual literature and expanded to include a focus on the bilingual practices of children as well as teachers. García (2009) describes translanguaging as a strategy that bilinguals use in their everyday communication to make and share meaning; shape, mediate, and learn from experience; and engage socially with the world. These strategies include language mixing and, in the context of deaf children, the alternate and simultaneous use of sign and spoken language. These layered language practices are an expected and natural aspect of dynamic bilingual language use and, as such, a feature of the linguistic complexity of home and school experience.

Creese and Blackledge (2010) illustrate translanguaging in practice in different multilingual educational contexts in the United Kingdom. In one example, they describe a teacher's communication with parents about the school timetable. The teacher alternates and integrates her use of both languages (Gujarati and English) to engage and include all the parents (p. 108). In the same school context, the children are observed to use both languages to talk about a learning activity and then to preference English for playful off-task chatter. Using these and other examples, they illustrate how the alternate and integrated use of two languages provides one complete message as the "boundaries between language's become permeable" (2010, p. 112).

Other reported examples of translanguaging in language classrooms suggest that students' use of their first language (L1) to talk about second language (L2) text not only helps understanding but also speeds up the pace of the activity and sharpens their focus on vocabulary and grammar issues (Swain & Lapkin, 2000). The benefits of translanguaging are often reported as multifold. The use of L1 to plan a joint writing activity in L2, for example, can facilitate the management of the task and the potential for detailed explanation and contributions, as well as the development of shared understanding of new vocabulary and grammar. Even with young, nursery-aged children (5–6 years), translanguaging enables them to share and grow their language knowledge as well as to interact socially. García and Li Wei (2014) give an example of young children translanguaging between English and Spanish. One child, not knowing the English word for "raining" but wanting to share something with his English-speaking classmates, improvises with the language that he does have and says that it is "washing." One of his bilingual friends asks him in Spanish if he meant "raining" and provides the English translation for him. This example is a poignant illustration of the extent to which, without direction, children can use their language resources flexibly to create and share meaning in their learning environment. Although translanguaging can be orchestrated for pedagogical purposes, it also occurs naturally in communication where there is a drive to engage and build understanding with others.

Li Wei (2011) suggests that there is more to translanguaging than these practices in which bilingual and multilingual speakers are routinely engaged. He argues that translanguaging requires decision-making and choosing and thus represents a critical and creative use of an individual's language skills repertoire. This concept is expanded in the work of Hornberger and Link (2012) who talk in terms of "discourse practices" to encompass knowledge of how to use one's languages, as well as knowledge of the languages themselves. This requires not only knowing how one's languages interact but also understanding how and when to deploy this interaction. This proposed cognitive aspect of translanguaging brings a multicompetency perspective to the study of bilingual language use that is fully explored in the following chapters. At this point, it suffices to recognize the creativity and criticality involved in the translanguaging practices of bilingual and multilingual children (Li Wei, 2011, p. 371).

Taking translanguaging theory into deaf education provides a lens through which to consider deaf children's language diversity and plurality in terms of what they are able to do with their languages, as well as what language(s) they know. This is a shift toward seeing language repertoire as a combined resource of language knowledge and abilities. Such a perspective provides a framework for analyzing the full repertoire of language skills that deaf children bring to the learning context and the different ways in which these skills are deployed.

DEAF CHILDREN'S TRANSLANGUAGING

Translanguaging theory provides a useful lens through which to explore the ways in which "deaf children organise and deploy their separate but interconnected language systems" (Plaza-Pust, 2014, p. 45). Such an exploration involves consideration of the movement across the modalities of sign, speech, and text that are a part of many deaf children's language experience. Some features of translanguaging are common across bimodal and unimodal bilingualism. However, the additional modality of a visual-spatial language within this interplay between languages, the increased emphasis on written language as more accessible than the spoken form and the augmented use of other multimodal resources-bring a different dynamic to translanguaging theory. The commonalities and particularities between bimodal and unimodal translanguaging are explored next.

Translanguaging and Code Switching

Translanguaging can occur in the bimodal bilingual context in the much the same way as the unimodal bilingual context in terms of the alternate use of two or more languages. One example of this can be seen in *code switching*. Translanguaging, as the deployment of a speaker's full linguistic repertoire, does not simply equate to code switching (Otheguy, García, & Reid, 2015). However, code switching is one of the behaviors within the repertoire that can occur among and between sign and spoken languages. An individual may stop speaking and start signing (or vice versa) for reasons of context, audience, or activity, just as in the case for two spoken languages. The reasons for code switching may be multifold. There are often social and cultural reasons, such as the need to accommodate deaf or hearing communication partners. In some contexts, a particular language choice may be an expression of identity or affiliation with a culture, community, or peer group. There may be pragmatic reasons as well, linked to language abilities. Code switching often enables learners to express something in one language that they do not have the skills or vocabulary for in the other. Children with cochlear implants (CIs), for example, have been observed to use sign language to talk about concepts and ideas that they are not yet able to express in spoken language (Rinaldi, Caselli, Onofrio, & Volterra, 2014; Walker & Tomblin, 2014). For deaf children, code switching is likely to be more constrained than for hearing bilinguals because of the impact of deafness and early language experience on the potential for sign and spoken language fluency. However, it is still a natural part of language behavior for bilingual and multilingual deaf children, whatever their language ability; as such, it must be considered an integral part of their language repertoire (De Quadros, Lillo-Martin, & Chen Pichler, 2016; Kusters, 2011).

Translanguaging and Code Blending

Translanguaging also occurs in the bimodal bilingual and multilingual contexts when items from a sign and a spoken language are blended and used simultaneously. The phenomena of blending sign and spoken language is usually considered a unique feature of the bimodal bilingual context. However, it has been argued that simultaneous code blending is also evident in utterances where aspects of two spoken languages are combined; for example, in the use of an idiom from one language glossed in another (Tracy, 2000).

In the bimodal bilingual context, the type of code blending may be, on the one hand, a natural result of contact between deaf and hearing people. This has been well-documented in sociolinguistic research (e.g., Lucas & Valli, 1992). A different version of code blending occurs when sign and spoken languages are combined intentionally for pedagogical purposes.

In the UK context, Sign-Supported English (SSE) is the catchall term to refer to both of these types of code blending, but there is an important distinction to be made between them in terms of context and audience. SSE that occurs as the natural result of contact between deaf and hearing interlocutors involves a variety of signing with substantial mixing and blending of English, such as the mouthing or fingerspelling of English words. Deaf and hearing children and adult use this type of code blending spontaneously, usually to ensure that both deaf and hearing parties can participate (Sutton-Spence & Woll, 1999). In an educational context, SSE is usually used to support the comprehension of spoken English and, in this case, involves the simultaneous production of grammatically correct spoken English and signs (usually meaning-carrying signs) borrowed from British Sign Language (BSL). In this context, the use of SSE tends to be spoken-language driven and the objective is to maintain the integrity of the spoken message. Whether its use is pedagogically driven or the result of language contact, the use of SSE serves to open up the communication for a mixed deaf/hearing audience and as such provides a rich example of translanguaging in this field.

SSE is unusual in being both a natural and contrived form of translanguaging (depending on the context and the communication partners). This sets it apart from other invented approaches to providing visual support for spoken English. Other more systematically codified language systems have been developed to provide visual support for spoken English. There are a number of international varieties, but all of them have in common the use of the main spoken language of the community accompanied by signs borrowed from the sign language of that community along with invented signs for certain grammatical features of the spoken language. In the UK context, for example, Signed English (SE) and Signed Exact English (SEE) both include signs borrowed from BSL and made up signs to convey morpho-syntactic aspects of spoken English such as apostrophe "s" or "ing" or "ed." The use of these systems is intended to provide a "through the air" experience of spoken English and support literacy development (Gaustad & Kelly, 2004; Mayer, 2007; Mayer & Akamatsu, 2000; Nielsen, Luetke, & Stryker, 2011).

Translanguaging Contexts

Translanguaging in the bimodal bilingual context can thus occur for different reasons and in different contexts. It may be a natural part of communication between deaf and hearing people and/or have a very specific pedagogical goal. It may involve the alternate use of sign and spoken and/or written language, the blended use of sign and spoken language, or the alternate use of sign and spoken and/or written language and a code-blend. In all of these cases, the emphasis is on the dynamic ways in which languages can be used together in a new form of utterance to make meaning. Translanguaging is not a shuttling between languages but instead conveys the creative ways in which "we are" with our languages in the world. Translanguaging is thus a natural and integral aspect of a bimodal bilingual language repertoire that can facilitate both learning and teaching in a number of different ways.

Deaf children's translanguaging enables them to contribute to learning activities by drawing on the language repertoire available to them. It is also in itself facilitative of language learning. For example, translanguaging allows deaf leaners to engage in dialogue in the learning context, even if they are not able to respond in the language that the teacher or peer has used. A child may understand a question in spoken English but be able to respond more fully in BSL or SSE, or through writing. The ability to draw on all of the skills within one's linguistic repertoire can potentially facilitate a greater and more complex contribution to dialogue in the classroom. Translanguaging thus affords opportunities to express new meanings not otherwise available in one language. This potential is evident when, for example, a deaf child uses a sign in the place of a spoken word that he or she does not know or has not yet learned, or fingerspells a word for which he or she does not know the sign.

These are particular examples of how switching between two languages can facilitate communication and comprehension. Blending features of sign and spoken language by using them together lends fluidity to this type of mixing as signs and spoken words are constantly interchanged and/or used together. The point is that translanguaging frees the learner to respond in the way that he or she can to sign or spoken language input.

Rinaldi observed deaf children to do just this in their separate and blended use of sign and spoken language to respond to test items regardless of the language of the assessment (Rinaldi & Caselli, 2009; Rinaldi et al., 2014). Klatter-Folmer et al. (2006) also found that the use of mixed sign and spoken language enabled deaf children to communicate with greater linguistic complexity than was available to them in either one of their languages. In this Dutch study of six deaf children's language development over three years, the children's bimodal bilingual competencies increased over time and the children's sign and spoken language skills continued to grow in the presence of the other. The children were reported to flexibly use and develop their languages according to context and audience. They did not limit their language use according to the hearing status of the adult, except with respect to the use of speech with the deaf native signer. Neither of these authors use the term "translanguaging," but both describe a critical and creative use of language repertoire and language competencies that traverse skills in either language. In both cases, and as with other bilinguals, deaf children communicate using all the means available to them. This does not remove the imperative to develop high levels of skills in sign and spoken languages, but encourages recognition of the potential of translanguaging to increase engagement in and enhance learning.

As well as enabling individuals to flexibly use and develop their language skills, translanguaging also facilitates dialogue around learning in mixed language environments. An example of this is given in Krausneker's (2008) description of a bimodal bilingual classroom in Vienna where deaf and hearing children with various cultural and linguistic backgrounds are learning together. Within this context, deaf children are taught Austrian Sign Language (OGS) as an L1 and German as the L2 using Sign-Supported German (LBG). Krausneker reports that the children are able to make accurate language choices according to their communication partner and differentiate clearly between languages and modalities for different learning activities. Reading aloud is done in LBG but OGS is used for the planning stage of writing, discussion, and translation. Krausneker also remarks on the children's language awareness and communicative sensitivity, describing the way in which they are able to correct one another's language mistakes.

Lindahl (2015) reports on pupil and teacher translanguaging in science lessons, where "sign language and Swedish integrate and interact" (p. 136). In this study, Lindahl illustrates how the classroom dialogue and meta-dialogue that is facilitated by translanguaging enables the shared development of scientific knowledge, engagement with scientific reasoning processes, and the negotiation of meaning in scientific discourse. She gives examples of how Swedish Sign Language, Signed Swedish (SSS), written Swedish, and fingerspelling are combined by the teacher and the pupils to enable fluid dialogue in the science classroom. She describes the powerful teaching and learning potential generated by the "spontaneous, dynamic and seamless language shifting, as well as cross-linguistic dialogue" (p. 137).

These examples illustrate the complex translanguaging of which deaf learners are capable as they move between and blend two dissimilar languages and forms of communication. A still more remarkable example concerns Chinese deaf learners who have to mediate three dissimilar languages as they learn spoken Cantonese, written Chinese (based on Mandarin), and Hong Kong Sign Language (Tang, Lam, & Yiu, 2014). This study reports on the language abilities (in three languages) of 20 deaf Chinese students in a mainstream program. The grammatical abilities of the children in each language were shown to be highly correlated. Furthermore, the length of time in the co-enrolment environment seemed to strengthen the relationships among the languages. The authors suggest that the transfer of skills between the languages can explain this finding. It is difficult to be certain of this, but it is nonetheless evidence of deaf children's potential to translanguage among three different language systems without detriment to the development of skills in any one language. As such, this is an example of exceptional translanguaging.

The translanguaging practices of bilingual and multilingual deaf and hearing children are dynamic: the way in which languages are used together will change over time according to context, preference, and abilities (García & Li Wei, 2014). For deaf children, the nature of deafness itself and how this is or is not mediated by hearing technologies presents particular and significant influencing factors. Specifically, the extent to which deaf children mix and blend sign and spoken language is likely to change over time according to their access and response to audiological intervention. The increased exposure to spoken language afforded by CIs, for example, will enhance children's language repertoire in terms of listening and speaking. The improved audiological experience, access to environmental sound, and enhanced potential for speech perception and production will naturally change individual translanguaging practices. This is evident in research that has demonstrated how children with CIs gravitate toward using more spoken English than sign language as they become more able to make use of the auditory input that the CI provides (Watson, Archbold, & Nikolopoulos, 2006). This is often a gradual—and certainly not an all or nothing—shift as many children continue to use sign language for particular social or learning situations (Wheeler, Archbold, Hardie, & Watson, 2009). Translanguaging continues, but the balance between the two languages changes as children continually adapt and deploy their language resources flexibly.

The question of language dominance and how to assess this is often debated in this context (Grosjean, 2001; Klatter-Folmer et al., 2006). However, language dominance is very difficult to define and, as a concept, can be construed in different ways (Dunn & Fox Tree, 2009). Overall language dominance may be evident as children illustrate a general preference for one language or the other in most communicative contexts. However, language dominance may also shift from moment to moment and be contingent on context, audience, and ability (Lillo-Martin, De Quadros, Pichler, & Fieldsteel, 2014). English, for example, may be the dominant language that a child uses to engage in a curriculum activity, but BSL may be the language used with a particular deaf communication partner. Contrariwise, English may be the medium for reading a book with an adult, but BSL may be the preferred means of talking about the events and characters in the story. In some contexts, such as the school playground or the family home environment, the dominant means of communication may well be the blended use of BSL and spoken English. Children may be translanguaging without a strong base in either one of their sign and spoken languages. Concepts of dominant and first or second language are therefore problematic. It is more useful to talk about repertoire and competency in terms of different communicative contexts. This will be explored in full in Chapter 6. In the case studies gathered as part of the Leeds University diversity study, parents and children talked in terms of situated language use, emphasizing communicative contexts and audience. Three of the children in this project spoke to the researchers about this (Swanwick et al., 2016):

I sign to my dad who is deaf, he is trying to learn names he can now say (says her name). My mum uses English and Punjabi both. I am learning Urdu from my Auntie and I can speak some now. When I talk to my friends on the phone I speak English. I use Facebook and sign with my deaf friends. When visits come some speak English and some Punjabi. I learn Arabic at Mosque, it's easy. I talk to my brother, he's hearing. I talk in English, he does not know

Punjabi. When my cousins come we talk in English because they don't really understand Punjabi. (Indira, aged 11)

We use Latvian sign language at home. I know some English; I use it with my sister. My mum understands some English. (Thomas, aged 8)

[We speak] Roma most of the time. Mum and dad sometimes speak to each other in Slovakian. My brother and sister [they are hearing] sometimes speak to mum and dad in Slovakian, I some times speak to my sister in English. I speak to [name of deaf brother] in Roma. I speak to my older brother in Roma. I speak to my younger brother in Roma or English. I sign to deaf friends or sign and speak at the same time. (Anne, aged 13)

Some of the parents in this project also elaborated on language use at home with reference to people and situations. Indira's mother explained that Punjabi and English were used at home, and homesign was used among the family to communicate with the father, who is deaf. Tomass' mother said that Latvian sign language was predominantly used in the home and the local community, where she has Latvian friends who are also deaf. She explained that Tomass' sister used some English with him and that she was herself learning English and BSL and sometimes used SSE. Anna's mother said that Romani, Slovakian, BSL, and English were used home but that most communication among the family was in Romani. BSL was sometimes used with Anna's younger deaf brother. Outside the home, the parents said that they used Slovakian for medical or school appointments because of the difficulties of interpretations from Romani.

Deaf children and their parents are clearly flexible in their language use and choices, and this changes over time. This is apparent in all families with different language mixes, preferences, and experience of deafness (A. Baker & Van Den Bogaerde, 2008; A. Baker, Van Den Bogaerde, & Woll, 2005; Levesque, Brown, & Wigglesworth, 2014). These examples underline the value of focusing what is being done with the language resources available and the importance of recognizing translanguaging in context and the meaning-making that this facilitates.

TRANSLANGUAGING AND LITERACY

This exploration of sign and spoken language translanguaging has thus far concentrated on face-to-face communication among deaf and hearing children and adults. This has brought to light a new dimension of trans-languaging in terms of the blended (simultaneous) use of sign and spoken language that is unique to the bimodal bilingual context. The additional modality involved in sign and spoken language translanguaging extends the use of this term beyond current discussions in the unimodal bilingual literature. Extending this discussion to include bimodal bilingual literacy adds a further dimension.

Translanguaging around literacy events in the unimodal bilingual context usually involves reading or writing in one language and discussion in another or discussion in one language and writing in another. In some cases, two languages may be used to talk about a text in a third language, or texts written in two languages may be discussed in a third language (Martínez-Roldán & Sayer, 2006). Whatever the language combination, the objective of transnational literacy practices is to help learners use the linguistic resources that they have to comprehend and work with text and, at the same time, valorize the language and cultural affiliations that they bring to the classroom (Hornberger & Link, 2012).

In these activities, translanguaging takes place in a number of ways and is supportive of the literacy learning process. To give an example, students writing in their L2 often bring features of their L1 (such as language structures or turns of phrase) into their writing. This maintains the flow and cohesion of the writing process and facilitates the communication of meaning through text. Translanguaging can also scaffold the writing process. When searching for a synonym of a word in an L2, for example, it sometimes helps to move back into L1 and see what synonyms are available as a way of stimulating the repertoire that one has in L2 (Canagarajah, 2011).

Translanguaging around literacy learning activities also occurs in the bimodal bilingual context, but the language blending that this type of bilingualism affords add a further layer of complexity that is unique to this context. This complexity centers on the interaction between the different modalities of sign, spoken, and written languages that occur within a literacy activity and the potential constraints that deaf children experience in terms of access to the spoken form of the written language that do not normally pertain for hearing bilingual learners. These issues do not preclude the relevance of translanguaging theory to the bimodal bilingual context; rather, they explain and shape translanguaging behaviors.

Translanguaging in any biliteracy context entails dialogue about text (reading) or as part of the process of producing text (writing) where two or more languages are in play (Hornberger & Link, 2012). Dialogue as the mediator for literacy learning may occur in the language of the text, or another language, or involve both languages. Dynamic translanguaging may therefore be happening in different ways across spoken and written languages. For bimodal bilingual deaf children, dialogue around reading and writing activities may take place in spoken or sign language and is very likely to involve the alternate and blended use of both languages. Translanguaging in the bimodal bilingual context can thus be conceptualized as a number of different types of language interaction.

Sign Language and Written Language

Translanguaging takes place when sign language is the main medium for literacy instruction. In this context, attention is alternated between sign and written language. Written language is the objective in terms of a reading or writing outcome, and sign language is the language of the dialogue and interaction in the classroom around the literacy activity. Typical illustrations of this type of translanguaging are seen in contrastive analysis and translation activities where the use of sign language to mediate literacy learning facilitates the construction and negotiation of meaning along with the development of metalinguistic skills and language awareness (Evans, 2004; Kelman & Branco, 2009; Swanwick, 2001, 2002; Wilbur, 2000).

Sign Language, Written Language, and Spoken Language

The role of spoken language in translanguaging will be contingent on individual spoken language skills. When spoken language comes into play in bimodal bilingual literacy activities, translanguaging becomes yet more layered. Spoken language can be part of bimodal bilingual literacy as part of the dialogue around the reading or writing activity. This may be for reading aloud, providing a spoken model of the written form, or as a means of directly linking written words and phrases to their spoken equivalent. In these activities, the use of sign and speech may be alternated (everything is repeated in both languages), used in parallel (with simultaneous interpretation), or combined through the use of fingerpselling or one of the blended forms of communication, such as SSE or SSS.

There are examples of all of these approaches in the literature, and ideas are changing. The sequential and parallel approaches that aim to keep sign, spoken, and written language separate, as proposed in the model by R. E. Johnson et al. (1989), are less frequently reported. This perhaps reflects a growing critique of the "one language at a time" approach, recognition of the increasingly diversity and fluidity of deaf children language repertoires, and the language opportunities and constraints of teaching and learning within mainstream settings. The most prevalent form of translanguaging, where spoken language is part of the learning and teaching dynamic, comprises the various ways in which items from sign and spoken language can be combined (as seen with SSE, SEE, and SE) to provide an visual representation of English (Mayer & Akamatsu 2000; Power, Hyde, & Leigh 2008).

Alongside these invented systems, fingerspelling plays a central part in the translanguaging dynamic because of its hybrid nature as a natural part of the lexicon of sign language and an accessible means of presenting a visual representation of written graphemes (Alvarado, Puente, & Herrera, 2008; Haptonstall-Nykaza & Schick, 2007; Padden, 2006; Roos, 2013). Fingerspelling is a method of spelling out the written version of words using a handshape for each letter. As a feature of sign languages, it is used to spell out names of people and places for which there is no sign or to clarify a new, unknown, or regional sign (Sutton-Spence & Woll, 1999). Because fingerspelling can be used in conjunction with speech-reading and mouthing, its use can provide a phonological bridge between the sounds and spellings of words. This compensates to some extent for the difficulties that deaf children experience with the decoding component of the reading process (Emmorey & Petrich, 2012; Harris & Terlektsi, 2011).

Writing as Translanguaging

These examples illustrate the relevance of translanguaging theory to bimodal bilingualism by demonstrating the interactions among sign, spoken, and written languages in the context of literacy development. Although the focus thus far has been on the dialogic nature of translanguaging in terms of observable classroom interaction, we should remember that dialogue in languaging and translanguaging theory is construed as internal "workings out" as well as face-to-face interaction among peers and adults.

As for hearing bilingual learners, bimodal bilingual deaf children translanguage "internally" as they use their own knowledge of one language to mediate learning in the other. Taking this further, it can be argued that writing *is* translanguaging for bimodal bilingual deaf children. Research suggests that bimodal bilingual deaf children draw on and combine their different linguistic resources to construct written text (Niederberger, 2008). It is argued that the influence or interaction between languages accounts for the lexical and structural features of sign language often evident in deaf children's writing (Koutsoubou, Herman, & Woll, 2006; Menéndez, 2010; Plaza-Pust & Morales-López, 2008a). Another way of conceptualizing this is as translanguaging where knowledge of two languages is pooled to create something new. This creative process may involve blending features of sign and written language at a linguistic or a pragmatic level (Niederberger, 2008; Wilbur, 2000).

Application of translanguaging theory to the bimodal bilingual context places the spotlight on ways in which sign, spoken, and written languages interact in "multiple, complex, and fluid ways" (Hornberger, 1990, p. 213). These interactions have been variously described in the deaf education literature as evidence of "language transfer" or as a "the pooling of resources" and as "language influence" (Holzinger & Fellinger, 2014; Ormel & Geizen, 2014; Plaza-Pust, 2014). Translanguaging theory facilitates a perspective that encompasses these different perspectives to provide a focus on learning and the central role of (external and internal) dialogue in this process. This perspective also accents the agency of the learner in the meaning-making process and the underlying competencies involved in the critical and creative use of his or her language resources in complex and challenging language learning contexts. These cross-language competencies and how we might conceptualize these resources as individual linguistic repertoires will be further discussed in the next chapter.

LANGUAGE AS RESOURCE

Translanguaging provides a perspective on deaf children's plural and diverse use of languages that focuses on those language practices of deaf children that are "readily observable" (García, 2009, p. 44). Placing children's language practices at the center of the discussion encourages a shift away from attention to language policy and ideology and offers new ways of looking at the ways in which deaf children use sign and spoken language for meaning-making in their daily lives. Translanguaging theory encompasses all that we understand about language mixing (switching and blending) and the associated concepts of interference, borrowing, and transfer influence and reconceptualize these behaviors as "multiple discursive practices that constitute languaging" (García, 2009, p. 40). This perspective reconciles the hitherto problematic positioning of sign and spoken language as either L1 or L2 and opens up spaces for more fluid and plural "practices and voices" in deaf education (Hornberger, 2014, p. 265).

This new way of looking has the potential to transform pedagogy in deaf education. Awareness of deaf children's translanguaging practices will help practitioners to understand fully the language resources that children bring to the learning context and to harness these to enhance learning. This understanding entails the ability to recognize the full range of linguistic and communicative language resources that deaf children "possess and deploy" (Blommaert, 2010, p. 102). Knowledge of individual skills in separate languages provides one piece of this picture, but to really know individual potential entails an understanding of individual repertoire. What this means in terms of deaf children's languages, modalities, and practices is explored in the next chapter.

6 Multicompetency and Repertoire

The overview of languaging and translanguaging theory in Chapters 4 and 5 proposes different ways of looking at deaf children's language skills and abilities in the learning context. The focus on language in use accents the critical and creative ways in which deaf children use their diverse language resources to make meaning and reveals language knowledge, awareness, and skills that traverse languages. In this chapter, the nature of these abilities is further explored in terms of multicompetency and repertoire. These concepts facilitate a perspective on the totality of an individual's linguistic knowledge and a holistic view of individual language resources.

DEFINITIONS OF MULTICOMPETENCY

The application of theories of languaging and translanguaging to bimodal bilingual deaf children brings to light ways in which they deploy their diverse language resources to engage with others and make meaning. Analysis of children's languaging and translanguaging behaviors encourages new understandings of bimodal bilingualism and learning that look beyond the use and development of two separate language systems to ways in which bilinguals critically and creatively deploy the language skills that they have (Bialystok, 2007, 2009*b*). This ability includes language knowledge, awareness, processing, and behaviors that do not pertain to one particular language. This multiplicity of abilities can be better described as *multicompetency*.

Multicompetency is a term originally introduced by Cook (1991) to describe the "compound state of a mind with two grammars" (p. 112). The development of this concept signified an important step change from a view of languages as separate entities in the mind to the idea of one merged language system that comprises everything that a person knows about all of their languages. The concept of multicompetency, as expanded by Cook (1992, 2008), refers to the skilful ability to manipulate the communicative context and make decisions about language use based on knowledge of the languages and cultures in play.

Much of the psycholinguistic research prior to this was based on the notion of languages as separate entities. Concepts of "interference," "transfer," and "interlanguage" were predicated on the assumption that languages exist separately in the mind (see, e.g., Weinreich, 1953). As research into bilingualism has evolved, this construct has been critiqued as a monolingual and fractional view of bilingualism that does not recognize the "equal but different communicative competences of bilingual individuals" (Grosjean, 1996, p. 22). A more holistic view of bilingualism proposes individual bilingual ability to be an integrated whole that cannot easily be deconstructed into separate parts. This school of thought posits that the bilingual person is not the sum of two complete or incomplete monolinguals; rather, he or she has a unique and specific linguistic configuration. The coexistence and constant interaction of two or more languages produces a different but complete language system (Grosjean, 2008, p. 13).

The concept of multicompetency offers a view that what a person knows and understands about language is more than the sum of their two (or more) languages (Cook & Li Wei, 2016). The current use of the term "multicompetence" thus implies the existence of a merged language system. This construct includes the extended cognitive and social competences that bilingual people have by dint of learning, knowing, and using two or more languages in different contexts. In the cognitive domain, multicompetency has been explored in terms of metalinguistic awareness (Bialystok & Barac, 2012), executive function (Adesope, Lavin, Thompson, & Ungerleider, 2010), working memory (Marian & Schroeder, 2012), and divergent thinking and creativity (Kharkhurin, 2008). Social competences include increased communicative confidence, adaptivity or flexibility, emotional stability, and empathy (Dewaele, Petrides, & Furnham, 2008; Li Wei & Dewaele, 2012). This is not an exhaustive list but illustrates the extent to which multicompetency can be identified and described across cognitive and social domains.

The concept of multicompetency encompasses process-orientated and usage-orientated perspectives on language (Herdina & Jessner, 2002). Language is practice and activity (usage) as well as a cognitive tool (process) for learning (Canagarajah, 2007). The concept of translanguaging, as one example of multicompetency, integrates notions of process and usage by bringing attention to what we do and how we communicate and act in the world using the linguistic resources at our disposal (Swain & Deters, 2007). To use one's available language resources meaningfully involves both "knowing and doing" (García & Li Wei, 2014, p. 11). This perspective emphasizes the sociocultural contexts of language use and the importance of cultural as well as linguistic knowledge in bilingual communicative acts (Li Wei, 2011). In order to deploy adequately one's bilingual language resources in a given situation, some knowledge and understanding of the cultural norms and conventions of the communicative context are needed. This context sensitivity, it is argued, should be included within a usage-oriented framework of multicompetence (Alptekin, 2010). Multicompetency is thus the cognitive and social wherewithal that underpins this "knowing and doing." The dynamic language practices of individuals, such as translanguaging, are observable manifestations of multicompetency (Hall, Cheng, & Carlson, 2006).

MULTICOMPETENCY AND REPERTOIRE

The term "language resources" has thus far been used in this text to refer to knowledge, skills, and behaviors within and across languages that, in their totality, constitute multicompetency. The use of the term "repertoire" is proposed here as more in keeping with the concept of multicompetency as one complete language system. Repertoire suggests a singular entity that consists of plural skills. A language repertoire comprises a set of integrated skills across languages rather than separate skills embedded within one system or separately and underlying a number of systems.

Early discussions of repertoire in the 1960s were influenced by the work of Gumperz (1964), who used this term to explain the aggregated verbal strategies of speech communities used to interact and make meaning (Hymes & Gumperz, 1986). Repertoire, although considered to constitute different languages and forms of communication, is conceptualized as one "behavioral whole" (Gumperz, 1964, p. 140). Concepts of multicompetency and repertoire overlap: it is not possible to delineate categorically between what one knows about language and how one uses language. Repertoire, as an assemblage of language skills, includes the ability to make "critical and creative" choices about language use (García & Li Wei, 2014, p. 10). These choices, which are contingent on abilities, require the social and cognitive understandings and processes associated with multicompetence.

The concept of repertoire in the 21st century has evolved to keep pace with the expanding linguistic diversity and language practices of communities where the interaction across and between social groupings and cultures gives rise to increasingly dynamic and mobile language practices (Vertovec, 2007). The increasing superdiverse nature of societies where language and cultural networks intermingle to form new networks, the global mobility of languages, and the diversity of language experiences and resources of individuals have expanded the concept of repertoire from communities to individuals (Blommaert & Backus, 2012). It is within this context that the concept of translanguaging as a way of galvanizing individual communicative resources and as evidence of multicompetency has gained currency. Repertoire is the multidimensional constellation of linguist resources, values, and practices that are the preserve of the language user. These resources are "attached to an individual life and a life experience" (Blommaert, 2008, p. 16) and all of the "constructs and narratives therein" (Blackledge & Creese, 2010, p. 224). Translanguaging draws on this repertoire to enable the generation of new communicative acts (Li Wei, 2011).

The concept of repertoire provides a framework to explore linguistic practices in a way that does not "imagine languages as clear cut entities" (Busch, 2012, p. 507). Studying linguistic repertoire is therefore complex because it involves understanding the whole ecology of a communicative context and understanding "the complexes of resources people actually posses and deploy" (Blommaert, 2010, p. 102). This necessarily includes a focus on the observable ways in which individuals use language in different spheres of life.

Individual repertoire is not marked by geographical, community, or cultural boundaries but is the result of diverse language experience and learning that can range from formal (classroom) learning to the informal ways in which we "brush with" languages in our everyday lives. In the context of deaf children, repertoire thus comprises ways of knowing and using use sign and spoken/written languages that are shaped by personal biographies and that are constantly in flux. A bimodal bilingual repertoire does not imply complete or finished knowledge of a sign and/or spoken language but a changing "patchwork of competencies and skills" (Blommaert & Backus, 2012, p. 1). Deaf children's language repertoires move with their lives, for example, as they learn to read and write, learn to decipher spoken language through a cochlear implant (CI), learn how to adjust their British Sign Language (BSL) register, recognize a spoken language accent, develop speech-reading skills in noisy environment, and learn new slang in the playground or curriculum-specific vocabulary in the classroom.

Repertoire cannot be captured through the discrete description of skills in separate languages. Instead, it involves seeing how resources and knowledge interact and are combined. Busch (2012) describes a study that sought to achieve a description of repertoire with "language portraits." In this study, schoolchildren were asked to paint all their languages on a blank body silhouette using different colors to identify not only different languages but also different varieties of languages that the children themselves identified. The methodology used here serves to illustrate the multidimensional properties of language repertoire and how this might be conceptualized in superdiverse contexts. Gumperz's original ideas about repertoire as a whole is borne out in this research as the portraits and discussion around them illustrate that languages and language varieties are understood in relation to each other and not as separate entities. Furthermore, repertoire in terms of languages practices are attached to life experience, identity, and affiliation. Repertoire is thus both cognitive and emotional and, as such, an intensely individual, fluid, and dynamic expression of different ways of being in the world with others.

A Dynamic System

Because our ways of being in the world change all the time, we perpetually develop new repertoires as we act in different ways and in response to new situations. This is a dynamic process in which repertoire can be conceptualized as a "soft assembled" set of resources, used in different ways for different purposes (Larsen-Freeman & Cameron, 2008). A complex systems perspective recognizes that the language knowledge and resources within our repertoire operate dynamically as one interconnected systems. This is a fluid and transformative process. 'Learners actively transform their linguistic worlds; they do not just conform to them' (2008, p. 159). Making meaning involves the constant adaptation of linguistic resources according to internal, physical, emotional, and cognitive as well as external, environmental, contextual, and social influences. When we are languaging and/or translanguaging, we are constantly adapting to these influences by soft assembling our language resources and transforming our linguistic repertoire in the process.

Within this definition, repertoire describes the constellation of linguist and cultural resources, values, and practices that deaf children bring to communicative acts (Li Wei, 2011). Repertoire amounts to more than the sum of sign and spoken language varieties that deaf children may draw on. Rather, it refers to the diverse ways in which these linguistic resources are deployed in the service of making meaning and the creation of new utterances through the use of different language varieties, dialect, registers, genres, and modalities (Blommaert, 2010; Busch, 2012).

To engage with this adaptive and dynamic system in the educational context requires an understanding of the social, immediate, and historical contexts within which learners use and develop their languages. This means that we, as educators, need to be aware of learners' histories, orientations, intentions, thoughts, and feelings. Furthermore, we need to be able to notice how learners adapt their language repertoire to fit changing communicative situations.

In the context of deaf education, this involves understanding all the factors that influence language experience and being cognizant of the additional challenges that deafness imposes on the development of language abilities while also recognizing the linguistic and cultural competencies and repertoires that deaf children bring to the learning context.

DEAF CHILDREN'S MULTICOMPETENCY

Working with a view of deaf children as multicompetent implies a shift away from the idea of two separate languages in one mind or of two different, separate sets of competencies. This is a different way of approaching bilingualism and multilingualism in deaf education. Discussions of bimodal bilingualism more usually conceptualize sign and spoken languages as two separate entities and envisage the interaction between them as transfer across two language systems rather than as an integration of competencies within one repertoire (Holzinger & Fellinger, 2014; Mayer & Wells, 1996). This perspective has engendered a view of bimodal bilingualism as theoretically problematic because of the dissimilar nature of the languages involved. The research questions within this paradigm have focused on whether or not transfer between sign and written languages can occur. This has not been a very useful question because it has eclipsed attention to the actual language repertoires of bimodal bilingual deaf children and how children draw on these repertoires to make meaning. The focus on two separate languages has also raised questions of language equivalence, balance, and dominance (Knoors & Marschark, 2012) that, again, detract from seeing the breadth of individual language abilities.

A multicompetency view shifts the focus of attention from the equivalence between an individual's languages to the complete linguistic repertoire of an individual and the dynamic and complex system surrounding his or her language use. This perspective recognizes that a bilingual repertoire is more than the sum of two sets of separate language skills. It also widens the assessment and measuring lens to include attention to the way in which children galvanize and adapt their existing language resources and develop new resources to make meaning. This involves noticing everything in the learner's linguistic repertoire and judging competency in terms of not only the knowledge of, understanding of, and abilities in sign and spoken languages but also in terms of how they operate within and transform their linguistic world. Attention to repertoire and situated use of language involves consideration of the individual and internal influences on language practices as well as the influences of the closer and more distal environments within which language use is played out.

It is difficult to contemplate the language of a child until we know something of the context (Kanto, Huttunen, & Laakso, 2013; Paradis, 2010). Understanding the full ecology of a child's life delivers this rich contextual information and opens up approaches to language assessment, planning, and intervention that are individually matched and contextually relevant. Individually developing skills in sign and spoken language are by no means neglected in this paradigm; rather, they are seen within the holistic concepts of repertoire and multicompetency. To understand the language abilities of an individual involves the scrutiny and assessment of his or her languages as well as the potential of the mixed use of all languages.

Multicompetency in the context of deaf children can be thought of in a number of ways. One aspect of this is children's critical use of sign language, spoken language, and written language. This entails engagement with the mixed and blended use of sign and spoken languages in social and learning contexts, which in turn requires sensitivity to the different cultures in play in different communicative contexts. Multicompetency is evidenced in the way that deaf children translanguage in their face-to-face interactions and in their writing. It is also manifested in children's language and metalinguistic skills and in the communicative sensitivity and cultural awareness they bring to language acts.

Translanguaging as Evidence of Multicompetency

The way in which deaf learners organize their bimodal bilingual knowledge in their writing is a good example of translanguaging as multicompetency. Translanguaging in this context involves the creative use of repertoire to establish or express new meaning where sign, spoken, and written languages are all in play. These behaviors are observed in the research literature on bimodal bilingual deaf children's writing, although not usually described in terms of multicompetency. In a longitudinal study of bimodal bilingual deaf children's learning of written German, Plaza-Pust comments on language mixing in the children's writing (Plaza-Pust & Morales-Lopez, 2008a). In this study, Plaza-Pust observes the way in which bimodal bilingual deaf children construct their written German. Her findings suggest that learners use lexical and structural "borrowings" from German Sign Language (DGS) in an organized and systemic way to enable the expressions of complex meanings not (yet) available to them in their written German repertoire. In particular, there is evidence of the application of DGS word order to their writing and attempts to translate meaning from DGS (expressed spatially) into written German. This so-called "pooling of resources" (2014, p. 42) is evident across the literature on bimodal bilingual deaf children's writing and very much reminiscent of descriptions of translanguaging in unimodal bilingual contexts (Canagarajah, 2011; Velasco & García 2014).

Translanguaging as evidence of multicompetency can also be seen in deaf children's sign-to-written-language translation processes. These translation activities, common in bilingual classrooms, involve the complex process of analyzing and deconstructing a unit of meaning in sign language and reconstructing or mapping this on to a sequentially organized written language system (Evans, 2004; Koutsoubou, Herman, & Woll 2006; Swanwick, Kitchen & Clarke, 2012; Wilbur, 2000). The language competencies required for this translanguaging act amount to more than the children's knowledge of the two separate languages. Such activities involve "tacit knowledge about the equivalency of languages at a deeper level" (Plaza-Pust, 2008a, p. 129). Multicompetency would seem an appropriate term to capture the language knowledge, skills, and experience at work here and in other examples of deaf children's creative use of their language repertoire in the writing process.

Translanguaging in face-to-face interaction has already been discussed in Chapter 5 in terms of the alternate and blended use of features of sign and spoken languages according to context, purpose, and audience. Deaf children's translanguaging in face-to-face interaction is a further illustration of multicompetency and of the galvanizing of repertoire. This is evident, for example, in the ways in which deaf children naturally blend features of sign and spoken languages in their use of Sign-Supported English (SSE) to include deaf and hearing interlocutors (Sutton-Spence & Woll, 1999). This particular type of blending usually involves the use of signs from BSL in English word order with either the use of voice or mouthing of English words. Fingerspelling is also likely to be used more frequently in this context to spell out English names and terms that do not have a sign equivalent or where clarification is needed for a hearing (or nonfluent sign language) audience.

Deaf children also use and respond to the blended use of sign and spoken languages in the educational context. They are able to respond to adult use of SSE in the classroom and other sign systems (Humphries & MacDougall, 2000). They also use these systems themselves to demonstrate their knowledge of the morpho-syntactic features of English with no detriment to their sign or spoken language learning (Mayer & Akamatsu 2000; Power, Hyde, & Leigh, 2008). Children's ability to produce features of sign and spoken language simultaneously, which involves the selection and use of two lexical items at the same time from two different languages, is evidently a crucial part of the bimodal bilingual repertoire. As such, this constitutes an important and visible feature of deaf children's multicompetency. Within their linguistic repertoire, deaf children have the skills to blend features of sign and spoken languages in natural and contrived situations and for different social and academic purposes. Language blending is thus in itself a stable element of the repertoire that allows for the extended and creative use of language that might not otherwise be available in only the sign or spoken form.

Bimodal bilingual deaf children deploy their language repertoire in different ways from moment to moment and in different contexts. By way of example, the case study here shows how Samia, during the course of one school day, draws on and combines her skills of listening, speaking, and signing to participate in different learning contexts. The abilities that she is able to demonstrate in each language can, of course, be assessed individually but the underlying competency that facilitates the deployment of her repertoire of skills needs also to be recognized.

CASE STUDY: SAMIA

Samia has a profound, bilateral, sensorineural hearing loss. She has a unilateral CI and also wears a hearing aid on the left ear. Samia attends a school for the deaf that is co-located within a mainstream secondary school. The school for the deaf has a bimodal bilingual approach providing English and BSL as languages of learning and to access the curriculum. Samia joins her mainstream class for about 50% of the time-tabled week where she uses an FM (radio aid) system to support her access to the spoken language of the classroom and where educational support is provided by a communication support worker. In this context, the curriculum is delivered in spoken English with simultaneous BSL interpretation. Samia switches her attention between the speaker and the signer in class. Samia is able to switch between BSL, spoken English and SSE depending on the context and who she is communicating with.

The conceptualization of translanguaging as multicompetency reverses concepts of language deficit to a more asset-focused view of deaf children's language abilities and behaviors (Antia, 2015). This perspective also recognizes SSE and other manually coded systems as integral to a bimodal bilingual repertoire and as evidence of critical and creative use of language resources. This reframes the mixed use of a sign and a spoken language as an essential part of meaning-making, rather than a compromised means of communication where neither sign or spoken language is fully represented (Knoors & Marschark, 2012). How this can be taken forward in pedagogical terms is discussed in Chapters 7 and 8.

Language Interaction

The way in which deaf children mix and blend their languages and modalities in particular contexts offers tangible examples of translanguaging as multicompetence. Less visible is the interaction in bimodal bilingual language processing that takes place. This developing area of bimodal bilingual research explores the extent to which the use of one language triggers the activation of the other language. There is emerging evidence of sign language activation during visual word recognition (Morford, Wilkinson, Villwock, Piñar, & Kroll, 2011; Ormel et al., 2012). As with unimodal bilinguals, this leads to questions about the cognitive benefits of this activity or "exercise" in the brain (Bialystok, 2009a; Bialystok, Craik, & Luk, 2012). Studies of these benefits in deaf children are only just beginning to emerge. Findings suggest some benefits in terms of a shared and total vocabulary and enhanced cognitive control (Hermans, Ormel & Knoors, 2010; Ormel & Geizen, 2014; Tang, Lam, & Yiu, 2014). The interaction between children's sign and spoken languages, evident on several levels, thus serves not only to develop both languages but also to extend linguistic repertoire, resources, and dynamic individual multicompetency.

Tang et al. (2014) describe this interaction as a "scaffolding" effect (p. 331) in their study of bimodal bilingual deaf children's linguistic competencies in Hong Kong. In this learning context, deaf children are learning spoken Cantonese, written Chinese, and Hong Kong Sign Language (HKSL). Chinese in Hong Kong is based on Mandarin grammar but pronounced in Cantonese. Assessment of the three languages in question revealed a correlation between the developing grammars of each language: the more sustained the input from each language, the stronger the relationship. Although Tang et al. (2014) use these results to revisit the debate about language transfer between dissimilar languages, this could be construed more helpfully as evidence of shared competency across languages. The language repertoire is dynamic; constantly developing new language knowledge in one domain seemingly scaffolds or supports growth in another. As well as providing an interesting illustration of the relationship between repertoire and multicompetence, this study illustrates very well the complex dynamics at work in this exceptional language learning context. The variability of language experience is contingent on multiple factors, some of which are unique to the deaf bimodal bilingual context (level of hearing loss; type of amplification; parental hearing status; age; and duration of exposure to spoken Cantonese, written Chinese, and HKSL). The important question for pedagogy here is whether these competencies are the result of language interaction or a reflection of the rich and supportive multilingual learning environment.

Metalinguistic Awareness

The bimodal bilingual learning and communicative situations that some deaf children experience would seem to require a degree of mental agility that stretches beyond the unimodal bilingual experience. The various experiences of bimodal bilingual language use described earlier and the examples of the diverse and resourceful ways in which deaf children exploit their linguistic repertoire might lead us to expect an underlying analytical orientation to language. This aspect of multicompetency is usually described in the bilingual literature as metalinguistic or language awareness and is argued to be one of the cognitive advantages of being bilingual (C. Baker, 2011; Bialystok, 2009b).

Research into this aspect of bilingualism became established during the 1960s, after the seminal Peal and Lambert (1961) study of bilingual children's mental flexibility and concept formation. The knowledge of two or more languages, it is argued, affords the opportunity to notice language as well as to use it and thus to treat language as an "object of thought" (García, 2009, p. 95). To know two (or more) different ways to describe our world or things in our world presents choices and a critical perspective on language that we may not experience as a monolingual speaker. Vygotsky spoke of this as the ability to see one's language "as a particular system among many" (Vygotsky, 1962, p. 110).

This aspect of multicompetency is actually required of bimodal bilingual deaf children in all aspects of their lives, and particularly in the school context, as they move between sign, spoken, and written language use. If we look at a typical school experience, we can see that alongside the breadth of language exposure and use, sign and spoken languages are also in themselves subjects of study and the focus of comparative analysis and translation activities.

CASE STUDY: JOSH

Josh has a bilateral profound sensorineural hearing loss and wears bilateral hearing aids, which are FM enabled. Josh attends a designated resourced provision center within a large mainstream school. He is educated for some of the time in a small group taught by a Teacher of the Deaf (ToD), and he joins his mainstream class for more than 60% of the time-tabled week where he has a ToD and Teaching Assistant (TA) support. The school has a bilingual approach, and both BSL and English are used throughout the school day. Josh is learning BSL and English, and the curriculum is taught through BSL and the two different languages are used at different times and for different purposes throughout the school day. As part of his language education, Josh is taught about the differences between English and BSL and routinely engages in translation activities and comparative analysis of BSL and written English stories.

The experience that Josh has, in terms of moving between different languages and forms of communication, is not an unusual one for a deaf learner. Bimodal bilingual deaf children are often exposed to different languages and modalities in the classroom and are able to differentiate and respond accordingly. In bilingual classrooms, teachers frequently alternate (Humphries & MacDougall, 2000) and/or blend their own language use in their teaching according to the task, the context, and the language competencies of the teaching group (Andrews & Rusher, 2010; Mayer & Akamatsu, 2000; Power et al., 2008; Swanwick, 2001). Bimodal bilingual deaf children are thus frequently exposed to and expected to respond to a dynamic language situation where sign language, spoken language, sign-supported speech, text, and fingerspelling may be used sequentially or simultaneously (Krausneker, 2008; Tang et al., 2014).

It is therefore not surprising that bimodal bilingual deaf children are able to talk about, compare, and contrast their different languages. Sometimes this type of metatalk forms part of a teaching activity. For example, deaf children are often involved in translation activities, which require substantial metalinguistic skills (Jessner, 2008). This might be done as a straight translation from a story in BSL into written English (Evans, 2004; Swanwick, 2002), through contrastive analysis activities that help children to make connections between sign and written forms of expression, or through a "preview, view, review" teaching sequence that involves preparatory discussion in sign language followed by a writing activity and a review. in sign language (Andrews & Rusher, 2010; DeLana, Gentry, & Andrews, 2007; Rudner et al., 2015). Deaf children also compare and contrast their languages naturally and, when asked, can talk about their experience of sign and spoken and written language use (Gregory, Smith, & Wells, 1997; Sutherland & Young, 2007; Wheeler, Archbold, Gregory, & Skipp, 2007).

The process of writing involves metalinguistic awareness for all children. The organization and control of the written language code requires levels of analysis beyond those normally required for face-to-face interaction (Torrance & Olson, 1991). For bimodal bilingual deaf children, the process of writing brings the spoken, signed, and written forms into an interaction (McQuarrie & Abbott, 2013). The very act of composing written texts can involve the analysis of and translation between sign and written forms of language (Swanwick, Kitchen, & Clarke, 2012). This requires an ability to analyze meanings in one language and judge how they may best be expressed in another (Bialystok, 1991). Interestingly, writing activities that involve translation from sign into written language have been found to have positive effects on deaf children's writing in terms of planning, organization, and text content (Koutsoubou, Herman, & Woll, 2007; van Beijsterveldt & van Hell, 2009).

Whether these metalinguistic abilities can be described as an advantage of being bimodal and bilingual or simply as a part of the bimodal bilingual experience is debatable for deaf children. What is important here is that these skills are recognized as one aspect of bimodal bilingual multicompetency. As such, they need to be fostered in the educational context for the advantages of being bilingual to be realized (Bialystok, 2004).

Communicative Sensitivity

Certain social competencies also govern the deployment of bimodal bilingual repertoire in different communicative contexts. We all use our understanding of people and intention to constantly navigate and monitor language choices, use, and response. Communicative sensitivity as another aspect of multicompetency does not pertain to any one of our individual languages but instead constitutes a global ability to make judgments and choices about language according to the situation and the communication partners involved. These choices will be, to some extent, contingent on the language resources available, but awareness of context and audience is still a guiding factor. This again focuses on the language assets that deaf children bring to the learning context to recognize multicompetency in exceptional circumstances and as potential evidence of the enhanced social cognition that bimodal bilingualism affords (Tomasuolo, Valeri, Di Renzo, Pasqualetti, & Volterra, 2013).

Communicative sensitivity can be recognized in the way in which bimodal bilingual children are able to respond to the language choice of others flexibly, spontaneously, and from an early age. This is evident in the ways in which deaf children switch and blend languages to accommodate mixed deaf and hearing interlocutors (de Quadros, Lillo-Martin, & Chen Pichler, 2014; Lillo-Martin, De Quadros, Pichler, & Fieldsteel, 2014; Plaza-Pust, 2014; Rinaldi, Caselli, Onofrio, & Volterra, 2014). More often than not, this accommodation is done very much "on the fly" because the complexities of the language situation mean that there is rarely a clear delineation between who uses sign or spoken language, or sign-supported speech, at any given time. Exceptionally, for deaf children with deaf parents or siblings, sign language may be used for much of the communication at home. However, for most deaf children, in hearing families there is likely to be a mixture of sign, spoken, and sign-supported speech in use and no clear cut pattern of language use related to specific people (Klatter-Folmer, van Hout, Kolen, & Verhoeven, 2006).

As well as being sensitive to the communication needs or preferences of others, deaf children exercise communicative sensitivity in terms of their own language use because they have to adjust and monitor their use of spoken and sign language according to the constraints on their communication. A noisy listening environment or obscured visual access to the sign language user, the teacher, or an interpreter are examples of some of the obstacles that may need navigating in learning contexts and that will influence how an individual may decide to interact. This self-awareness is an important aspect of multicompetency that demonstrates how adaptive individual repertoires need to be in response to any given communicative situation. Sutherland and Young (2014) capture some pertinent examples of this where, through the shared review of video diaries, children comment on particular instances of language use as well as on how their language use had changed over time.

The case study here further demonstrates this awareness and sensitivity to self as well as others. In this example, Alice adjusts her use of language according to what she needs and with what she is comfortable. This is evidenced by the choices that she makes about her CI use in the learning context as well as at home. What comes through from this are the number of permutations of language exposure and use that a bimodal bilingual deaf children may encounter in one school day.

CASE STUDY: ALICE

Alice has a profound bilateral sensorineural hearing loss and has a CI that she was initially reluctant to wear until she started attending school. Now she wears it consistently during the school day, where she accesses the mainstream curriculum mostly through spoken English. English is the language spoken at home, but Alice's parents and some of her extended family have good BSL skills. Alice's mother will follow her lead in her choice of communication. On weekends, Alice often chooses not to wear her implant in the morning, to have a "quiet time" and use BSL to communicate at home. However, when she is going out, she will put her device on and switch to spoken English or SSE.

Cultural Awareness

A further aspect of multicompetency that is very much linked to communicative sensitivity is cultural awareness. Culture is conceptualized here in the broadest sense, as in the behaviors, beliefs, values, shared experiences, and ways of knowing that an individual shares with others (Bruner, 1990; Grosjean, 2008). The intention here is to recognize the various cultures in play in interactions between deaf and hearing children, not to make a binary delineation between deaf and hearing cultures (or deaf and hearing worlds) or to assume children as "belonging" to one particular cultural group (Ford & Kent, 2013; Ladd, 2002; Padden

& Humphries, 2005). Culture is thus conceptualized not as fixed values, identities, or ideologies pertaining to any one community but rather as a "repertoire of strategies for action" influenced by individual biographies and experience (Kramsch, 2011, p. 313).

In bimodal bilingual children, we have already seen that language use and language identities are constantly in flux. Cultural identity is equally fluid as children shift between identities and affiliations as the situation demands (I. Leigh, Maxwell-McCaw, Bat-Chava, & Christiansen, 2009; McIlroy & Storbeck, 2011). As Monaghan et al. (2003) remind us in their exposition of deaf identifies, there are many ways to be deaf. This is borne out in studies of deaf people with plural identities and cultural affiliations. For example, the work of Atkin et al. (2002) with Asian (mainly Pakistani Muslim) deaf young people found their identifications to be "multiple, complex and contingent" (p. 1757) as they talked about themselves as being "deaf but being other things as well" (p. 1768).

The layering of culture and the elusiveness of a monolithic deaf/hearing stance is evident throughout the literature on deaf children who, moment by moment, may associate with the culture of being a teenager (Punch & Hyde, 2011), being a member of a deaf family (Padden & Humphries, 2005), being part of a school for the deaf community (Anglin-Jaffe, 2013), or part of a mainstream school community (Jarvis, Iantaffi, & Sinka, 2003). This is by no means an exhaustive list. Studies that explore deaf children's own perspectives on this issue, however, are scare. Wheeler et al. (2007) offer a particularly pertinent example in their study. They examined the experience of cochlear implantation for young adolescents. When the young people were asked about their identity, it was clear that they had no fixed conceptions in terms of conventional descriptors. They described flexible communication practices ("With my deaf friends I sign, with the others I talk") and fluid identities ("Some days deaf, some days hearing"; p. 8).

Cultural awareness in these terms thus implies a subtle understanding of another person's behaviors, attitudes, and values, that allows one to see the communicative situation through their eyes. As deaf children deploy their sign, spoken, and sometimes written language skills to accommodate diverse audiences in diverse communicative situations, they are making these cultural judgments: whether to use or not use voice or touch to gain attention; to use features of sign and spoken languages simultaneously; to use the vernacular or the conventional sign or word; to write things down or fingerspell, these are all choices informed by a cultural understanding of different ways to be in the world and to make meaning. The final case study presented here provides a colorful illustration of this aspect of multicompetency that allows Indira the fluidity of movement between different aspects of her daily life at home and at school.

CASE STUDY: INDIRA

Indira is an eleven-year-old girl from a family whose origins are in Pakistan. Her father and her younger brother are also deaf. Indira has a bilateral, profound sensorineural hearing loss. She was fitted with hearing aids at four months. She consistently wears her hearing aids and began using a radio aid in class when she was five years old. She was fitted with a single CI when she was eleven and continues to use her hearing aid. Indira understands and uses spoken English, Punjabi, Urdu, and BSL. She also uses SSE and some homesign, and she reads Arabic. In school, she uses mainly spoken English and SSE with her deaf friends. She understands, but does not use much BSL, depending on whom she is with.

OPPORTUNITIES FOR PEDAGOGY

This chapter has discussed concepts of multicompetency and repertoire and explored the extent to which they apply to the context of bimodal bilingual deaf children. Using examples from the research and illustrative case studies, different aspects of multicompetency have been identified to illustrate the relationships among translanguaging, multicompetency, and repertoire. A multicompetency perspective offers insights into deaf children's language and repertoires that are often eclipsed in the literature by a focus on issues of language fluency, academic attainment, and literacy levels. These issues are important, but they are not the only measures of what an individual can do with the language resources at his or her disposal. A focus on multicompetency brings different questions about deaf children's language and learning to the literature. Instead of asking whether bimodal bilingualism is an appropriate pathway for learning, attention is directed toward the investigation of the language resources of individual children and strategies for enhancing and exploiting these.

To be or not to be bimodal and bilingual is not the question. Instead, the task is to develop educational approaches that recognize, respond to, and deploy deaf children's diverse and differentiated language competencies. This entails extending the measurement of bimodal bilingual deaf children's language abilities beyond monolingual norms to develop language profiles that reflect the full range of language competencies of an individual. Pedagogically, we need to develop teaching approaches that develop multicompetent individuals and, as educators, "soft assemble" our classroom tools and approaches to respond flexibility to the increasing linguistic and cultural heterogeneity and dynamic linguistic repertoires that deaf children bring to the learning context. The challenge that this presents for pedagogy is the description and assessment of children's full repertoire of language skills and the provision of appropriate language intervention and support for individuals.

7 A Pedagogical Framework

The preceding chapters have reviewed the knowledge available about deaf children's bimodal bilingualism and learning and extended this knowledge by exploring deaf children's multilingual language experiences and lives. This review has raised further questions about how well we understand the diverse and plural language repertoires of deaf children and how they can be brought into play in the learning context. The concepts of languaging and translanguaging have been introduced as ways of examining how deaf children use language for learning. These ideas need to be developed to explore how teachers' languaging and translanguaging can help children learn. The competencies involved in the layered use of sign, spoken, and written languages have been explored within an asset-focused model of deaf children's language diversity.

The use of translanguaging theory facilitates a new perspective on deaf children's language repertoire and competencies. The concepts of language and translanguaging embody an essentially dialogic view of how we each interact with the people and the activity that surround us. We learn to make sense of the world through seeing ideas in relationship to each other, through interchange of perspective, and through questioning (Wegerif, 2011). This perspective brings language and learning together by considering language as a tool for meaning-making. To further explore the relationship between language and learning, this chapter proposes a pedagogical framework that privileges the dialogic nature of learning and teaching and the role of language as "the tool of all tools" to facilitate this process (Mercer & Littleton, 2007). This framework is based on a dialogic theory of learning that embraces language diversity and plurality in deaf education. Building on established work on classroom talk in deaf education, the issues around dialogue are explored in the light of current learning contexts and contemporary understandings of children's diverse and plural use of sign and spoken languages. Within this context, the languaging and translanguaging practices of learners and teachers are explained as central to the learning and teaching process and as pillars of a pedagogical approach.

Discussions of "how to teach deaf children" are very often dominated by a preoccupation with issues of language policy or educational placement (mainstream or special education). Furthermore, discussions of learning and teaching in deaf education are frequently couched in terms of "instruction" and do not really fully explore the process as a two-way exchange (see, e.g., Moores, 2001). As a result, the wealth of information available on deaf children's language learning, literacy and numeracy development, and curriculum learning rarely intersects with discussions of classroom practice. There are increasing efforts in the field to make this connection (e.g., Easterbrooks & Beal-Alvarez, 2013; Knoors & Marschark, 2014, 2015), but there is still no sense of a coherent pedagogy. One can locate theoretical work about deafness and language development, reading, cognition, and so forth and, in different places, find descriptions of practice. However, attention to the theory and practice of education that asks what learning means, what it involves, and how successful learning can take place in the classroom is missing in the literature. There is less research on how to teach deaf students than how they learn (Marschark & Hauser, 2012, p. 120).

The following discussion addresses this lacuna by arguing for a pedagogical framework. This framework rests on a dialogic view of learning that is seated within a sociocultural paradigm. Connections are made between what has been learned about deaf children's diverse and plural language repertoires and practices and what is known about effective classroom practice to suggest a workable pedagogy for deaf education.

A SOCIOCULTURAL PERSPECTIVE

A dialogic theory of learning is grounded in sociocultural ideas about development and learning that we associate with theorists such as Vygotsky (1978), Bruner (1978), and others who have developed educational applications of this work (Linell, 2009; Mercer, 1995; Wells, 1999). Within a sociocultural perspective, social interaction is at the center of learning and the means through which we acquire the cultural tools to make meaning. This perspective rests on an understanding that learning does not take place in a vacuum. Rather, learning occurs in, and is unavoidably shaped by, our cultural and historical context. Learning comes about through interpersonal interaction with others and the social and cultural values, beliefs, and norms of the environment.

The construction of knowledge is thus a social activity on many levels. This activity is serviced by language as the most powerful cultural tool in the human repertoire for making sense and sharing experience (Wells, 1999). We learn, not just as a result of action in the world, but through action that is mediated by language as the most "ubiquitous, flexible and creative of all the meaning-making tools available" (Mercer & Littleton, 2007, p. 2). The nature of this mediation may be social, such as through discussion, collaboration, and argument with others, or solitary, as we privately reflect and reason on experience. This is a perpetually transformative experience because the process of mediation changes understanding, which in turn transforms how we approach a new experience or argument. We might see this in terms of the process of thinking through a problem (internally or with others), where we solve the problem but also develop our approach to problem-solving. Similarly, when we are learning a new language and overcome vocabulary or grammatical problems, we are at the same time expanding our experience of how to learn a language (Halliday, 1993). In both examples, we are learning about the process of learning itself and continually transforming the cognitive processes involved in mediating learning. This way of conceptualizing the learning process provides a helpful lens through which to consider deaf children's languaging, translanguaging, and learning in the classroom.

A sociocultural theory of learning focuses attention on the way in which interaction, at a number of levels, mediates learning and the role of language within this. There have been different explorations of this that have influenced educational practice. The most well known of these applications is Vygotsky's (1978) notion of the zone of proximal development (ZPD). In what Wells (1999) describes as his "legacy for teachers," Vygotsky's notion of the ZPD encapsulates how the potential for learning is created and realized through interaction. The ZPD is conceptualized as the zone between what a child can do with or without help from an adult or expert peer; that is, the difference between their actual developmental level and their potential.

Subsequent elaborations of this concept have influenced the development of dynamic models of assessment and focused attention on exactly what type of help or guidance is needed to ensure that learning is meaningful. In the classroom context, "scaffolding" is used to talk about what that guidance may entail (Bruner, 1978; Wood, Wood, Griffiths, & Howarth, 1986). Scaffolding is a metaphor for the structures, or steps, put in place to enable learners to succeed. The metaphor of the structure is important because it represents guidance that provides incremental levels and supports that are tuned to or contingent on the needs of the learner. The temporary nature of scaffolding (to get a particular job done) also suggests that, through guidance and over time, learning becomes secure and the need for support falls away. Scaffolding may comprise many different sources of guidance, including direct support from those around us, our experience, engagement with cultural activities and artifacts, and our own mental "workings out." Much of the educational research associated with these sociocultural concepts has focused on teacher talk and classroom interaction. A distinctive research domain has emerged from this interest that focuses on dialogue as shared inquiry and the collaborative construction of knowledge in education. As Mercer and Littleton suggest (2007), a socioconstructivist approach is more than a theoretical position: it has true application to contemporary education by providing an explanatory account of how interaction—specifically dialogue—in the classroom can transform learning and teaching.

In the context of deaf education, a socioconstructivist approach lends a perspective that embraces the diverse experiences that deaf children may bring to the learning context. The central principle of a socioconstructivist model of learning and teaching is to provide an environment that enables learners to bring their language and cultural "tool-kit" into play so that they can actively engage in learning, develop as individuals, and participate in society (Wells, 1999, p. 335). To achieve this aim in the context of deaf education requires a critical look at how teaching and learning is organized to enable shared inquiry and the collaborative building of knowledge. This involves the establishment of a learning community that is hospitable to individual difference in terms of language and culture, as well as learning styles, and that provides guidance and challenge in equal measure. To apply this theoretical framework in the classroom with deaf learners, it is helpful to develop further the focus on interaction and on dialogue in particular as the centerpiece of a pedagogical approach.

A DIALOGIC THEORY OF LEARNING

A dialogic theory of learning is grounded in the sociocultural view that we learn in the context of cultural and historical relationships brought into play through interaction. That is to say, we learn across difference, where the juxtaposition of different perspectives opens up spaces for new meanings to emerge. Dialogue in its broadest sense thus refers to the interplay of different perspectives (the view and the counterview) that changes what and how we know (Wegeriff, 2011). In this sense, dialogue is not just how we learn; it is how we are in the world. Dialogue represents "a continuous, developmental communicative interchange through which we stand to gain a fuller apprehension of the world, ourselves, and one another" (Burbules, 1993, p. 8).

Dialogue is usually construed as occurring between two or more people (my voice and your voice), but it can equally refer to an interchange between the self and the cultural, social voice of our environment. Bakhtin's work on the dialogic nature of literature (1981) and of language itself suggests a distinction between the authoritative and the persuasive voice (Bakhtin, 1986). He uses this distinction to differentiate between monologic, or instructive, voice and the dialogic voice that offers other perspectives. A dialogic theory of learning privileges the persuasive voice that provides possibilities for developing thinking skills, language, and subject knowledge through talk. This type of voice does not presuppose ready-made answers but engages learners in a collective search for meaning (Reznitskaya & Gregory, 2013; Sedova, Salamounova, & Svaricek, 2014). This view of dialogue rests on an assumption that knowledge is neither absolute (there is no one truth) or completely subjective (there is no shared understanding) but that it is negotiated and constructed as a result of the dialogical processes of examination, reflection, and judgment (Kuhn, Cheney, & Weinstock, 2000).

The attraction of a dialogic theory of learning as a basis for a pedagogical framework lies first in the fact that it is a transformative theory of learning. It is an approach that encompasses learning, and learning how to learn, that can be readily applied to many aspects of our own experience. As we interact with others, listen to ourselves, and witness new perspectives, we are learning, but we are also honing our learning skills and changing our thinking and that of others. Our understanding is transformed, and, as learners, we are transformed, as is our identity as learners. At the same time, the social context of the learning activity and the learning of others are transformed. This continual and dynamic stretching and expanding of new knowledge has no fixed or end point. The individual and society are in constant dialogue, "each creating, and being created by, the other" (Wells, 1999, p. 332). In the context of deaf education, this offers a dynamic way to look at teaching and learning that is not limited to one fixed methodology. As an approach, it also integrates attention to learning skills, alongside the learning of language and curriculum content.

A dialogic theory of learning is also a holistic one. Learning and teaching cannot be separated where there is attention to dialogue. The very focus on the nature and quality of interaction that supports learning brings all communicative partners into focus. This rounded and inclusive view of learning extends beyond the focus on dialogue among children and adults to take account of the cultural context of learning: the interaction between school as part of a society and a culture and how learning in constructed within this context. In this sense, a dialogic approach embraces an ecological perspective, recognizing that learning is influenced by the more distal, social, and environmental experiences of the individuals as well as by proximal, day-to-day relationships. A holistic and ecological framework provides scope for the recognition of the range of influences on deaf children's learning. For example, the issues associated with being a deaf learner in a mainstream classroom setting are recognized, but do not detract from attention to the quality of interaction within the classroom among deaf learners and their teachers.

A dialogic theory of learning is also an optimistic one: through a focus on dialogue, it is easy to envisage how approaches to learning and teaching can be improved to be more effective. As educators, we have the latitude to set up classrooms and provide the right sort of classroom talk to facilitate learning. Working with dialogue potentially gives teachers agency to explore ways in which they can enhance learning. Although it is not always possible to influence the language skills and experiences of deaf children, within the learning context, teachers can develop dialogic approaches that effectively support learning. A dialogic approach is evidence-based and readily applicable to the context of deaf education (Brown & Palincsar, 1989; Mortimer & Scott, 2003; Nystrand, Wu, Gamoran, Zeiser, & Long, 2003; Rojas-Drummond & Mercer, 2003). It is an approach to learning and teaching that shifts attention from issues of language policy to language use in the classroom and provides indicators of what can be changed, on a day-to-day basis, to make learning more effective. It is an approach that places change and improvement in the hands of practitioners and encourages attention to language competencies rather than barriers to learning.

A DIALOGIC APPROACH

A dialogic theory of learning is one that can and has been applied and examined in classroom practice. Over the past two decades, this has been explored by a number of educational researchers who have distilled principles of how this theory of learning can be brought into being in practice. Wells offers, in very broad terms, a dialogical conceptualization of learning and teaching that centers on ways in which knowledge is co-constructed between learners and teachers through shared activities (1999). This approach, he argues, reconciles the tension between the individual development and cultural reproduction that education seeks to realize by focusing on the growth and development of teachers and learners. He envisions a community of inquiry that enables the dual transformation of the individual and the cultural context whereby:

- activities undertaken are such that, although chosen by the teacher for their cumulative contributions to an understanding of the central theme, they allow for groups of students to make them their own and progressively to exercise more choice over how they are conducted
- activities involve a combination of action and reflection, of group work, individual reading and writing, and whole-class discussion
- goals are made explicit, and the relationship between these goals and the operations by means of which they are to be achieved is made the subject of discussion
- there are frequent opportunities for students to express their beliefs and opinions, to calibrate them with those of their peers, and the change them in the light of persuasive argument or further information. (Wells, 1999, p. 229)

Wells suggests that these characteristics of educational practice provide the context for teacher talk that scaffolds learning and is contingent on students' interests, abilities, and learning potential. Although considered quite progressive at one time, these principles still hold true in terms of good educational practice despite an increasingly crowded curriculum and a preoccupation with attainment data.

The work that Wells and others have done to bring Vygotsky's theories of learning, and in particular his conception of the ZPD, into the classroom has stimulated an extensive field of research into the educational function of classroom talk (Alexander, 2001, 2008*b*; Gutierrez, 1993; Howe & Littleton, 2010; Mercer, 1995, 2000; Nystrand et al., 2003; Scott, 2008; Sharpe, 2008). This substantial body of work has explored ways in which teachers can open up the dialogic space by bringing together different perspectives to facilitate thinking, creativity, and learning.

Mercer and Littlewood (2007) suggest a number of strategies in their "thinking together" project. In this study, teachers and children were encouraged to develop shared ground rules for exploratory talk in the classroom. The children were also given explicit guidance about how to use dialogue to think together and solve problems. Mercer and Littlewood argue that engaging children in this "interthinking" (p. 57) served to make dialogue more visible and opened the children's eyes to the power of language as a tool for building knowledge with others. At the heart of this work is the emphasis on language as a tool for working things out, either through solitary thinking or with others in a social context. The dialogic environment seeks to make the most of this tool to shape learning and sharpen thinking.

Alexander's description of dialogic teaching emerged from his research comparing primary classrooms across five different countries and is among the most well-known (2001). His observations of classroom talk in different cultural contexts illuminates different ways in which teachers shape dialogue in the classroom to foster learning. Through analysis of these observations, he conceptualizes the notion of dialogic teaching to refer to the reciprocal and participative interaction between teachers and pupils that develops the learners' thinking and understanding.

Other more detailed indictors of dialogic teaching include an emphasis on the use of challenging, authentic, and open-ended questioning (Gayle, Preiss, & Allen, 2006); the facilitation of coherent dialogue that is contingent on the contributions of others (Nystrand et al., 2003); and the generation of exploratory talk (Mercer & Dawes, 2008). Reznitskaya et al. (2009), in their analysis, identify that while engaging in dialogue with pupils, teachers also have a crucial mediating role in making visible the connections between student ideas. A further layer of complexity is added in bilingual and multilingual learning contexts, where all of these indicators imply the dynamic use of different languages and forms of communication to realize effective dialogue (Gutiérrez, Baquedano-López, Alvarez, & Chiu, 1999).

There is some overlap across different typologies of dialogic teaching, but it is possible to draw general principles of a dialogic approach from the research. It is fundamentally an approach that centers on the activity of knowing and how, through dialogue, children learn subject knowledge and language and learn about themselves as learners and about the world of others.

Although some researchers have argued that dialogic teaching is difficult to sustain (Billings & Fitzgerald, 2002; Lefstein, 2008; Mercer & Howe, 2012; Sedova et al., 2014), there is substantial evidence of its efficacy. The positive effects of dialogic teaching have been noted in terms of the learning of subject knowledge, particularly science (Mason, 2001; Scott, Ametller, Mortimer, & Emberton, 2010), and the development of metacognitive skills (Daniel et al., 2005), argumentation skills (Resnitskaya et al., 2009), and problem-solving skills (Sams & Mercer, 2006).

A PEDAGOGICAL FRAMEWORK FOR DEAF EDUCATION

A dialogic theory of learning is a transformative, holistic, and optimistic one. The educational approach is hospitable to the diverse sign and spoken language practices and the cultural and linguistic experiences of deaf children. The congruence between this approach and translanguaging theory provides a powerful basis for a pedagogical framework. Both perspectives are located in a sociocultural theory of mind that construes language as a cognitive tool for mediating learning and the development of new understandings to make and shape meaning. Both theoretical approaches recognize that our language actions shape, and are shaped by, experience and knowledge and that our language experience and knowledge cannot be divorced from our language actions (Blommaert & Rampton, 2011). Both theories accent the power of language as a discursive tool (García, 2009) and construe meaning-making as a dialogic process that comes about as we engage in the "to and fro" of perspectives through solitary or social reflection (Bakhtin, 1981).

The integration of these two concepts provides the foundations for a pedagogical framework for deaf education that is based on theories of how we construct meaning and learn through dialogue. Within this framework, languaging is conceptualized as the external or internal discourse that mediates this learning (Lantolf & Thorne, 2006). This discourse can only be effective if it is truly dialogic; that is, if it offers an interplay of different perspectives and a space for new meanings to emerge (Gutierrez, 1993; Gutiérrez et al., 1999). Dialogic teaching, as the centerpiece of this framework, necessitates an understanding of the language repertoires in play and how they can be channeled to unlock dialogue in the classroom. In bilingual and multilingual contexts, this implies attention to the layered use of different languages to make meaning, framed here as translanguaging (García & Li Wei, 2014). Dialogism and translanguaging are therefore interdependent aspects of this framework: dialogic teaching is facilitated through translanguaging, and translanguaging, by its very nature, is dialogic.

A pedagogical framework for deaf education is thus proposed that is situated within a sociocultural perspective, adopts a dialogic theory of learning, and encompasses the concepts and practices of translanguaging. The question is, what can such a framework offer to enhance established theory and practice of learning and teaching in deaf education?

First, this approach does not offer a prescribed methodology or a list of teaching strategies. Rather, it suggests directions and priorities for practice and provides a framework for developing a classroom approach that is responsive to some of the big questions in deaf education. It is an approach that encourages practitioners to think about what is understood by "learning" and how learning takes place. This brings into focus not only what is being in taught in school and how, but also the classroom relationships and interactions that are fostered in this context (Alexander, 2008a). This reflection involves a step back from the day-to-day classroom decisions in deaf education and encourages instead the development of a rationale to underpin classroom actions. Deaf education practitioners are often most anxious about making the language of the classroom accessible to deaf learners, and this can obscure thinking about what learning they are trying to promote and how this can best be realized. The very question of how children learn has become somewhat lost in a focus on communication and access. A dialogic approach addresses this by ensuring that language, communication, and learning are approached in an integrated way.

A Focus on How Language Is Used

Clarity in the way in which we, as practitioners, think about learning facilitates a learner-oriented and critical use of language in the classroom. A focus on how language is used in the classroom is pertinent to all the different contexts for learning that deaf children encounter. In a mainstream context, this includes the complexes of interaction between learners, mainstream teachers, deaf education practitioners (teachers of the deaf educational interpreters, teaching assistants), and peer group. In a special school setting, the dynamics of interaction may be less complex. However, attention to how language is used in the classroom is equally pertinent to ensure that the more intensive language experiences that a special school context can offer are maximized for learning. For any learning context, a dialogic perspective potentially opens up an integrated view of deaf children's curriculum learning, language learning, and their experience of learning about learning.

Mayer, Akamatsu, and Stewart (2002) recognize the importance of attention to dialogue. In their exposition of exemplary practice, they argue that the reconceptualization of education as dialogue side-steps prescriptive approaches to language use, emphasizing instead the quality of discourse and the meaning-making potential of classroom talk. They do not talk about translanguaging as such, but they do recognize the range of ways in which teachers and pupils might use and combine sign and spoken languages to engage in meaningful conversation. This openness to different ways of communicating in the classroom still needs to be channeled so that language use is mindful of and responsive to the learners' interest and ability. An effective dialogic approach will recognize and be responsive to the diverse repertoires of deaf children and thus be finely tuned to scaffold individual learning. As Knoors and Marschark point out (2014), the ability to make one's communication contingent on the communicative and linguistic preferences of individuals requires considerable language dexterity and flexibility on the part of teachers.

First, deaf children's language repertoires and competencies have to be known, and, second, this knowledge has to be deployed in a nuanced way to achieve dialogically organized learning and teaching experiences.

For bimodal bilingual learners, translanguaging will be a natural part of these learning and teaching experiences as both children and adults find creative ways to make meaning using the language resources that they have. Earlier chapters have illustrated how children's dynamic use of language resources, including their translanguaging, facilitates dialogue and provides a means through which individuals position themselves and express self and identity (García & Li Wei, 2014, p. 9). Translanguaging thus enables social and/or solitary talk as a tool for learning and also allows learners to culturally and linguistically "be themselves" in the learning context. Translanguaging therefore allows for the fluidity of communication in the learning context and the flexible and dynamic expression of individual identities from moment to moment. For bimodal bilingual deaf children, translanguaging will be the lynch pin for a successful dialogic approach, one that involves the whole learner and all of the linguistic and cultural resources that he or she brings to meaning-making.

A Response to Linguistic Diversity and Plurality

A dialogic approach offers a pragmatic and optimistic response to linguistic diversity and plurality in deaf education. The focus on learning and on how language use in the classroom supports learning affords an inclusive perspective on languages in use and individual repertoire. The recognition that meaning-making involves the dynamic use of language eschews a preoccupation with any one particular language methodology (sign bilingual, total communication, auditory-oral). These principles cut across all approaches that simply entail noticing what language resources children bring to the learning context and using and further shaping those resources in the process of building new understandings. This asset-focused approach may be diversely operationalized, but the core intention remains stable, grounded within a theory of learning not hitherto expressed within any of the language approaches in deaf education. The fundamental intention of establishing dialogue is an education goal, not just the means to an end, and it drives and informs flexible but mindful language use in the classroom.

THE BIG QUESTIONS IN DEAF EDUCATION

No single pedagogical framework will answer all the big questions in deaf education. However, a framework that provides a theoretical basis for classroom practice that integrates issues of learning and teaching and provides a foundation for the development of teaching approaches is a step in the right direction. Furthermore, a pedagogical framework that is sufficiently robust to respond to the range of issues that impact on learning and teaching in deaf education is worth a second glance. The final section of this chapter reviews the big issues and sets the agenda for evaluating the potential of a dialogic framework in deaf education.

Being Deaf in a School Environment

The pathology of deafness and how that influences the school learning experience is often placed as one of the earlier chapters in deaf education texts (see, e.g., Marschark & Hauser, 2012). This topic is usually placed at the front of discussions about learning, not to emphasize a deficit or medical position, but rather to spell out the reality of deafness as a disability (often invisible) and how this affects the social and academic experience of school. These issues pertain particularly to the mainstream experience, which is the reality for the majority of deaf learners. Even mild deafness in a school environment presents some very real physical issues, such as learning in noisy classrooms and being able to follow multiple conversations (Dockreill & Shield, 2006). There are also more subtle challenges associated with the fact that learning occurs not only from face-to-face interaction but also from hearing other children talk about their work, ask questions, and solve problems (Matthews & Reich, 1993). These learning issues are confounded by the fact that relationships in schools with other peers and adults, that often ease the school experience for many learners, are difficult to establish and maintain where the experience of being deaf is not shared or fully understood. The proper use of individual and whole-school hearing technologies can partially alleviate these issues. However, technology does not remove deafness or provide a complete solution for every child (Vermeulen, De Raeve, Langereis, & Snik, 2012). The next chapter explores how a dialogic approach can mitigate the impact of deafness on the learning experience to enable a positive academic and social experience of school, particularly in inclusive settings.

Language and Conceptual Knowledge

The impact of deafness on the early experience of language and interaction often means that deaf learners enter school without sign or spoken language fluency (Knoors, 2016; Marschark & Hauser, 2012). Furthermore, because interaction needs to be primarily face to face, many incidental opportunities for learning about the world through overhearing adult or peer commentary are compromised (Convertino, Borgna, Marschark, & Durkin, 2014; Marschark et al., 2012). Practitioners therefore need approaches to teaching in deaf education that can build language knowledge and skills while supporting the "back filling" of children's conceptual development. This is a rather bleak presentation of the facts but deliberately framed in this way to fully expose the learning issues and test the potential of a dialogic pedagogy. The evaluation of the potential of a dialogic pedagogy will need to take into account the diversity of deaf children's language experience and the dynamics of sign and spoken language use that are present in a classroom. The next chapter will explore how a dialogic approach can build on the language resources that deaf children bring to learning to enrich language experience and develop world knowledge by enhancing meaningful communication and shared meaning-making at home and at school.

Learning Styles

When language development is disrupted, cognitive development is also delayed (Cormier, Schembri, Vinson, & Orfanidou, 2012; Mayberry, 2007). Furthermore, it is argued that the very the experience of deafness shapes the development of children's cognitive profiles or learning styles (Marschark et al., 2016; Marschark & Hauser, 2008). This may be evident in terms of preferences for auditory and visual information, sensitivity to peripheral stimulation (and tendency to be drawn off task), and differences in terms of attention and memory skills (Dye & Hauser, 2014; Marschark et al., 2005). In addition, deaf learners often struggle to develop essential learning skills such as the ability to organize their learning, solve problems, make predictions, see generalizations, and make connections between concepts (Marschark & Wauters, 2011). This is in part explained by early language experience and lack of prior knowledge. However, these problems are sometimes exacerbated by the lack of opportunities provided in school to work on and tackle new problems independently (Marschark, Spencer, Adams, & Sapere, 2011).

A pedagogical approach for deaf education must alleviate these teaching issues and effectively support children's learning, but also facilitate the development of thinking skills and learning how to learn. The next chapter explores how a dialogic approach can provide the scaffolding for learning that presents opportunities for pupils to practice "working things out" and how this approach might accommodate the different cognitive profiles of deaf learners.

Literacy

Deaf children's literacy development is the most researched and published issue in deaf education, and the questions are myriad regarding routes to literacy for deaf children (Trezek, Paul, & Wang, 2011). Because of deaf children's language experience, learning to read already presents a universal challenge, and, as they move through the educational system, being able to read to learn presents a still greater hurdle (Swanwick et al., 2012).

To develop effective practice, an approach is needed that enables deaf children to draw on the sign and spoken language skills available to them, activate their prior knowledge, and use their phonological skills and vocabulary knowledge to gain meaning from text (Convertino et al., 2014). There is already some evidence of the potential of a dialogic approach for this area of learning. Positive results have been found when a structured dialogic approach is introduced with young deaf children around picture book sharing. In both sign and spoken language contexts, the children show gains in their receptive vocabulary development (Fung, Chow, & McBride-Chang, 2005; Trussell & Easterbrooks, 2014). Furthermore, it is argued that an approach that focuses on developing fruitful interaction and dialogue around story reading lends itself to training with parents and thus has application at home as well as in school. The next chapter explores the extent to which a dialogic approach can support the development of early reading skills and strategies and promote the more sophisticated skills needed to engage with a breadth of curriculum knowledge through text.

Social and Emotional Maturity

The impact that childhood deafness has on early language experience and interaction can also mean that deaf learners entering school may be less socially and emotionally mature than their hearing peers (Calderon & Greenberg, 2011; Langereis & Vermeulen, 2015; Rieffe, 2012). This lack of maturity can manifest itself in a number of ways in the school context and can adversely affect learning. School is an inherently social milieu, and it is very hard to be a successful learner if you just do not know how to interact socially, behave appropriately, and manage emotions in this environment. To be able to work and play with others and navigate the school environment requires an understanding of others and some social skills (Wauters & Knoors, 2008). Successful learning is also affected by individual confidence, expectation, and self-esteem (Hintermair, 2015). The next chapter explores dialogic ways of teaching and talking with deaf children that embrace and respond to these social and emotional issues to enhance the all-round school experience for deaf learners.

THE LEARNING CONTEXT

The contexts for deaf children's learning are probably more diverse than for hearing children. The two main possibilities are special schools and inclusive (mainstream) settings, but there are various models of inclusive practice that present very different learning opportunities. Depending on the assessment of individual learning and language needs and parental preference, some deaf children may be placed in mainstream schools with individual itinerant support. The majority (78%) of deaf children are educated in this context in the United Kingdom. Children who need more support for learning than can be provided by a visiting teacher are usually educated within a resourced mainstream school for deaf children where there are other deaf learners and a specialist teaching staff (Salter, 2015). Placement in a school for the deaf promises customized and specialist teaching and a fully accessible social community for deaf learners.

In all of these locations, the important question to be asked is who is doing the talking and the teaching in the classroom. It is important to know how deaf learners are accessing the specialist curriculum knowledge in school and whether their learning is mediated by another adult, a teacher of the deaf, an interpreter, a teaching assistant, or any combination of these (Marschark, Sapere, Convertino, & Pelz, 2008). This configuration is crucial in terms of the talk around learning that deaf children experience and the extent to which this talk is meaningful. The next chapter will explore the extent to which a dialogic approach can be responsive to different learning contexts and facilitate learning in both face-to-face and mediated learning experiences.

COMMUNITIES OF PRACTICE

Finally, taking a broader view of the learning context, a question that surfaces frequently in deaf education is how to bring research and practice closer together (Swanwick & Marschark, 2010). This issue is not easily solved through research publications, conferences, and seminar activities. These valuable dissemination activities have a place but frequently only facilitate (as the word dissemination suggests) one-way communication. Real exchange comes through dialogue, through the juxtaposition of different perspectives that makes way for something new. In true dialogue, it is hard to say who is thinking (Wegeriff, 20011). A dialogic approach is therefore not only about the classroom but also about the communities surrounding the child (home, school, education, research) and how they talk to each other and build new understandings (Engeström, 2001; Wenger, 1998). The next chapter will explore how the principles of a dialogic approach can be taken beyond the classroom to develop the synergy between research and practice and transformational conversations among learners, parents, educators, and researchers (Swanwick, 2015).

This chapter has set out the theoretical basis of a dialogic approach and begun to argue its relevance for deaf education. The practical application of a dialogic pedagogy has to take into account the big questions in deaf education about developing practice and research. Professionals in this field now have so much information about deafness itself, deaf children's language and social development, cognition, learning styles, literacy development, technologies, and contexts for learning. However, although this is knowledge, it is not necessarily "know-how." The following chapter seeks to adjust that balance by orientating the questions from "what do we know about" to "what can we do about" the school experience, language and learning, social development, and effective teaching. Exploring these questions within a dialogic framework does not privilege any one particular language or modality approach. As such, it provides an emancipatory perspective on practice that underlines the quality of the dialogue and talk around learning. The next chapter will explore how this quality is defined and how it can be achieved in the context of deaf education.

8 Teaching and Talking with Deaf Children

The previous chapter offered a conceptual framework for pedagogy in deaf education that situates the quality of interaction as central to the learning process and embraces deaf learners' rich and varied language practices. This chapter explores how such a framework might work in practice and delivers an approach that is responsive to the diverse learning needs of deaf children and contexts for learning, one that facilitates successful school experience and achievement. Ways in which a dialogic approach have thus far been explored in deaf education are taken forward to explore how such practices can be developed and enhanced by translanguaging. Practical teaching strategies are suggested that draw on successful approaches in the wider field of language learning but also take account of the particular learning experience and contexts of deaf children. This practice-orientated chapter demonstrates the broad, inclusive, and responsive nature of a dialogic pedagogical framework that brings together the best of practice in deaf education and eschews a "one-size-fits-all" mentality.

CLASSROOM TALK IN DEAF EDUCATION

The title of this chapter is a deliberate reference to the most extensive piece of research that has been done in deaf education on classroom interaction and, as such, the cornerstone of this discussion of practice (Wood, Wood, Griffiths, & Howarth, 1986). This study by David Wood and colleagues examined classroom interactions between deaf children and their hearing teachers. The research focused on spoken language interaction and did not consider the bimodal bilingual context. Nonetheless, there is a lot to be learned from this work about classroom talk when reviewed within a perspective that embraces language diversity and plurality and that promotes quality of interaction over issues of modality. This retrospective is prompted by an identified gap in the literature, where discussions of teaching practices have focused primarily on communication and not learning and where there has been little guidance in terms of pedagogy (Knoors & Marschark, 2014, 2015; Mayer, 2016). As Mayer, Akamatsu, and Stewart (2002) suggest, we have perhaps "lost the forest for the trees" (2002, p. 231). Hence, a back-to-basics focus on interaction and learning and how this can be facilitated, but not led, by modality issues.

The research by Wood et al. (1986) on ways in which adult talk in the classroom facilitates learning opened the door to thinking about dialogue in deaf education, even though this was not the zeitgeist of the time. Woods et al. explored "conversational partnerships" between teachers and deaf children and looked at what features of teacher-talk encouraged children's engagement and participation in learning. With a specific focus on questioning, they identified how different styles of interaction could be deployed for different teaching objectives and outcomes. Most importantly, they advocated the need for teachers' awareness of and readiness to evaluate their own teaching styles vis-a-vis their teaching objectives (p. 179). The central concepts about classroom conversation to take forward from this extensive work are those of "contingency" and "control." *Contingency* describes adult talk that helps learning by being finely tuned to the interests and developing competencies (this can mean knowledge and/or skills) of the individual. Typical examples of this are seen in early interactions, where parents imbue their child's communication with intention and respond appropriately. *Control* is concerned with reciprocal roles in a conversation and the adults' ability to relinquish their control of dialogue to enable pupils to initiate and develop their contribution. Pupil loquacity and engagement is enhanced by contingent communication but inhibited where the conversation is overdirected. In the Wood et al. (1986) study, it was found that adults' style of conversation with deaf children tended to be on the more controlling side. This control was most often characterized by repair strategies, such as asking for repetitions, and the use of closed yes/no questions. These controlling communication behaviors were observed to be used more frequently than strategies such as phatic comments, that indicate interest but leave space for a response (see full discussion in Swanwick, 2015).The findings from this seminal work about how teachers mange conversational flow to support learning in the classroom are still salient today.

Changes to contexts for learning and increasing individual language diversity have made the issues of classroom interaction even more dynamic. Research into classroom conversation in these more linguistically complex contexts that is not hijacked by policy issues is only just beginning to emerge (Marschark & Lee, 2014). The work available on classroom communication between deaf learners and adults and among deaf and hearing children is often referenced to questions of successful inclusive education (see, e.g., discussions in Marschark, Knoors & Tang, 2014). Understandably, the inclusion agenda has prompted a reevaluation of what is understood by successful learning and how, as practitioners, we recognize and plan for it. Measuring learning outcomes provides some information about how pupils are doing in any one educational context.

Finding out what pupils know and what they can do is a relatively tangible aim. Examining teaching methods to identify quality education is more exacting. Knoors and Renting (2000) took an approach to this that focused on learner engagement in terms of their emotional well-being and involvement in learning. Using Laevers' (1994) framework for measuring learner involvement in whole-class and small-group conversation, they found that group size and the scaffolding provided for a learning activity were among influencing factors for the degree of learner involvement.

These more general pointers about the quality of educational experience re-open the question of what kind of classroom communication enables deaf children's learning in current educational contexts. Kelman and Branco (2009) identify the nuances of classroom communication between deaf learners and their teachers as important contributors to successful inclusive education. Congruent with a dialogic theory of learning, they argue that the social and academic experiences of education are intertwined and that successful interaction responds to the identities and cultures of individuals as well as to the learning goals. Their observations of bilingual classes, where teachers of the deaf were co-teaching with mainstream specialist subject teachers, reveal that meta-communication is as important as the content of the dialogue in facilitating pupils' engagement in learning. They conclude that communication behaviors (such as touch, gesture, posture, and intonation) and classroom organization (the use of space) that demonstrate an emotional and practical commitment to the pupils enhance the inclusive learning experience of deaf pupils. This attention to the social and emotional aspects of learning adds a further dynamic to the features of classroom talk considered in the Wood et al. study (1986).

Dialogue among children, as well as between children and adults, in the classroom also needs to be considered. Much of classroom learning is acquired through peer interaction. This relies on being able to follow and contribute to group discussion and have a shared understanding of the curriculum vocabulary or terminology in use. Both of these prerequisites can be problematic for deaf children (Dye & Hauser, 2014). Partaking in group discussions can easily break down, particularly in subject areas such as science where there exists a particular discourse and where familiar words are frequently used in an unfamiliar scientific context (Molander, Halldén, & Lindahl, 2010).

This growing body of work since the study by Wood et al. (1986) has re-established a focus on the quality of interaction in the classroom. The conclusions so far point to the potential facilitative nature of the right kind of dialogue among deaf and hearing learners and their teachers (Knoors

& Marschark, 2014). Studies that explicitly refer to a dialogic approach provide positive indications of its efficacy in terms of the quality of teaching and learning (Mayer et al., 2002) and learner engagement (Trussell & Easterbrooks, 2014). Dialogic inquiry is shown to be particularly useful for assessment and evaluation purposes (Mayer et al., 2002) and to have a valuable role in facilitating language diversity and multiple identities in the classroom (Mudgett-DeCaro & Hurwitz, 1997). A pedagogical framework for deaf education that builds on and extends this work will be based on a broad conceptualization of dialogue as an interaction between ourselves and the world that leads to understanding as well as to the "to and fro" of ideas in conversation with others. Working with this definition, the first question to ask is what constitutes dialogue and good dialogic teaching in the classroom; the second question concerns how such dialogic teaching can be achieved in deaf education in light of the issues of language and learning issues discussed in previous chapters.

DIALOGIC TEACHING

The principles of dialogic teaching have been extensively reviewed in the work of Robin Alexander (2008a). Alexander's work focuses on primary education, but parallel issues have been explored in the context of secondary subject teaching (G. Kelly & Brown, 2002; Mercer, 2008; Mercer & Dawes, 2008; Scott, Mortimer, & Aguiar, 2006). Alexander studied interaction in primary classrooms during the 1980s and 1990s. He conducted comparative studies of primary education across five cultures (1995, 2001). Through this exploration of pedagogy, he developed indicators of dialogic teaching that are predicated on the notion that talk lies at the center of successful teaching and learning.

Of all the tools for cultural and pedagogical intervention in human development and learning, talk is the most pervasive in its use and powerful in its possibilities. Talk vitally mediates the cognitive and cultural spaces between adult and child, among children themselves, between teacher and learner, between society and the individual, between what the child knows and understands, and what he or she has yet to know and understand (Alexander, 2008*b*). Dialogic teaching in Alexander's terms involves a focus on the nature of talk in teaching and its use in building the spirit of inquiry in the classroom and supporting understanding (2003). It is not a single set method but an approach that is based on several important principles. These principles are explored in the following sections.

Principles of Dialogic Teaching

- *Collective*: adults and children address learning tasks together
- *Reciprocal*: adults and children listen to each other, share ideas, and consider alternative viewpoints
- *Supportive*: children articulate their ideas freely, without fear of embarrassment over "wrong" answers, and they help each other to reach common understandings
- *Cumulative*: adults and children build on their own and each other's ideas and chain them into coherent lines of thinking and inquiry
- *Purposeful*: adults plan and steer talk with specific goals in view

(Alexander, 2008*a* p. 28)

The principles of dialogic teaching that Alexander distilled from his observations of primary classrooms are congruent with the issues that have thus far been identified regarding classroom talk in deaf education. Learning is successful in this context when it is facilitated through engagement and shared exploration and discovery (Knoors & Renting, 2000), where there is attention to reciprocity and contingency in communication and space for learners to contribute (Woods et al., 1986), and where the social emotional needs and identities of learners are recognized and supported (Kelman & Branco, 2009). Effective classroom dialogue supports the development of communication skills but also scaffolds curriculum learning by being embedded in the discourse of the subject (Molander et al, 2010). This congruence provides some alignment with the big questions in deaf education about language, knowledge, and belonging.

The principles of dialogic teaching underpin what Alexander refers to as *dialogic teaching repertoires*. These repertoires are indicators of types of talk that facilitate interaction and support learning. He proposes a number of kinds of talk and behaviors that children should be helped to develop and use in dialogic classrooms. In this analysis, Alexander construes children's repertoires in dialogic classrooms in terms of "talk for everyday life" and "learning talk" (2008*a*, p. 38–39). Within each of these categories, he suggests the types of talk that should be encouraged (Table 8.1).

In addition, he outlines the type of teacher talk and teaching styles that encourage participation and that transform learning (Table 8.2). In this taxonomy, Alexander includes familiar strategies of rote, recitation, instruction, and exposition but gives special attention to defining the nature of discussion and scaffolded dialogue.

Table 8.1 Children's Repertoires in Dialogic Classrooms

Children's Repertoires in Dialogic Classrooms	Types of Talk
Talk for everyday life: empowers and supports everyday human interaction	transactional talk • expository talk • interrogatory talk • exploratory talk • expressive talk • evaluative talk
Learning talk: facilitates engagement in learning	narrate • explain • analyze • speculate • imagine • explore • evaluate • discuss • argue • justify • ask questions

Table 8.2 Teacher Repertoires in Dialogic Classrooms

Teachers' Repertoire	
Discussion	The open exchange of views and information in order to explore issues, test ideas, and tackle problems
	Led by one person (teacher or pupils) or undertaken by the group collectively
Scaffolded dialogue	Interactions that encourage children to think in different ways
	Questions that require much more than simple recall
	Answers that are followed-up and built on rather than merely received
	Feedback that informs and leads thinking forward as well as encourages
	Contributions that are extended rather than fragmented
	Exchanges that chain together into coherent and developing lines of enquiry
	Classroom organization, climate, and relationships that make all this possible

Alexander proposes that discussion and scaffolded dialogue can be organized in any number of ways and should be varied to exploit the different potential of whole-class teaching, group work, and one-to-one interaction.

This outline of principles and repertoire is adapted from Alexander's (2008a) pamphlet "Towards Dialogic Teaching," in which the nuances of these repertoires are discussed in detail and indicators are suggested for the development and evaluation of dialogic practice. In this publication, the research evidence that underpins this approach is presented and extensive professional development material is provided. This adapted summary provides a way to think about dialogic teaching in deaf education classrooms.

Before doing so, it is important to acknowledge that not all classroom talk can be dialogic and neither would this be appropriate (Scott et al., 2006). What is important is awareness of how talk is used in the classroom and the potential of different approaches. To be mindful of types

Table 8.3 Distinction Between Authoritative and Dialogic Talk

Types of Talk	Characteristics	Outcomes
Authoritative talk (Information transmitting)	One voice/closed	Fixed outcome
	Usually response to teacher/adult	Tends to discourage intervention
	Often single/detached words	Conveys information
	Often direct assertions	Often uses closed questions
		Usually factual statements
		Selectively involves other voices
Dialogic talk (Discovering meaning)	Several voices/open	Generative outcome
	Often spontaneous contribution	Open to debate and challenge
	or in response to other voices	Intended to generate meaning or
	Often whole ideas/phrases	stimulate thinking
	Often tentative suggestions	Often uses open questions
	Open to interpretation and development by others	Aims to sustain dialogue
		Represents other voices

Adapted from Mortimer & Scott, 2003.

of talk and their effect is already a powerful facility for teachers. Scott et al. (2006) make this point in their exploration of the tension between authoritative and dialogic talk and the way in which they are "intimately connected" in science classrooms (p. 622). The contrast between these two types of classroom talk, set out in Table 8.3, has resonances with the early work of Wood et al. (1986) with regards to control in classroom conversation. Decisions to open up or close down dialogue in the classroom require teachers to be flexible in their approach and to make informed judgments according to the needs of the learners, the teaching objectives, and the learning context.

DIALOGISM AND LANGUAGE DIVERSITY

The pedagogical models explored thus far have not been developed with deaf children in mind. They nonetheless provide a framework for practice. The challenges for the deaf education context are how to engender the different types of talk that support learning while recognizing the plural and diverse language repertoires of deaf learners and their teachers.

To meet this challenge means examining how the linguistic resources of the classroom can be used to provide dialogically organized teaching. This question has been explored in other (hearing) bilingual contexts, and, although multilingual language pedagogies for hearing learners cannot be directly applied, some of the teaching principles are relevant for deaf learners. Furthermore, as evidenced in Chapter 3, the increasing linguistic diversity of deaf children is in some ways closing the gap between the deaf and hearing bilingual pedagogies. For example, the foreign language learning model, in which children take up the learning of an additional language from a different societal and national context, usually in secondary school (such as French, Spanish, German in the United Kingdom), is relevant to some deaf children. Models of second language instruction can also be applied in part to deaf children whose home language is different from the majority language (such as Punjabi in British Asian communities).

The main differences in both of these cases are, first, that the use of sign language and forms of communication that mix sign and spoken languages, may be an additional aspect of children's language repertoire at home and/or at school. Second, levels of fluency in different languages will be influenced by the experience of deafness itself in addition to the individual and contextual influences that pertain to all language learners. This difference may extend concepts of heteroglossia in terms of the different linguistic profiles that are present in different contexts but should not categorically separate deaf and hearing bilingual learners.

For deaf children, as for hearing children, the language issues are complex, and their experience of bilingualism is dynamic (Cummins, 2006,

2007; García, 2009). There is, therefore, very likely to be common ground for the development of practice in terms of the dynamic use of language in the classroom and the particular role of translanguaging.

THE ROLE OF TRANSLANGUAGING IN DIALOGUE

The development of research and practice on plurilingual pedagogies has become increasingly focused on the quality of learning that can be provided through the dynamic and fluid use of languages in the classroom and, in particular, the role of translanguaging. The principles of dynamic and plurilingual pedagogies align very closely with those of dialogic teaching: language is expected to be used in a planned and mindful way that is responsive to the diverse language practices of children and supports language development and curriculum learning (García & Flores, 2012). To achieve this in plurilingual contexts, translanguaging plays a big part.

Translanguaging, as discussed in Chapter 5, conceptualizes children's fluid and dynamic language practices. The original use of this term, however, described an emancipatory approach to using two languages in the classroom that embodies a move from "solitudes" toward "synergies" in language education (Lewis, Jones, & Baker, 2012, p. 3). Translanguaging in the teaching context involves recognition of the dynamic and layered language practices of multilingual speakers that adapt for and re-emerge through meaning-making (García & Li Wei, 2014). In this context, translanguaging supports quality interaction in the classroom around language tasks and/or curriculum learning. As a dynamic way of using two (or more) languages, translanguaging offers opportunities for extensive exposure to different languages as well as supported attention to how different languages are structured. Translanguaging makes collaborative, peer-to-peer, and teacher-centered learning activities accessible to children with diverse language profiles within one classroom. Blackledge and Creese (2010) outline a number of principles that helpfully guide this type of language action in the classroom. They suggest that translanguaging as a teaching strategy should be underpinned by the recognition of individual linguistic repertoire as one set of resources and of individual (and institutional) identity and culture. They specify that a translanguaging approach should entail the specific use of different language competencies according to context, task, and audience; the use of languages side by side; and attention to the momentum of the conversation or learning task (pp. 112–113).

In practical terms, translanguaging encompasses the many different ways in which languages can be used together (alternately or simultaneously) to ensure the fluidity, inclusivity, and accessibility of communication in the classroom that enables learning to take place. Translanguaging includes the use of translation and rephrasing, as well as strategies of language switching and blending, but it is not synonymous with any single one of these practices. There are a growing number of studies that report on the way in which teachers use translanguaging strategies to develop children's language skills and curriculum knowledge while also recognizing and validating individual cultural and linguistic identities (Celic & Seltzer, 2012; Gort & Sembiante, 2015; Martin-Beltrán, 2014; Probyn, 2015). These studies illustrate different ways in which translanguaging opens up and makes accessible classroom discourse and is contingent on and expands multilingual repertoires that facilitate dialogue and the co-construction of knowledge among linguistically diverse peers.

The taxonomy of translanguaging teaching strategies emerging from this research is readily applicable to the diverse and plural deaf education contexts and the proposed dialogic framework. The congruence between translanguaging strategies and dialogic principles is shown in Table 8.4, with specific reference to sign and spoken language translanguaging. A distinction is made in this framework between *code blending* to refer to the simultaneous use of features of sign and spoken languages that occurs in the use of manually coded language varieties (such as sign-supported English) and *code switching* to refer to alternate use of languages and language varieties. Code switching in this case can include a switch between sign and/or spoken/written languages and a code blend.

Table 8.4 Bimodal Bilingual Translanguaging and Dialogic Pedagogy

Translanguaging Strategies (Teacher)	Teaching Examples	Dialogic Principles
Use two languages side by side to • compare and contrast languages • model language structures	Look at an English text as a group and discuss ways in which it could be recast in BSL; negotiate choices of language structures and vocabulary to agree an equivalent BSL version.	Provides opportunities for pupils to reflect on and talk about language. Makes visible the structure of different languages and the understandings of the learners. Encourages individual contributions according to their own language repertoires Provides opportunities for pupils to analyse, speculate, evaluate, discuss, argue and justify
Use students' preferred language to contextualize and plan learning activities	Prepare students for viewing a film in English with subtitles by discussing in BSL what they already know about the topic of the film, the storyline, and the characters; what new English vocabulary they are likely to encounter; anticipate any questions they might have	Facilitates discussion and open exchange of views and information Poses questions that require extended answers that are followed-up and developed Allows for feedback that informs and leads thinking Encourages contributions that are extended rather than fragmented and exchanges that result in a coherent whole
Use one language to model learning strategies for the other (e.g., "This is a way of remembering French irregular verbs")		Encourages children to think in different ways Provides opportunities for pupils to engage in "learning talk"

(continued)

Table 8.4 Continued

Translanguaging Strategies (Teacher)	Teaching Examples	Dialogic Principles
Invite contributions in student's preferred language	Lead a whole-class question-and-answer problem-solving activity in either BSL or English with interpreter support where pupils are asked to contribute their ideas in either spoken English/SSE or BSL. Recast each student contribution back to the whole group in the other language and note the gist of each idea on the board	Provides multiple entry points to dialogue and is hospitable to individual cultural and linguistic identities Encourages learners to listen to each other and respect alternative viewpoints Brings multivoicedness to the learning Allows for spontaneous contribution and response to other voices Fosters a hospitable classroom climate and working relationships
Draw on the pupil's home language (where this is not the majority language) as part of the learning activity	Discuss an English story in BSL Invite pupils to share home signs or words for the new and important vocabulary	Values and deploys the full repertoire of individuals and in particular the home language Allows pupils and teachers to learn from each other (co-learning)
Code switch between languages to • check understanding • negotiate meaning • extend the classroom discussion	Discuss a math problem in British Sign Language (BSL) as a class or group; use written English and fingerspelling to point out new math terminology; set new problems for pupils to solve in pairs or groups in BSL or English preferred	Builds a community of practice in the classroom

• introduce new curriculum knowledge • model new language structures • work with learners with different language repertoires	Introduce a new language structure using written English combined with spoken English and fingerspelling to model a range of examples; regularly check individual and group understanding in BSL Demonstrate to the whole class a science procedure in spoken English with interpreter support; follow-up in small group work in BSL or spoken English to fit individual language profiles	Incudes all learners Keeps the task moving forward and conversation flowing Allows for sustained dialogue that represents other voices
Code-blend features of two or more languages to • manage discussion among a linguistically diverse group • introduce new content knowledge and language • make a connection between two languages • model new language structures	Use Sign-Supported English (SSE) to introduce a new topic to a mixed deaf and hearing group and facilitate whole-class discussion Use SSE to facilitate a group discussion among a group of deaf learners with different sign and spoken language repertoires Use SSE for reading aloud during a shared reading task to support access to and understanding of spoken English and make a connection between the spoken word and the text	Facilitates one-to-one or group discussion Facilitates one-to-one or group scaffolded dialogue Provides opportunities for pupils to discuss and question Encourages pupils to listen To and respect alternative viewpoints

BIMODAL BILINGUAL TRANSLANGUAGING
AND DIALOGIC PEDAGOGY

This outline framework suggests how translanguaging can be used in the deaf education classroom as a way of drawing on all the linguistic resources of individuals to support and scaffold learning through a dialogic approach. The strategies and examples comprise ways of making meaning, shaping experiences, and gaining understanding and knowledge with two languages (Baker, 2011, p. 288). These illustrations are not exhaustive. Many different constellations of language use will extend this preliminary framework. As a starting point, this model stimulates ways of thinking about how dialogic teaching can be achieved with deaf learners in diverse and plural contexts. The strategies illustrate how the purposeful use of two or more languages can respond to the language and communication dynamics of the environment and maintain the fluidity of interaction. Most importantly, this framework privileges manner above mode. It is orientated toward achieving quality of interaction and exploring the use of different languages and forms of communication to foster this quality. As way of working, this implies an acceptance of the various different ways that children and adults mix and blend sign and spoken languages to make meaning in different contexts and for different audiences. As a framework for teaching, this model focuses on teacher strategies. However, it is recognized that such practices facilitate learner translanguaging strategies and that this dynamic interplay facilitates learning.

The principles and practical application of translanguaging offer an optimistic perspective on language use in deaf education classroom. The proposed framework for pedagogy conceptualizes translanguaging as a means of "unlocking" classroom dialogue and learning by allowing interaction to flow and all learners to participate. Within this approach, realization of the language or curriculum learning objectives is supported, not constrained, by the language repertoires in play. The open and hospitable nature of this approach does not suggest that "anything goes" in terms of classroom language use. Using translanguaging to facilitate dialogic teaching requires informed and careful planning.

PLANNING FOR TEACHING AND TALKING WITH DEAF CHILDREN

Whether in diverse and plural or monolingual learning contexts, teaching and talking with deaf children needs careful planning that is informed by knowledge of the learners and the learning context (Knoors & Marschark, 2012). This implies knowing the learning profiles of individuals and understanding the full ecology of the child's life in terms of the proximal and more distal influences on his or her learning. These factors, and the ecology of the classroom, will have a bearing on language use and talk among all learners and their teachers. These influences will impinge on the organization of learning and the dynamics of different teaching scenarios such as group work, pair work, and pupil- and teacher-led inquiry (Knoors & Marschark, 2014).

In terms of language use, the decisions that teachers make should be based on an understanding of what language resources the individual brings to learning and how well pupils are learning from different types of language input. Assumptions can too often be made about the most accessible language for learning for deaf learners (Marschark et al., 2005). Such assumptions need to be replaced by informed judgment about individual language competences. Decisions about how language use can be optimized will rest on the extent to which classroom talk can be made accessible through visual communication, hearing technologies, assistive listening devices, and classroom acoustics. The questions that teachers might usefully ask as part of the planning process are:

- What do I know about individual language experience and repertoire?
- What do I know about the language ecology of the classroom?

Many deaf children are still developing competency in sign and/or spoken language even at the high school level, and so the balance of opportunities for supported language learning as well as learning through language needs to be planned individually. The clarity of teaching objectives is crucial because the approach to a language learning activity and a curriculum learning activity will involve completely different types of dialogue, learning activities, and classroom management. Questions that might help teachers to clarify these objectives are:

- What are my learning objectives? Are they language- or curriculum-focused, or a combination of both?
- What types of classroom talk will support these objectives?
- How can this kind of talk be facilitated through teacher and pupil language use in the classroom?

For discussion and dialogue to flow in the classroom, it is not only the nuances of language use that teachers need to achieve, but also the match of the activity to the learning styles of each individual learner. Dialogue requires skills and experience in terms of participation. Some deaf learners may need additional scaffolding to solve problems through dialogue, such as worked examples, or a steer toward relevant information (Borgna, Convertino, Marschark, Morrison, & Rizzolo, 2011). Learners may need activities to be broken down into small steps. Others may need preparatory work that provides contextual support for the activity and helps them to draw on their prior knowledge of a topic (Marschark & Wauters, 2011). Steps may also need to be taken to ensure a physically hospitable learning environment in order to mediate the acoustic demands of group and peer-work activity and the visual business of the classroom (Dye & Hauser, 2014). Deaf learners often experience more authoritative than dialogic talk in the classroom and so getting them used to thinking about, planning, and taking control of their own learning will be an important part of this process. Questions that might guide teachers or planning for these issues are:

- What are the learning styles of the learners (strengths and weaknesses)?
- What support do learners need to participate in dialogic activities?

Dialogue also relies on positive relationships in the classroom among learners, as well as between learners and adults. Indeed, a dialogic approach is predicated on respect for the perspectives of others. This involves understanding alternative positions and viewpoints and knowing how to respond appropriately (e.g., with empathy but not emotion). Deaf learners sometimes lack these skills in social participation and miss essential nonverbal information or nuances of meaning that give information about what others think and how they are feeling (Most & Aviner, 2009). These factors can inhibit the development of friendships in school and social participation. Activities thus need to be managed to promote self-image and the development of positive classroom relationships (Martin, Bat-Chava, Lalwani, & Waltzman, 2011). Questions to help teachers plan for this are:

- What are the social and emotional needs of individuals that may inhibit classroom relationships and dialogue?
- How can these be anticipated, supported, and accommodated to facilitate successful dialogue in the classroom?

Part of the planning process involves thinking about when and how engagement and learning will be monitored. This will include a focus on individual dynamic assessment for learning and summative assessment that measures what has been learned, what progress has been made, and how successful the learning activity was. Checking in on learners allows for targeted individual support and adjustment to the task or the outcomes to ensure that the experience is successful. Ongoing monitoring also gives information about how individuals are learning, and this informs future planning. Summative assessment is less dynamic but provides information about the outcome of the activity in terms of the learning objectives and its overall success, and it tracks learner progress over time. Both of these types of assessment are instrumental in terms of planning learning and assessing progress in school. At the same time, teachers need to build an evidence base of what works in terms of pedagogy and evaluate the potential of dialogic teaching and translanguaging to enhance children's learning and progress in school. Ways of approaching this will be discussed in Chapter 9.

Questions that guide decisions about assessment approaches are:

- What do I want to know in terms of formative and summative task assessment?

- What are my formative strategies for "checking in" on and monitoring learning?
- What are my plans for summative assessment of the overall learning outcomes?

FROM SOLITUDES TO SYNERGY

Great strides have been made in the field of deaf education since the work by Wood et al. (1986) in terms of understanding bimodal bilingualism (and to some extent multilingualism). The extent of this learning affords recognition that teaching and talking with deaf children entails many languages and forms of communication. Pedagogies are therefore needed that are inclusive of all deaf children, relevant to any language and modality, and build on and transform individual repertoires.

There are compelling reasons to adopt a dialogic pedagogical approach in deaf education that encompasses translanguaging. The first is that this approach builds on pedagogical ideas already in development in terms of bimodal bilingual and multilingual deaf education and dialogic approaches (Akamatasu, Stewart, & Mayer, 2004; Lindahl, 2015; Mayer, 2016; Mayer et al., 2002; Swanwick, 2016). This approach also provides ways to develop the good practice already in place in deaf education. Dialogic teaching and translanguaging provide scope for directly teaching aspects of language such as phonics (Miller, Lederberg, & Easterbrooks, 2013) or vocabulary (Luckner & Cooke, 2010) and metalinguistic skills (Berent et al., 2007), as well as strategies for embedding language learning within classroom activities (Williams, 2012).

In terms of literacy development, dialogic teaching and translanguaging provide opportunities for work on early language and shared reading in school and at home (Aram, Most, & Mayafit, 2006; Swanwick & Watson, 2007). This way of working also facilitates the transition from face-to-face communication to reading and writing (Mayer, 2007) and supports learners in engaging in purposeful shared and independent writing activities (Antia, Reed, & Kreimeyer, 2005; Marschark, Lang, & Albertini, 2002). With regard to the wider curriculum, a dialogic approach facilitated by translanguaging, provides opportunities for teaching the knowledge content of the curriculum as well as technical language (R. Kelly, Lang, & Pagliaro, 2003; Kritzer, 2009; Pagliaro & Ansell, 2012). In particular, this approach facilitates the experience of engaging with the discursive practices of the different curriculum areas through use of argument, analysis, and problem-solving dialogue (Molander et al., 2010).

A dialogic approach will not be a panacea or one-step solution to all the challenges in deaf education. Its implementation will need to take into account the heterogeneous and complex nature of this population of learners who are likely to experience diverse challenges in terms of language and literacy, cognition, and social and emotional development. Its relevance will also need to be evaluated for the large proportion of this population (40%) who experience additional learning, physical, and cognitive difficulties associated with the etiologies of hearing loss (Knoors & Vervloed, 2011).

As well as understanding the needs of individual learners, the contexts for learning will also play a part. Deaf children are taught in different contexts where they will encounter a range of qualified—and less qualified—adults with different understandings of deafness and learning, curriculum specialisms, and expectations (Knoors & Marschark, 2014; Salter, 2015). Working dialogically will entail a significant shift in practice across some parts of the profession.

Mindful of these caveats, this approach can provide a way to develop practice that addresses key questions raised in Chapter 7 about language use in the classroom; the development of language and literacy skills, as well as curriculum knowledge; support for the cognitive profiles of deaf learners; and attention to their social and emotional needs in different learning contexts.

An approach that combines dialogic teaching and translanguaging provides the potential for synergy between what we know about language and what we know about learning in deaf education. It is an approach that offers a dynamic response to language diversity and plurality: it provides a structure for the critical and creative use of language repertoires in the classroom, values individual language and cultural identities, and facilitates the teaching of curriculum content and language in a way that fully engages individuals in the learning process. By privileging manner over mode, this approach deconstructs categorical dichotomies and inhibitors around sign and spoken language pedagogies and instead encourages a broad and inclusive perspective on language repertoire and competency that comprises a "dynamic plurilingual pedagogy" (García & Flores, 2012, p. 244).

9 Creating an Evidence Base for Practice

Concepts of plurality and diversity have been discussed in this book starting with a focus on individual language practices. These concepts have been developed to suggest approaches to pedagogy in deaf education. To further knowledge and understanding in both of these domains requires the development of an evidence base for research and practice. This chapter discusses the issues of creating an evidence base about deaf children's language plurality and diversity. This begins with consideration of what is meant by evidence and what we need to know about deaf children's language experience and use, and why. Approaches to building this knowledge base in the field of deaf education, the strides made thus far, and the outstanding questions are reviewed. Ways to extend the breadth and depth of knowledge in this area are discussed while drawing on methodological approaches from the wider field of language research. The importance of transactions between research and practice are underlined as central to the successful gathering of new knowledge and development of evidence-based practice.

EVIDENCE THAT EVALUATES PRACTICE

The priorities for evidence in education vary according to what questions are being asked about learning and the learning process. Most commonly, educators are concerned with evidence regarding the effectiveness of an approach, intervention, or teaching strategy. This kind of evidence is usually conceptualized in terms of outcomes, whether these be academic, developmental, or social (Davies, 1999; Pirrie, 2001). The search for this type of evidence as "proof" is usually articulated in terms of questions at the end of a process that focus on the impact or product of education and the need to evaluate how well something "works." In the context of bimodal bilingual deaf education, these types of questions are frequently asked about the impact of interventions designed to support children's early language development, their literacy learning, and their social and emotional adjustment or the effectiveness of hearing technologies (see Marschark, Knoors, & Tang, 2014). Evidence that one educational approach is more successful than another is also frequently called for in this field (Knoors & Marschark, 2012). One might question the extent to which measuring the outcomes of a whole approach, and all the complexities therein, can be useful. However, until the rigid categories between language approaches in deaf education dissolve, this unanswerable question is rehearsed.

EVIDENCE THAT INFORMS PRACTICE

In contrast to outcome-focused questions, process-focused questions seek evidence that inform practice and provide an insight into what is happening in the learning context. This focus seeks to reveal how children are learning and how adults can help them, so that the effectiveness (or not) of a particular teaching approach or interventions can be judged. This type of evidence often constitutes the rationale for decisions about actions or strategy in education, such as the implementation of a new curriculum or pedagogical approach. The design of a particular intervention or approach should also be based on this sort of evidence.

Educational practitioners should be informally collecting this sort of evidence all the time and adjusting their practice accordingly. The cumulative contextual and process evidence that they collect informs their decisions about what is needed in terms of intervention, change, or support. One would hope that this type of evidence informs all educational initiatives. Unfortunately, expediency sometimes compromises the establishment of a sound evidence base and top-down change, or the adoption of particular educational approach then occurs without this groundwork. In bimodal bilingual deaf education, this process-oriented approach to evidence has been crucial for developing an understanding of deaf children's sign language development, the nature of bimodal bilingual language processing and use, the relationship between sign language and literacy skills, and the changing nature of deaf children's language profiles. Without the growth of this evidence base, bilingual educational support for deaf children would never have developed.

Different types of methodologies tend to be associated with these different approaches to evidence. This should not be overgeneralized because all methodologies are dependent on the research question being asked. However, the groupings described by Spencer and Marschark (2010) are a helpful way to differentiate between types of approach. In the preface to their review of evidence-based practice, Spencer and Marschark identify the most commonly used research methods in educational research to be experimental, quasi-experimental, single-subject design, correlational, and qualitative (pp. 28–37). In their discussion of these different investigative processes, they, too, debate the nature of evidence and its provenance. They stress that no one design is any more useful than the next. The appropriateness of the research design rests on the nature of the research questions. The research questions emerge from gaps in the knowledge base.

In terms of deaf children's linguistic plurality and diversity, there are a number of gaps in our knowledge and competing priorities for evidence. There is a need for evidence that both informs and evaluates practice, but this cannot be achieved without first fully understanding individual experience and contexts for learning. Stepping into relatively unknown territory means that the bulk of the work to be done in the first instance is to gather information about individuals and their language learning contexts. Only then will it be possible to develop ways of working with deaf bilingual and multilingual children and their families (Atkin, Ahmad, & Jones, 2002; Steinberg, Bain, Li, Delgado, & Ruperto, 2003; Zaidman-Zait, 2007). This is not a straightforward task. As Crowe, McLeod, and Ching (2012) acknowledge, the "conceptualization of deaf people's multilingualism is complex" because of the multiple modalities and languages involved (p. 421). This makes it difficult to gather evidence about and accurately describe children's sign and spoken language diversity.

UNDERSTANDING INDIVIDUAL LANGUAGE PROFILES

Although some inroads have been made into understanding and describing deaf children's bimodal and bilingual language experiences (see Marschark, Knoors, & Tang, 2014; Swanwick, 2016), this work is only just extending to contemplate language plurality and diversity in deaf children's lives. A more in-depth understanding involves extending the bimodal bilingual knowledge base to embrace children's experience and use of multiple languages. This implies knowledge of the languages that deaf children are exposed to in different contexts, as well as understanding the diversity of individual repertoire and communicative competence in its broadest sense (Council of Europe, 2007). As discussed in Chapter 6, this means understanding not only children's sign, spoken, and written language abilities but also the way in which they deploy their different language resources to make meaning (Blackledge & Creese, 2010; Blommaert, 2010; Li Wei, 2011). This includes their "critical and creative" use of language (García & Li Wei, 2014, p. 10) and the ability to deploy communicative sensitivity, cultural awareness, and metalinguistic awareness to engage with and respond to the communicative context.

Developing the individual language profiles of deaf children also entails understanding their cultural identification and the diverse ways in which this may be manifested in a culturally diverse society (G. Leigh & Crowe, 2015). This information has to be gained from close-up studies of individuals and their lives. Where possible, insights are needed that draw on the voices of children and their parents, as well as on those in the educational context, in order to expose the "real-world language mosaic of deaf and hard-of-hearing students" (Sutherland & Young, 2007, p. 469). Only with this information can we begin to develop teaching practices, programs, and an educational infrastructure that is supportive of and responsive to individual diversity.

UNDERSTANDING LANGUAGE LANDSCAPES

Research with individuals needs to be set in the context of demographic work about deaf children's signed and spoken languages; that is, the wider "language landscape" (Crowe et al., 2012, p. 423). In the United Kingdom at the moment, we are short on information about the language demographics of schools and services for deaf children. The national survey data gathered by the Consortium for Research in Deaf Education make some inroads into this, but it is incomplete and sometimes confusing (CRIDE, 2015). There is no information about language use in the home context, and the focus of the survey makes it difficult to capture the diverse use of sign and spoken languages at home and at school. The structure of this survey is in development, but, at the time of writing, little is known about the language experiences and repertoires of deaf children in the United Kingdom. Schools and services make every attempt to supplement this national data with data collection methods of their own, but gathering information about language use in plural and diverse contexts and communities is complex and problematic (Mahon et al., 2011).

This dearth of demographic information about sign and spoken language plurality and diversity is not unique to the United Kingdom. Very little published data on deaf children's spoken and sign language plurilingualism exist that reaches beyond English-speaking populations (Crowe, McLeod et al., 2014; Hiddinga & Crasborn, 2011; Woll, Sutton-Spence, & Elton, 2001; Willoughby, 2012). At the same time, language diversity among deaf people is increasing, particularly among population subgroups that are already linguistically diverse and translocated, such as migrant and refugee communities (Knoors & Marschark, 2015; G. Leigh & Crowe, 2015; G. Leigh, Newall, & Newall, 2010).

LANGUAGE LANDSCAPES: METHODOLOGICAL APPROACHES

Different methodological approaches have been employed to address these knowledge gaps. In terms of language landscapes, board contextual knowledge about languages in use across a population can usually be gathered from national census data. These data do not, however, include data about deaf children and their families. The available sources of information for this group are more elusive. Research about national language landscapes that includes attention to deaf children and their families often come from national surveys. For example, the US Annual Survey of Deaf and Hard-of-Hearing Children and Youth collects information on language use at home and at school. The latest 2010 report from this survey showed that 82% of deaf children used English at home, 22% used Spanish, and that other spoken languages in use in that population included Arabic, Filipino, Chinese, Vietnamese, Korean, and Russian. There have only been cumulative reports from smaller-scale surveys since then. At the time of writing, this work was on hold (Gallaudet Research Institute, 2010).

The aforementioned CRIDE survey in the United Kingdom is another example of a survey of population demographics that collects some language information. The data in this survey go so far as to indicate that in schools in England approximately 13% of deaf children use a spoken language other than English. This is difficult to trust because, according to the UK national pupil database, this figure for all schoolchildren is nearer 15% (Strand, Malmberg, & Hall, 2015). The CRIDE survey asks questions about language use that are difficult for teachers to answer, it does not investigate language use at home, and there is missing pupil data. For these reasons, only a partial view of language diversity in the population of deaf schoolchildren is offered, and the figures given need to be interpreted with caution (Swanwick, Wright & Salter, 2016).

A small number of more in-depth and focused population-based studies about deaf children's language use are visible in the research literature. These tend to be limited to developing counties. The most extensive of these is the work by Crowe et al. (2012). This study extrapolated information about the cultural and linguist diversity of three-year-old deaf children from a national survey known as the LOCHI study (Ching et al., 2010). This is a longitudinal study of the audiological, speech, language, academic, and psychosocial outcomes of children with hearing loss across three states of Australia. Data for the 406 children in this study were collected via a written questionnaire completed by children's caregivers and educators. Information about participants' linguistic backgrounds, language use, and communication mode was collated from the full data set. This is the first national study that looks at the language diversity of a population-based sample of three-year-old children. This work is distinctive in its involvement of parents and caregivers in data collection.

Other reported population surveys have been carried out in the United States focusing on Hispanic deaf children (Delgado, 1984; Gernier De Garcia, 2000; Guiberson & Atkins, 2012), in Hungary (Kontra & Csizér, 2013), and in Norway (Arnesen et al., 2008). There are often problems getting complete demographic data. An example of this is seen in the population-based survey study by Albertorio, Holden-Pitt, and Rawlings (1999). The aim of this study was to develop a demographic profile of the Puerto Rican school-aged population. To achieve this, information was extrapolated from the US Annual Survey of Deaf and Hard-of-Hearing Children and Youth about 336 students in education on Puerto Rico. This methodology did not capture the full population, and there were particular gaps in the data about deaf children in inclusive settings. These difficulties, and those encountered in other population-based studies, compromise the knowledge base. It is therefore important that outcomes be reported with caveats so that skewed figures about particular populations do not become indelible facts in the literature. Other available language demographic studies have tended to focus predominantly on sign and spoken language use and have not explored deaf children's use of other languages at home and/or at school (Arnesen et al., 2008; Grimes, Thoutenhoofd, & Byrne, 2007; Mitchell, Young, Bachleda, & Karchmer, 2006).

Smaller scale language demographic studies, although they cannot be generalized to a whole population, can provide useful evidence about particular groups. Such studies broaden understandings of language diversity and can also provide insights into issues for data collection. The study by Mahon et al. (2011), for example, focuses on a group of 147 cochlear-implanted children at one London center. Patient records on this group were analyzed for information about languages used at home as well as audiological and educational placement data. The findings from this study show the propensity for language diversity among deaf children on the one hand (15 different home languages were identified across the group), but also on the variability of information available on children's language and communication. The authors acknowledge the difficulties of collecting information about language use at home and of identifying suitably sensitive measures of communicative competence for such a diverse group.

Population-based studies have the potential to provide a breadth of contextual information and to enable us to build a global knowledge base about deaf children's language diversity and plurality. Population-based surveys combined with national census date can go a long way to providing a comprehensive picture. However, there are a number of caveats. The first is that data are not available in many less economically developed countries. Second, survey methods do not always reach children's use and exposure to language beyond their school lives. Third, where studies do reach parents and families, the information gained has to be carefully interpreted because the use of languages at home by adults and siblings may not reflect individual language use (Willoughby, 2012).

INDIVIDUAL LANGUAGE PROFILES: METHODOLOGICAL APPROACHES

Language landscapes provide the context for understanding individual language experience. Information about individuals enables professionals to plan interventions and support with deaf children and families. To develop this aspect of professional practices requires the close-up scrutiny of individual language repertoires and competence. Collecting this type of evidence in plural and diverse contexts is not straightforward, not least because professionals and researchers rarely have skills in the home languages of the children and families that they are working with. One of the challenges for this field is to develop ways to gain information about the home language environment and culturally sensitive measures of language competence.

There are a number of examples of qualitative measures used in the research to gain in-depth information about language experience and use. Leigh and Crowe (2015) suggest "sensitive and culturally competent observation" alongside more formal language profiling (p. 84). Observation is a time-consuming but an invaluable means of understanding the language dynamics of plurilingual families of deaf children. Observed interactions between children and their parents can be highly structured around proficiency scales (e.g., McConkey-Robbins, Waltzman, & Green, 2004) or centered on naturally occurring communicative situations (e.g., De Quadros, Lillo-Martin, & Chen Pichler, 2016) depending on the nature of the evidence sought. Swanwick et al. (2016) conducted observations of children in communication with their parents and found that the depth of information that they gained about individual repertoire and competence brought different insights to and greatly enhanced the information solely available from school records and teacher report.

A number of questionnaires and interview schedules have been designed for use with multilingual families of deaf children. The bilingual family interview has been used with families of cochlear-implanted children (McConkey-Robbins, 2007). Home languages interview questions were developed for the LOCHI study (Crowe et al., 2012). Such schedules for children, families, and educators can provide insights into many different aspects of language experience, use, and ability and shed light on communication choices (Crowe, Fordham et al., 2014; Swanwick et al., 2016; Willoughby, 2012).

Collecting evidence about language proficiency is perhaps the most challenging aspect of research into plurality and diversity because of the breadth of language knowledge needed to do this properly and the absence of appropriately sensitive language measures for deaf children in different cultural contexts. A number of tools have been designed to develop multilingual language profiles through questionnaire. One example of this is the Language Experience and Proficiency Questionnaire (LEAP-Q) designed for adults to complete about their own language experience and proficiency (Marian, Blumenfeld, & Kaushanskaya, 2007). For children, the MacArthur-Bates Communicative Development Inventory is frequently reported as a useful profiling tool. This is a parent-report instrument designed to document children's communicative competence (Jackson-Maldonado, Marchman, & Fernald, 2013). The use of the Student Oral Language Observation Matrix (SOLOM) is also frequently reported. This profiling instrument is designed for use by teachers but can also be completed by parents about their children's proficiency in the home language (McConkey Robbins et al., 2004).

Measures such as these can be adapted for use in different languages and do not require professionals to have language-specific information. Instruments do exist that can measure aspects of deaf children's language competence (articulation and phonology) across a number of languages, but these require specific language knowledge (McLeod, Harrison, & McCormack, 2012).

Leigh and Crowe (2015) underline the importance of understanding individual linguistic and cultural diversity. They approach this challenge with optimistic creativity, offering numerous suggestions for collecting and understanding information about individuals and their families. Undaunted by the complexity of the diversity issues, they recommend using knowledge of other languages, where possible, but also emphasize the value of partnerships among professionals, communities, and families to collect data and develop this evidence base. They illustrate the value of shared endeavor in collecting language information in order to plan and implement appropriate interventions. This is underlined in the systematic review of published literature on the outcomes of multilingual children with hearing loss conducted by Crowe, McLeod et al. (2014). This review identifies only six studies that investigate children's language development and only four among these that give information about the home language. All of these use the SOLOM, which is not norm referenced, thus making it difficult to compare children's home language development to their monolingual peers.

ETHNOGRAPHIC APPROACHES

To develop further research methodologies that explore language plurality and diversity, there is some merit in looking to other social sciences methodologies. Anthropological research and the ethnographic methodologies associated with this interdisciplinary approach have much to offer in terms of developing an evidence base about language and culture to inform practice. In the field of deaf education studies, anthropological research is usually associated with the study of deaf communities, their history, and the socialization of deaf people (Senghas & Monaghan, 2002). Studies of deaf communities involve approaches to ethnography, and linguistic ethnography in particular, that can reveal a great deal about diverse (sign and spoken) language learning contexts and individual language experience. Ethnographic methodologies offer ways to look in depth at deaf children's family and school experiences in terms of language exposure and use. Such methodologies aim to get inside the everyday lived experiences of individuals, usually through interview and observational methods.

The aim of ethnographic interviewing is to reveal experience and response to that experience by combining unstructured and semi-structured interviewing techniques that encourage individuals to talk about their worlds in their own way (Walford, 2008). The recording and writing up of interview notes is considered an essential part of the analysis process, whereby the researcher immerses him- or herself in the life-worlds of the participants and seeks to interpret the meanings of their responses and actions and of surrounding events. The goal of this methodological approach is to gain and present an insider perspective. The ethnographic study by O'Connell and Deegan (2014) of children's language and schooling experiences illustrates an ethnographic exploration of personal narratives that might inform curriculum and policy development.

Within this paradigm, observational methods usually involve the researcher becoming a participant in the research context (the family, community, classroom, etc.) over an extended period. Being a part of an environment allows for immersion in the activities and the culture of the milieu and provides a close-up experience of interactions and behaviors. Minjeong (2012) used this approach to study the narrative practices of young deaf children. Through participant observation in two classrooms for six months, she collected samples of children's writing and drawing alongside video recordings of storytelling and story-writing events. This enabled her to analyze and identify the different classroom narrative practices that emerge in different social contexts.

Immersion in the family and school contexts of children's lives allows for the development of an insider view that is not normally accessible to researchers. The ethnographic study by Bruno and Lima (2015) provides a further illustration of this. Through immersion in the home and school contexts and the dialogue occurring between the two, they were able to describe language practices at home and at school. Their analysis identified siblings as mediators of communication in and between both contexts. Immersion in both contexts, and the interplay between them, enabled these researchers to develop an understanding of the relationship between communication practices and successful inclusion. The insights into intercultural dialogue gained from this study would not have been captured through conventional survey and interview techniques.

Linguistic Ethnography

Much can be learned from ethnographic approaches about the communication practices of families and communities. Evidence from ethnographic research about plurality and diversity can potentially be useful for educational planning. However, to develop the evidence base further, an in-depth knowledge of individual linguistic repertoire and competence is needed alongside an understanding of cultures and communities. Linguistic ethnography can potentially provide both types of evidence. Linguistic ethnography is a contemporary and still evolving approach that combines linguistic and ethnographic methods. A wealth of research has been undertaken under this umbrella since the term was first introduced and established as a field of study (Rampton, Maybin, & Roberts, 2015). Linguistic ethnography offers a new and interdisciplinary perspective on understanding everyday life, one that combines linguistic and ethnographic ways of questioning and seeing (Copland & Creese, 2015). This approach to inquiry was conceptualized as a way of bridging a gap in research methods to reach previously unreachable knowledge.

Linguistic ethnography offers much to the study of deaf children's language plurality and diversity as a way of finding out about the real-life contexts of language experience, use, repertoire, and competence. Linguistic ethnography in the context of deaf education and studies is usually associated with the study of deaf people's communicative practices and identities (Ladd, 2003). There is a growing body of work in this genre on the emergence of local sign languages and practices around the world (Friedner, 2014; Hoffmann-Dilloway, 2010; Kusters, 2014; Nonaka, 2014; Zeshan, 2011). It is also a methodology often used to bring deaf people's "voices" and "narratives" (including those of children) to the fore in research, policy, and practice (Cooper & Nguyên, 2015; G. Johnson, Pfister, & Vindrola-Padros, 2012; Sutton-Spence, 2010; Thumann-Prezioso, 2005; Van Herreweghe & Vermeerbergen, 2010). As an approach, it also lends itself to exploring interactions between deaf and hearing people in different contexts. Dickinson's (2010) study of sign language interpreters, Najarian's (2006) work on deaf women's negotiation of family and working lives, and Gesser's (2007) account of attitudes and communication behaviors among deaf and hearing people at Gallaudet University are all examples of this methodology in action.

Linguistic ethnography is characterized by openness to understanding the social context of language experience and use and a desire to analyze the linguistics therein. Emerson, Fretz, and Shaw (2011) describe this as a simultaneous process of opening up and tying down. Both these processes are essential in the endeavor to understand and respond to deaf children's language diversity in the educational context. Opening up perspectives on children's language experience and use allows us to see the full extent and dynamic nature of individual practices. Such an approach also enables an insight into how individual language practices are influenced by personal characteristics and abilities, motivations, and identities as well as social and cultural contexts.

Tying down is about exploring more specifically what is happening in terms of communication and interaction and what we can learn about individual language "assets and risks" in order to support development (Antia, 2015). At one level, this may involve any number of approaches to linguistic and discourse analysis, such as conversational analysis (Mahon, 2009), multimodal analysis techniques (Kusters, 2009; Millet & Estève, 2010; Poveda, Morgade, & Pulido, 2010; Poveda, Pulido, Morgade, Messina, & Hédlová, 2008), and textual analysis (Koutsoubou, 2010). In the educational context, this tying down also involves the use of standardized and custom assessment tools and protocols, such as the use of pragmatics profiles, development inventories, and formal and informal language assessments (Herman, 2015).

Bringing the two perspectives of linguistic ethnography and pedagogy together is rarely seen in deaf education and studies. This is not surprising because it is acknowledged in the wider research field that bringing a linguistic ethnographic approach to education creates an "uncomfortable disjuncture" in terms of the epistemological starting point and empirical approach (Rampton et al., 2015, p. 38). Educational research is usually carried out within a particular social construct of education and is often driven by questions of progress, achievement, and success. What we are looking for in educational research is often defined by professional experience and practice and a need to understand and evaluate learning and teaching in institutional terms. Linguistic ethnography, by contrast, seeks to look beyond institutional constructs to examine language use as a social practice embedded in context, and identities and meaning-making as shaped by relationships, histories, and individual repertoires. While recognizing these distinctions, it can be argued that these two perspectives need not be mutually exclusive. Indeed, the study of deaf children's language use, skills, and competencies (gained through conventional measures) can be enhanced by understanding children's different languages practices in different contexts.

The ecological approach to language planning developed at the University of Leeds aims to achieve exactly this sort of hybridization by enabling practitioners to gather data about the diverse contexts of children's sign and spoken language use as well as the extent of their language repertoire in terms of measurable skills and abilities (Swanwick et al., 2016).

Using this Language Planning protocol the Leeds Universty team developed an ecological methodology that sought to embrace both perspectives. This top-down and bottom-up approach was designed to collect a breadth and depth of information about deaf children's language plurality and diversity. Language demographic information was collected using national census and local authority survey data. The national data yielded information about the general population of a local authority district in terms of size, nationalities, ethnicities, and languages in use. The local data provided more detailed school population information in terms of numbers of deaf children on the education caseload, age ranges, and levels of deafness, children with cochlear implants (CIs), ethnicities, nationalities, and languages in use. Alongside the demographic data, individual pupil profiles were developed. The data collection methods for the individual studies involved the use of teacher reports and language assessment information; interviews with teachers, parents, and children; observations of children in school; and analysis of short video clips of children and their parents in conversation. Using this range of strategies enabled the development of rich case studies that described individual backgrounds; deafness, technologies use, and educational experience; language exposure and use at home and at school; and language abilities. The detailed research protocols used for this ecological approach are reported in Swanwick et al. (2016).

The combined demographic and case study approach adopted by this study provided some preliminary insights into deaf children's linguistic and cultural diversity in terms of individual experience and use of different languages within a superdiverse context.

The benefits of adopting a varifocal lens in order to develop evidence are seen in other studies that embrace ethnographic and pedagogical paradigms. Mouvet et al. (2013) adopted this dual focus to explore language practices among deaf children and their hearing parents and, specifically, how communication is influenced by maternal beliefs and ideologies about languages. The knowledge about situated language use that they amassed provides the context for describing and measuring individual pragmatic, linguistic, and communication skills in spoken Dutch and Flemish Sign Language. Further examples of the fruitful transaction between ethnographic and educational perspectives can be seen in the work of Bagga-Gupta and Gynne (2013) on the use of "chaining" in bimodal bilingual classrooms and the work of Roos (2014) on deaf children's use of fingerspelling with teachers and peers.

As with all research, the appropriateness of the methodology is contingent on the research questions. Although linguistic ethnography cannot directly answer the pedagogical questions in deaf education, it can help us to see "what is going on" in the classroom and in children's lives (Lefstein & Israeli, 2015, p. 203). Without this knowledge, any pedagogical approach or intervention is only based on a fraction of the full information needed. In terms of understanding deaf children's language diversity and learning, the interaction between ethnographic and pedagogic perspectives can potentially close the evidence gap. Ethnographic approaches provide ways to collect the evidence needed to design educational support and intervention. Pedagogical approaches provide ways to evaluate that intervention.

Approaches that seek to capture the reality of lived experience and document language use in real-life contexts are not without methodological concerns. There are particular issues in deaf education and studies that tax researchers. One very practical problem is how to work around the potential intrusive use of video recording, recognizing that this changes the communicative context and the dynamic between individuals. Having overcome this first hurdle and successfully collected data on sign and spoken language interaction, researchers are then faced with the question of how to develop a transcription system that fully brings to life the multimodal elements of sign and spoken language use and translanguaging practices of individuals (see Senghas & Monaghan, 2002, for a review). A number of approaches to analyzing multimodal conversations are reported in the literature, including the use of ELAN for analyzing language and creating transcriptions (Millet & Esteve, 2010) and ATLAS or NVivo for the analysis of interviews and field notes. However, capturing everything involved in communication in sign and spoken modalities, including the use of verbal, nonverbal, vocal, and gestural resources, greatly challenges the transcription and coding process.

A further methodological issue in ethnographic research centers on the relationships among deaf and hearing researchers and participants. Hearing researchers often (although not exclusively) explore deaf communities. This poses issues regarding insider–outsider status, the validity of interpreted interaction, and the equality of relationships (Dickinson, 2010; Young & Temple, 2014). These concerns are not unique to the deaf–hearing context. The question of who is qualified to do ethnographic research preoccupies much of the methodological discussion. Blackledge and Creese (2010), for example, underline the importance of a multilingual research team in their study of linguistic practices, ideologies, and identities in complementary school classrooms. A related issue is that of translation and voice in research involving sign and other unwritten languages (Stone & West, 2012). What and how to translate, and how to share such translations, is problematic in any context and even more so when the research questions themselves center on translation and interpretation issues (Roy & Metzger, 2014).

GROWING THE KNOWLEDGE BASE

This review of ways to collect evidence about deaf children's plural and diverse language use points to a number of positives: there is a growing knowledge base and more awareness of the questions that need to be asked to further extend this. Creative and novel approaches are developing to build this evidence base that traverse academic disciplines and methodological paradigms. This endeavor reflects recognition of the need to change from working from belief to working from trustworthy evidence (Spencer & Marschark, 2010).

However, there remains a lot of work to be done to advance this area of research as language and cultural diversity in deaf children increases on a global scale (Knoors & Marschark, 2015). The priorities in terms of growing the evidence base for practice center on knowing more about the context and the individual and all of the complexities therein (Kanto, Huttunen, & Laakso, 2013; Paradis, 2010). To understand anything of the language potential requires knowledge of any languages used and of the potential of the mixed use of languages (Rinaldi, Caselli et al., 2014). It is imperative that this knowledge base continues to be developed and that this evidence is translated into educational practice. For this to be realized, the evidence needs to be process-orientated (what is happening) and outcomes-orientated (what works) if we are ultimately to provide appropriate education for all deaf children.

The approaches reviewed here have been largely qualitative (interview, case study, survey, observation). Setting up the conditions for experimental, quasi-experimental, and correlation research remain problematic in terms of the size and diversity of the populations under investigation. Furthermore, the questions being asked about language plurality and diversity do not (at the moment) lend themselves to these methodologies. There is room, however, for the development of more single-subject design studies (e.g. Gann, Gaines, Antia, Umbreit, & Liaupsin, 2015) and longitudinal work as approaches that offer the potential for focusing on specific groups (De Quadros, Lillo-Martin, & Chen Pichler, 2014, 2015). Diversification of methodologies would help to shift the balance of research endeavor toward more outcomes-focused questions and to bring the language and pedagogy questions closer together. Whatever the research approach, working collaboratively with parents, teachers, and young people must be at the core of these activities. It is only through an understanding of language plurality and diversity across the full ecology of children's lives that meaningful intervention and support strategies can be developed.

10 Unlocking Learning

      The journey through this book began by reviewing what we know and what we do in deaf education and concludes by envisioning what we *could* know and *could* do. As a book about language plurality and diversity, it is hoped that the readership extends to a wide audience interested in the diverse and sometimes exceptional language experiences of bilingual and multilingual children. The first chapter sought to include readers with little experience of deaf education and studies by navigating the sometimes inaccessible and perplexing discourses in this field. The second chapter, outlined the work undertaken hitherto to understand and describe bimodal bilingualism and what this means for children is learning. The third chapter extended the questions about bimodal bilingualism to multilingual contexts and the plural language experiences of deaf children. These first three chapters prepared the ground and provided the rationale for fresh perspectives on language and learning. The fourth chapter encouraged new ways of looking at and thinking about language and presented the language and learning issues for deaf children in a new light. This perspective was explored through Chapter 5, which revealed synergies between deaf and hearing bilingual and multilingual learners. Chapter 6 envisages an asset-focused approach to language diversity and plurality in deaf education. The theoretical underpinning of Chapters 4, 5, and 6 provided the foundations for a pedagogical framework. The application of this approach was explored in Chapter 8. Chapter 9 combined caution with creativity, placing evidence as central to continued work in this area.

This final chapter reflects on the questions posed at the start of the text and the theoretical framework underpinning the ideas discussed. This chapter summarizes the shift in perspective that this texts brings to deaf education and studies and the contribution that it makes to the wider field of language education and research. Ways forward are suggested, anticipating future opportunities and challenges for research and practice.

THE RESEARCH QUESTIONS

Two questions were posed at the start of this book. The first of these was concerned with how to understand and describe deaf children's language use and experience in terms of current concepts of language plurality and diversity. The second asked how knowledge of and a different perspective on deaf children's language diversity and pluralism can inform pedagogy. The exploration of these two fundamental questions about deaf children's language and their learning can be concpetualised as as one big question about how language can mediate learning for deaf children. This would have been too big a question to contemplate in the first instance. Elucidation of the issues of language plurality and diversity was an essential first step before the learning issues could be properly analyzed. That done, approaches to language use in education were proposed that unlock learning for deaf children. These approaches build on established work in the wider field of language education and research but address the exceptional case of bilingual and multilingual deaf children.

The use of the phrase "unlocking learning" is a deliberate reference to a very early call for bilingual education for deaf children (Johnson,

Liddell, & Erting, 1989). This iconic discussion paper by scholars at Gallaudet University called for a new approach to deaf education that ensured children's access to curricular content through delivery in sign language. The model proposed at that time recommended sign language to be considered as deaf children's first language and for English to be learned through reading and writing. Although this "one-size-fits-all" model now seems too restrictive and out of sync with more dynamic approaches to bilingualism, the concept of "unlocking learning" remains powerful. It implies the pre-existence of potential and focuses on language as the key. To unlock learning requires an understanding of the learning process and the role of language in that process. The theoretical perspectives taken in this text accent this connection.

THEORETICAL PERSPECTIVES

The theoretical perspectives on bilingualism and learning that provide the footings for this book connect issues in deaf education with current thinking in the wider field of language and learning. The approach taken to bilingualism encompasses the plural and dynamic nature of deaf children's bilingual bimodal and multilingual language experience. The work that has been accomplished to develop understandings of bimodal bilingualism is taken forward to include the experiences of deaf children who use multiple languages and the diverse ways in which they use sign and spoken languages to make meaning for different purpose and in different contexts. The act of meaning creation is at the heart of this approach that focuses on what children can do with language and how they use language to interact with others. This attention to languaging reframes language ability as linguistic action. Language abilities are only meaningful in so far as they enable learners to be in, and to act on, the world. The sum of children's language knowledge and competencies is conceptualized as *repertoire*, that is, as an integrated whole with many linguistic and cultural dimensions. The notion of an integrated linguistic competency replaces the troubled questions of language transfer in the deaf education literature with the concept of a fluid and dynamic interplay between languages that generates novel and creative ways to make meaning. This theoretical approach offers a perspective on language use that recognizes the seamless ways in which languages can be used together to make meaning. The concept of translanguaging that encapsulates this fluidity in the hearing bilingual research is relevant to the context of deaf learners, notwithstanding caveats regarding the experience of deafness and the modality issues.

Learning is theorized in this text from a sociocultural perspective that places interaction at the heart of the learning process. Learning takes place not just as a result of "being" in the world, but also as a result of action in the world, action that is mediated by language. Within this paradigm, interaction refers not only to dialogue with others but also with the social and cultural values, beliefs, and norms of the environment. Dialogue can be construed as social talk, collaboration, or argument with others or as solitary reflection on experience and reasoning of action. Through this lens, learning is envisaged as a truly creative and transformative process through which we perpetually use knowledge and resources (our cultural tools) to develop new knowledge and resources. As we learn, we continue to learn about the process of learning itself. Dialogue is the fuel for this process, whether this is spontaneous or designed, social or internal. Dialogue provides the contrast of two or more perspectives that reveals a question to be explored or a space for something new to emerge. Dialogue is more than a conversation; it is the vehicle for examination, reflection, and judgment and for the negotiation of meaning among individuals and their social and cultural contexts. A dialogic theory of learning thus involves all of the communication partners involved. This perspective on learning also embraces the full ecology of a child's life and all the influences on learning therein. It is a theoretical perspective that positions language as central and languaging as the bedrock of learning.

DIALOGY IN DEAF EDUCATION

Current pedagogies in deaf education do not articulate how learning might take place. They impose a particular language diet for deaf learners but do not elucidate how any one particular regime might facilitate individual learning. The pedagogies that are prevalent in this field are underpinned by important concepts of inclusivity, equality, and access but not by theories of learning. In contrast, a dialogic pedagogical framework is underpinned by a theory of learning that does not prescribe any particular language menu in the classroom. As a pedagogical framework, it does not espouse any one particular language hypothesis (auditory-oral, sign bilingual, total communication [TC]) and is applicable to any deaf child in any learning context. As a pedagogy that facilitates language development and engagement with the curriculum, it is responsive to two of the main challenges in deaf education. The hospitable nature of this pedagogy, which emphasizes participation, engagement, and sensitivity to individual learner identity, also speaks to the emotional and social issues associated with deaf children's school experiences. This approach to pedagogy does not attach a singular approach to language use in the classroom. Instead, it involves thinking critically about language use and how to use language as a mediating tool to facilitate dialogue. It affords teachers the professional integrity to attune and respond to the discrepancies between the language demands of the learning context and the language resources of the individual and adjust their language use accordingly.

TRANSLANGUAGING IN DEAF EDUCATION

Translanguaging is not the next new approach to language distribution in the deaf education classroom; neither is it a methodology, philosophy, or a policy. Translanguaging certainly does not equate to TC, SimCom, or Sign-Supported Speech. Translanguaging denotes a rational way for describing the way in which deaf children use two or more languages in their daily lives. It is also a way of planning how to use the dynamic language repertoires in play in the learning context. As discussed in previous chapters, deaf children translanguage all the time, without confusion, regardless of the nature of the language input or the language policy in place. Children's translanguaging practices do not put their language development trajectories (in sign and/or spoken language) at risk. These practices enable children to "get on and do things" with the language resources that they have, and they do not compromise or inhibit the development of skills in their separate languages. Deaf children and other bilingual children, may well be translanguaging without a strong base in either of their languages. Although language fluency must be a priority, eschewing translanguaging while waiting for this base to develop is not practical. Children will do what they can with what they have. It is up to researchers and educators to keep up.

Translanguaging involves the integrated use of the languages, communication conventions, semiotic resources and cultures that we know to make meaning. It allows for fluidity of communication and expression of and responsivity to the identities and intentions in play. Translanguaging acts create new utterances that combine the language resources available. One language is not switched off as the other is switched on. The translanguaging acts of teachers may also be intuitive responses to individuals' translanguaging skills. These strategies constitute a powerful teaching tool. Translanguaging for pedagogical reasons should, however, be mindful. Teachers need to be aware of their own practices, articulate the decisions that guide them, and be able to evaluate their effect on children's learning.

Embracing concepts of dialogy and translanguaging opens doors to communication, learning, and teaching in plural and diverse learning contexts. In the classroom context, dialogy focuses attention on the quality of interaction and how this facilitates learning. Translanguaging (pupil and/or teacher) makes this interaction possible. Through dialogue, pupils can be supported to develop their language skills as well as extend their curriculum knowledge. Translanguaging enables the fluid movement between the use of languages to do something else and noticing language as an object of study. Teacher translanguaging enables the modeling of fluent language use but also the analysis of one language through another. The opportunities that translanguaging unlocks for dialogue in the classroom, as well as among children, their peers, their families, and their communities, are infinite. This emancipatory approach brings both opportunities and challenges to deaf education and research.

A COHERENT PEDAGOGY

The synthesis of the principles of dialogy and translanguaging offers a coherent and inclusive pedagogy in deaf education that is neither prescriptive nor divisive. A pedagogy that is concerned with the nature of talk in education is one that is relevant to any learning context, all learners, and all professionals involved in supporting learning. There is no hiding place from talk, whatever the language policy of the setting, the learning profiles of the student, the technologies in use, or the make-up of the support team. This is not a pedagogy only relevant to bilingual and multilingual pupils. It is a pedagogy that is relevant to all learners and especially hospitable to children for whom language learning and curriculum access present challenges. A linguistically dynamic and dialogic pedagogy implies the fine-tuning of language input and support that all deaf pupils need. As an approach that embodies empathy and cultural sensitivity, it has the potential to alleviate some of the social and emotional demands of school life and improve individual self-esteem and sense of belonging. The focus of this approach turns the argument about language in deaf education on its head by privileging attention to *how* language is used, rather than *what* language is used. There is no place in a linguistically dynamic and dialogic pedagogy for dogma about one language or the other. Only an open approach to language repertoire can facilitate a diverse and nuanced use of language in the classroom that is attuned to individual needs and the demands of context.

The coherence in this approach lies not only in its relevance across the field of deaf education. It represents a way of working that is congruent with the language practices of deaf children in contexts beyond the classroom and, in particular, within home, family, and close community settings. This presents a real opportunity to establish consistency of approach and shared understanding between schools and families; to value and build on the language practices in the home; and to provide support to families that is contingent on their linguistic and cultural identities, affiliations, and behaviors.

Finally, while recognizing the exceptional languages issues in deaf education, it is refreshing to contemplate a pedagogy that is recognizable across the wider field of language education and research. Deaf education encompasses specialist knowledge and questions about language, but it should not be considered a silo. This approach opens up the wider dialogue between deaf and language education. This is potentially transformative for both fields as new perspectives, evidence, pedagogical ideas, and challenges emerge.

AN ASSETS-BASED PERSPECTIVE

The risks to deaf children's educational progress and socialization are well-documented throughout the deaf education literature. The assets that deaf children bring to the learning context are less visible in the literature. To take an assets-focused approach is not to underplay the challenges to linguistic, cognitive, and social development that deaf children encounter (Antia, 2015). The intention is instead to bring to light the linguistic, cognitive, and social resources that deaf children do bring to the learning context. These resources become increasingly evident when we begin to analyze how deaf children exploit their linguistic repertory and competencies to make meaning with others and participate in diverse social and cultural contexts. Concentrating on language action, or languaging, exposes these resources and reveals what individuals can do with the language skills available to them to be with others and act on the world. Translanguaging enhances the languaging capacity of individuals by increasing the meaning-making potential of the total language repertoire. The next step for research and practice, beyond the contemplation of these assets, is to develop ways to identify, develop, and integrate them into pedagogy.

PROFESSIONAL DEVELOPMENT AND TRAINING

One of the challenges for practice that this approach presents concerns the training and development of practitioners. Although specialist training for teachers of the deaf already exists in the United Kingdom, these are not the only adults who engage in talk with deaf children in the school context. Some deaf children will be taught directly by a teacher of the deaf with the specialist skills and language expertise needed to facilitate talk that supports learning. However, teaching assistants and communication support workers, for whom there are no established training routes, support the majority of deaf children in mainstream classrooms. Furthermore, mainstream teachers do not usually have any prior experience of deaf children, and there is no compulsory deaf awareness component to their training. There are two issues here. The first is that a deaf child may be in a learning context where none of the practitioners has the skills and experience to create a dialogic learning experience. The second issue is that, even where a dialogue in the classroom is designed to facilitate learning, the deaf pupil may not be able to access this experience. Dialogue between the mainstream teacher and the class, or among a small group, may be mediated by another adult (through English, or sign language) so that direct person-to-person engagement is compromised. This is a training and professional development issue for all practitioners involved in teaching and talking with deaf children.

To equip teachers to embrace a linguistically dynamic and dialogic pedagogy, training courses need to help them think critically about language and dialogue across all the domains of their work. This requires an approach to training that provides a broad knowledge base in terms of deafness, development, language, learning, and technologies, but one that helps teachers to draw on this knowledge base to work dialogically and use language mindfully in the classroom. Enabling teachers to make these connections between theory and practice helps them to articulate the reasons for what they do in the classroom and make informed choices about developing teaching approaches or interventions. Knowledge on its own does not shape the teacher, and for experience to be meaningful there has to be reflection. The role of training is therefore to impart knowledge and provide opportunities for teachers to reflect critically on their experiences.

An effective way to create this critical orientation to language use and dialogy is to incorporate activities in training that challenge teacher's perceptions and assumptions about individual language repertoire and use and that invite teachers to examine their own language repertoire in action in teaching situations. One approach to this is to have teachers film themselves working with a group of deaf children with different sign and spoken language skills and abilities and ask them to analyze their language use during the teaching activity. This processes is enlightening and sometimes surprising for teachers as they reflect on the different ways in which their communication does, or does not, facilitate learning. This activity can produce some remarkable insights from teachers and transform their narrative about their own translanguaging in the classroom (Swanwick, 2015). The use of observation and filmed interactions between children and their peers, teachers, and parents is an invaluable tool in training for developing teacher's skills in seeing and describing an individual language repertoire and competency, as well as in analyzing and evaluating dialogy and translanguaging in action.

NEW METHODOLOGIES

A second challenge is the development of an evidence base to inform and evaluate practice. As professionals in the field of deaf education, we do not want another educational approach to be rolled out that is based on belief and ideology and not on evidence, or that that divides the field and that does not serve the full population of deaf school children. The development of evidence needs to be built into this way of working. Collecting evidence in deaf education does not have to involve randomized controlled trials or large-scale testing. The evidenced collected by Wood et al. (1986) on teaching and talking with deaf children was collected through classroom observation and the analysis of classroom interaction, as is the case with many other seminal studies in education (Alexander, 1995; Tizard & Hughes, 1984; Tough, 1977; Wells, 1986). Teachers' engagement with evidence is invaluable in this endeavor because they have the day-to-day, close-up experience of language, learning, and individual development. These insights can be developed as research evidence in many different ways through partnerships between practitioners and researchers. Practitioner secondment, action research partnerships, and collaborative language planning are just three examples of how this synergy can be successfully created through partnership methodologies (Swanwick, 2015). For an area of research that is so new, the development of methodologies will be an iterative process. The challenge ahead is to shape and hone tools that gather reliable and comprehensive language demographic information and to develop methods for perceiving and describing the language repertoires and competencies of individuals.

THE CONTINUING DIALOGUE

This book opened with two research questions. In true dialogic form, the answers to these questions open up new questions and areas for exploration: "If an answer does not give rise to a new question it falls out of the dialogue" (Bakhtin, 1986, p. 168).

The new questions that emerge embrace research and practice issues and very much set a working agenda that needs to be a transaction between both. The area of exploration centers on translanguaging as representing a shift in perspective from language to language in action and as the mechanism for unlocking participation and learning in linguistically plural and diverse contexts. Questions for the future need to guide the development of a deeper understanding of sign and spoken language translanguaging and how this facilitates communication, participation, and belonging in deaf children's lives.

The meaning of translanguaging in the context of deaf children has been explored for the first time in this text, and this has established that the dynamic and fluid use of sign and spoken languages is increasingly a natural part of communication among deaf children in the contexts of home and school. The work done so far raises profound issues about how children and their families engage in multilingual and multimodal meaning-making in exceptional circumstances. To take this forward, further exploration is needed of the linguistic and cultural dynamics of deaf children's translanguaging in home and school contexts as sites for the transmission of knowledge, values, and affiliation. The ways in which sign and spoken languages are used together for different purposes and in different contexts need to be fully identified. The role of different artifacts and actors in translanguaging acts also need to be analyzed to develop understandings of how translanguaging is mediated by technologies, individuals, and discourses in different cultural milieu. This will involve the development of data collection methods described in Chapter 9 as well as established approaches to observation and interviews with deaf children, their families, and teachers. More extensive data collection and the use of analysis tools such as ELAN will enable the full description of translanguaging practices linguistically, but also in terms of motivation, enactment, and impact.

To begin to categorize translanguaging practices and analyze the potential of these practices to enhance learning, a clear distinction needs to be made between individual and pedagogical translanguaging. In individual terms, the study of translanguaging needs to further explore the ways in which deaf children draw on their sign and spoken language repertoires to make meaning. Pedagogically, research is needed into translanguaging as the critical use of two or more languages in the classroom as a means of unlocking dialogue to facilitate learning. This ongoing work will extend understandings of different ways in which linguistic and cultural identities can be expressed and transformed in nuanced ways through the creative use of individual linguistic repertory. It will also develop understandings of what it means to be deaf and to be other things, such as bilingual and/or multilingual (Atkin et al., 2002). For learners and the adults who help them, the role of technology as a factor in translanguaging practices also needs to be understood. Such an endeavor will inform approaches to language support and intervention for all children who use multiple languages in their daily lives.

This text has argued for a dynamic view of language in deaf education that focuses on language as a mediating tool for learning and transcends established language ideologies. Adopting this perspective has exposed issues of diversity and plurality in deaf children's lives, identified gaps in the research, and opened up fresh ideas for pedagogy that are coherent and theoretically sound. The focus on languaging has revealed deaf children's language potential and how this potential is enacted in home and school contexts. Examining the languaging of deaf children, their families, friends, and teachers has enriched understandings of the nature of sign and spoken language interactions and how such interactions, through dialogue, support learning. With dialogue at the center, the proposed framework for pedagogy is limitless in terms of its scope for development and its application to diverse language and learning profiles in diverse contexts.

Although focused primarily on the language and learning experiences of deaf children, it is hoped that this book has begun a dialogue of its own between the field of deaf education and studies and the wider field of language education and research that is "a continuous, developmental communicative interchange through which we stand to gain a fuller apprehension of the world, ourselves, and one another" (Burbules, 1993, p. 8).

The study of people's languages and communication should embrace exceptional circumstances and contexts so that knowledge about human potential for language can continue to grow. If the aim of scholarship is to learn from, challenge, and expand established thinking, then studies of exceptional situations need to be analyzed within a wider context. This is an argument for a continued dialogue about plural and diverse language experience and use that includes sign, spoken, and written modalities and all the multiplicities therein.

REFERENCES

Adesope, O. O., Lavin, T., Thompson, T., & Ungerleider, C. (2010). A systematic review and meta-analysis of the cognitive correlates of bilingualism. *Review of Educational Research, 80*(2), 207–245. doi:10.3102/0034654310368803

Ahlgren, I. (1994). Sign language as the first langauge. In I. Ahlgren & K. Hyltenstam (Eds.), *Bilingualism in deaf education* (pp. 55–60). Hamburg, Germany: Signum Verlag.

Akamatsu, T., Stewart, D., & Becker, B. J. (2000). Documenting English syntactic development in face-to-face signed communication. *American Annals of the Deaf, 145*(5), 452–463.

Akamatsu, C. T., Stewart, D. A., & Mayer, C. (2002). Is it time to look beyond teachers' signing behavior?. *Sign Language Studies, 2*(3), 230–254.

Albertorio, J. R., Holden-Pitt, L., & Rawlings, B. (1999). Preliminary results of the annual survey of deaf and hard of hearing children and youth in Puerto Rico: The first wave. *American Annals of the Deaf, 144*(5), 386–394.

Alexander, R. J. (1995). *Versions of primary education.* London: Routledge.

Alexander, R. J. (2001). *Culture and pedagogy: International comparisons in primary education.* Oxford: Blackwell.

Alexander, R. J. (2003). Oracy, literacy and pedagogy: International pespectives. In E. Bearne, H. Dombey, & T. Grainger (Eds.), *Interactions in language and literacy in the classroom* (pp. 23–35). Milton Keynes, UK: Milton Keynes Open University Press.

Alexander, R. J. (2008a). *Towards dialogic teaching: Rethinking classroom talk* (4th ed.). Cambridge: Dialogos.

Alexander, R. J. (2008b). *Essays on pedagogy.* New York/London: Routledge.

Allsop, L., Woll, B., & Brauti, J. M. (1994). International Sign: The creation of an international deaf community and sign language. *Sign Language Research,* 171–118.

Alptekin, C. (2010). Redefining multicompetence for bilingualism and ELF. *International Journal of Applied Linguistics,* 20(1), 95–110. doi:10.1111/j.1473-4192.2009.00230.x.

Alvarado, J. M., Puente, A., & Herrera, V. (2008). Visual and phonological coding in working memory and orthographic skills of deaf children using Chilean sign language. *American Annals of the Deaf,* 152(5), 467–479.

Anderson, Y. (1994). Deaf people as a linguistic minority. In I. Ahlgren & K. Hyltenstam (Eds.), *Bilingualism in deaf education* (pp. 9–14). Hamburg, Germany: Signum Verlag.

Andrews, J., & Rusher, M. (2010). Codeswitching techniques: Evidence-based instructional practices for the ASL/English bilingual classroom. *American Annals of the Deaf,* 155(4), 407–424.

Anglin-Jaffe, H. (2013). Signs of resistance: Peer learning of sign languages within "oral" schools for the deaf. *Studies in Philosophy and Education,* 32(3), 261–271. doi:10.1007/s11217-012-9350-3.

Antia, S. (2015). Enhancing academic and social outcomes: Balancing individual, family, and school assets and risks for deaf and hard-of-hearing students in general education. In H. Knoors & M. Marschark (Eds.), *Educating deaf learners: Creating a global evidence base* (pp. 527–546). New York: Oxford University Press.

Antia, S., & Kreimeyer, K. H. (2001). The role of interpreters in inclusive classrooms. *American Annals of the Deaf,* 146(4), 355–365.

Antia, S., & Metz, K. (2014). Co-enrollment in the United States: A critical analysis of benefits and challenges. In M. Marschark, G. Tang, & H. Knoors (Eds.), *Bilingualism and bilingual deaf education* (pp. 424–444). New York/Oxford: Oxford University Press.

Antia, S., Reed, S., & Kreimeyer, K. H. (2005). Written language of deaf and hard-of-hearing students in public schools. *Journal of Deaf Studies and Deaf Education,* 10(3), 244–255. doi:10.1093/deafed/eni026.

Aragão, R. (2011). Beliefs and emotions in foreign language learning. *System,* 39(3), 302–313. doi:10.1016/j.system.2011.07.003.

Aram, D., Most, T., & Mayafit, H. (2006). Contributions of mother-child storybook telling and joint writing to literacy development in kindergartners with hearing loss. *Language, Speech, and Hearing Services in Schools, 37*(3), 209–223. doi:10.1044/0161-1461(2006/023).

Archbold, S. (2010). *Deaf education: Changed by cochlear implantation?* (PhD thesis), Radboud University, Nijmegen.

Archbold, S. (2015). Being a deaf student: Changes in characteristics and needs. In H. Knoors & M. Marschark (Eds.), *Educating deaf learners: Creating a global evidence base* (pp. 23–46). New York: Oxford University Press.

Archbold, S., & Mayer, C. (2012). Deaf education: The impact of cochlear implantation? *Deafness & Education International, 14*(1), 2–15. doi:10.1179/1557069X12Y.0000000003.

Arnesen, K., Enerstvedt, R. T., Engen, E. A., Engen, T., Høie, G., & Vonen, A. M. (2008). The linguistic milieu of Norwegian children with hearing loss. *American Annals of the Deaf, 153*(1), 65–77.

Atkin, K., Ahmad, W. I. U., & Jones, L. (2002). Young South Asian deaf people and their families: Negotiating relationships and identities. *Sociology of Health and Illness, 24*(1), 21–45.

Bagga-Gupta, S., & Gynne, A. (2013). Young people's languaging and social positioning: Chaining in "bilingual" educational settings in Sweden. *Linguistics and Education, 24*(4), 479.

Baker, A., & Van Den Bogaerde, B. (2008). Code-mixing in signs and words in input to and putput from children. In C. Plaza-Pust & E. Morales-Lopez (Eds.), *Sign bilingualism: Language development, interaction, and maintenance in sign language contact situations* (pp. 1–28). Amsterdam: John Benjamins.

Baker, A., Van Den Bogaerde, B., & Woll, B. (2005). Methods and procedures in sign language acquisition studies. *Sign Language and Linguistics, 8*(1–2), 7–58.

Baker, C. (2011). *Foundations of bilingual education and bilingualism* (5th ed.). Clevedon, UK: Multilingual Matters.

Bakhtin, M. (1981). *Dialogic imagination: Four essays* (vol. 1). Austin: University of Texas Press.

Bakhtin, M. (1986). *Speech genres and other late essays* (V. W. McGee., Trans.). Austin: University of Texas Press.

Barnum, M. (1984). In support of bilingual/bicultural education for deaf children. *American Annals of the Deaf, 129*(5), 404–408. doi:10.1353/aad.2012.0945.

Bauman, H. D., & Murray, J. (2009). Reframing: From hearing loss to deaf gain. *Deaf Studies Digital Journal, 1*(1).

Bebko, J. M., Calderon, R., & Treder, R. (2003). The Language Proficiency Profile-2: Assessment of the Global Communication Skills of Deaf Children Across

Languages and Modalities of Expression. *Journal of Deaf Studies and Deaf Education*, 8(4), 438–451. doi:10.1093/deafed/eng034.

Becker, A. L. (1995). *Beyond translation: Essays toward a modern philology*. Ann Arbor: University of Michigan Press.

Berent, G. P., Kelly, R. R., Aldersley, S., Schmitz, K. L., Khalsa, B. K., Panara, J., & Keenan, S. (2007). Focus-on-form instructional methods promote deaf college students' improvement in English grammar. *Journal of Deaf Studies and Deaf Education*, 12(1), 8–24. doi:10.1093/deafed/enl009.

Bezemer, J., & Kress, G. (2008). Writing in multimodal texts. *Written Communication*, 25(2), 166.

Bialystok, E. (1991). *Language processing in bilingual children*. Cambridge: Cambridge University Press.

Bialystok, E. (2004). The impact of bilingualism on language and literacy development. In T. K. Bhatia & W. C. Ritchie (Eds.), *The handbook of bilingualism* (pp. 577–601). Oxford: Blackwell.

Bialystok, E. (2007). Language acquisition and bilingualism: Consequences for a multilingual society. *Applied Psycholinguistics*, 28(03), 393–397. doi:10.1017/S0142716407070208

Bialystok, E. (2009a). Bilingualism: The good, the bad, and the indifferent. *Bilingualism: Language and Cognition*, 12(1), 3–11. doi:10.1017/S1366728908003477

Bialystok, E., & Barac, R. (2012). Emerging bilingualism: Dissociating advantages for metalinguistic awareness and executive control. *Cognition*, 122(1), 67–73. doi:10.1016/j.cognition.2011.08.003

Bialystok, E., Craik, F. I. M., & Luk, G. (2012). Bilingualism: Consequences for mind and brain. *Trends in Cognitive Sciences*, 16(4), 240–250. doi:10.1016/j.tics.2012.03.001

Billings, L., & Fitzgerald, J. (2002). Dialogic discussion and the Paideia Seminar. *American Educational Research Journal*, 39(4), 907–941. doi:10.3102/00028312039004905

Blackledge, A., & Creese, A. (2009). Meaning-making as dialogic process: Official and carnival lives in the language classroom. *Journal of Language, Identity & Education*, 8(4), 236–253. doi:10.1080/15348450903130413

Blackledge, A., & Creese, A. (2010). *Multilingualism: A critical perspective*. London: Continuum.

Blommaert, J. (2008). Language, asylum, and the national order. *Urban Language & Literacies*, 50, 2–21.

Blommaert, J. (2010). *The sociolinguistics of globalization*. Cambridge: Cambridge University Press.

Blommaert, J., & Backus, A. (2012). Superdiverse repertoires and the individual. *Tilburg Papers in Culture Studies*, 24.

Blommaert, J., & Rampton, B. (2011). Language and superdiversity. *Diversities*, 13(2), 1–21.

Böhme, D., Boll, F., Schmitt, C., & Müller, C. (2014). Gesture as interactive expressive movement: Inter-affectivity in face-to-face communication. In C. Müller, A. Cienki, E. Fricke, S. H. Ladewig, D. McNeill, & J. Bressem (Eds.), *Body-language communication: An international handbook on multimodality in human interaction* (Vol. 1, pp. 2112–2124). Berlin: Mouton de Gruyter.

Boons, T., Brokx, J. P. L., Dhooge, I., Frijns, J. H. M., Peeraer, L., Vermeulen, A., van Wieringen, A. (2012). Predictors of spoken language development following pediatric cochlear implantation. *Ear and Hearing, 33*(5), 617–639. doi:10.1097/AUD.0b013e3182503e47

Boothroyd, A. (2002). Room acoustics and speech perception. Retrieved June 28, 2014, from http://www-rohan.sdsu.edu/~aboothro/files/Papers_on_RoomAcoustics/

Borgna, G., Convertino, C., Marschark, M., Morrison, C., & Rizzolo, K. (2011). Enhancing deaf students' learning from sign language and text: Metacognition, modality, and the effectiveness of content scaffolding. *Journal of Deaf Studies and Deaf Education, 16*(1), 79–100. doi:10.1093/deafed/enq036

Botha, R. (2007). On homesign systems as a potential window on language evolution. *Language and Communication, 27*(1), 41–53. doi:10.1016/j.langcom.2005.10.001

Bourdieu, P. (2000). *Pascalian meditations*. Cambridge: Polity Press in association with Blackwell Publishers.

Bowen, S. K. (2008). Coenrollment for students who are deaf or hard of hearing: Friendship patterns and social interactions. *American Annals of the Deaf, 153*(3), 285–293.

British Academy. (2013). *Multilingual Britain*. Windsor: Cumberland Lodge

British Society of Audiology. (1988). Descriptors for pure tone audiograms. *British Journal of Audiology* , 22, 123

Bronfenbrenner, U. (1979). *The ecology of human development: Experiments by nature and design*. Cambridge, MA: Harvard University Press.

Bronfenbrenner, U. (1992). *Ecological systems theory*. London: Jessica Kingsley.

Bronfenbrenner, U. (2005). *Making human beings human: Bioecological perspectives on human development*. London: Sage.

Brooks, L., Swain, M., Lapkin, S., & Knouzi, I. (2010). Mediating between scientific and spontaneous concepts through languaging. *Language Awareness, 19*(2), 89–110. doi:10.1080/09658410903440755

Brown, A. L., & Palincsar, A. S. (1989). Guided co-operative learning and indivdiual knowledge acquisition. In L. B. Resnick (Ed.), *Knowing, learning and instruction* (pp. 393–451). Hillsdale, NJ: Lawrence Erlbaum.

Bruner, J. S. (1960). *The process of education*. Cambridge, MA: Harvard University Press.

Bruner, J. S. (1966). *Toward a theory of instruction*. Cambridge, MA: Belknap.

Bruner, J. S. (1978). The role of dialogue in language acquisition. In A. Sinclair, R. J. Jarvelle & W. J. M. Levelt (Eds.), *The child's concept of language* (pp. 241–256). New York: Springer-Verlag.

Bruner, J. S. (1990). *Acts of meaning*. Cambridge, MA: Harvard University Press.

Bruno, M. M. G., & Lima, J. M. (2015). Ways of communication and inclusion of the Kaiowá deaf children in family and school: An ethnographic study. *Revista Brasileira de Educação Especial, 21*(1), 127–142. doi:10.1590/s1413-65382115000100009

Burbules, N. C. (1993). *Dialogue in teaching: Theory and practice* (Vol. 10). New York/London: Teachers College Press.

Busch, B. (2012). The linguistic repertoire revisited. *Applied Linguistics, 33*(5), 503–523. doi:10.1093/applin/ams056.

Calderon, R., & Greenberg, M. T. (2011). Social and emotional development of deaf children: Family, school, and program effects. In M. Marschark & P. Spencer (Eds.), *The Oxford handbook of deaf studies, language, and education* (2nd ed., Vol. 1, pp. 188–199). New York: Oxford University Press.

Cambra, C. (1997). The attitude of hearing students towards the integration of deaf students in the classroom. *Deafness and Education, 21*(2), 21–25.

Canagarajah, A. S. (2007). The ecology of global English. *International Multilingual Research Journal, 1*(2), 89–100. doi:10.1080/15257770701495299

Canagarajah, A. S. (2011). Codemeshing in academic writing: Identifying teachable strategies of translanguaging. *Modern Language Journal, 95*(3), 401–417. doi:10.1111/j.1540-4781.2011.01207.x

Castellanos, I., Pisoni, D., Kronenberger, W., & Beer, J. (2016). Neurocognitive function in deaf children with cochlear-implants: Early development and long-term outcomes. In M. Marschark & P. Spencer (Eds.), *The Oxford handbook of deaf studies in language* (pp. 264–275). New York: Oxford University Press.

Celic, C., & Seltzer, K. (2012). Translanguaging: A CUNY-NYSIEB guide for educators Retrieved January, 2015, from http://www.cuny-nysieb.org

Chamberlain, C., & Mayberry, R. I. (2000). Theorizing about the relation between American Sign Language and reading. In J. P. Morford & R. I. Mayberry (Eds.), *Language acquisition by eye* (pp. 221–260). Hillside, NJ: Lawrence Erlbaum.

Chen Pichler, D., & Koulidobrova, H. (2015). Acquisition of sign language as a second language. In M. Marschark & P. Spencer (Eds.), *The Oxford handbook of deaf studies: Language and language development* (pp. 218–230). New York: Oxford University Press.

Ching, T., Crowe, K., Martin, V., Day, J., Mahler, N., Youn, S.Orsini, J. (2010). Language development and everyday functioning of children with hearing loss assessed at 3 years of age. *International Journal of Speech-Language Pathology, 12*(2), 124–131. doi:10.3109/17549500903577022

Ching, T., Van Wanrooy, E., Hill, M., & Incerti, P. (2006). Performance in children with hearing aids or cochlear implants: Bilateral stimulation and binaural hearing. *International Journal of Audiology, 45*(SUPPL. 1), S108–S112. doi:10.1080/14992020600783087

Christensen, K. M. (2010). *Ethical considerations in educating children who are deaf or hard of hearing.* Washington DC: Gallaudet University Press.

Cline, T., & Mahon, M. (2010). Deafness in a multilingual society: A review of research for practice. *Educational and Child Psychology, 27*(2), 41–49.

CRIDE [Consortium for Research into Deaf Education]. 2015. Report on 2015 survey on educational provision for deaf children in England. London: NDCS. [Accessed 30th January 2016]. Available from http://www.ndcs.org.uk/professional_support/national_data/cride.html

Conrad, R. (1979). *The deaf school child: Language and cognitive function.* London: Harper & Row.

Convertino, C., Borgna, G., Marschark, M., & Durkin, A. (2014). Word and world knowledge among deaf learners with and without cochlear implants. *Journal of Deaf Studies and Deaf Education, 19*(4), 471–483. doi:10.1093/deafed/enu024

Cook, V. (1991). The poverty-of-the-stimulus argument and multicompetence. *Second Language Research, 7*(2), 103–117. doi:10.1177/026765839100700203

Cook, V. (1992). Evidence for multicompetence. *Language Learning, 42*(4), 557–591. doi:10.1111/j.1467-1770.1992.tb01044.x

Cook, V. (2008). *Second language learning and language teaching.* London: Hodder Education.

Cook, V., & Li Wei (Eds.). (2016). *Cambridge handbook of linguistic multicompetence.* Cambridge: Cambridge University Press.

Cooper, A. C., & Nguyên, T.(2015). Signed language community-researcher collaboration in Viêt Nam: Challenging language ideologies, creating social change. *Journal of Linguistic Anthropology, 25*(2), 105–127. doi:10.1111/jola.12081

Copland, F., & Creese, A. (2015). *Linguistic ethnography: Collecting, analysing and presenting data.* London: Sage.

Cormier, K., Schembri, A., Vinson, D., & Orfanidou, E. (2012). First language acquisition differs from second language acquisition in prelingually deaf signers: Evidence from sensitivity to grammaticality judgement in British Sign Language. *Cognition, 124*(1), 50–65.

Council of Europe. (2001). *Common European framework of reference for languages: Learning, teaching, assessment.* Cambridge: Cambridge University Press.

Council of Europe. (2007). *From linguistic diversity to plurilingual education: Guide for the development of language education policies in Europe.* Strasbourg: Council of Europe. Cambridge: Cambridge University Press

Creese, A., & Blackledge, A. (2010). Translanguaging in the bilingual classroom: A pedagogy for learning and teaching? *Modern Language Journal, 94*(1), 103–115.

Crowe, K., Fordham, L., McLeod, S., & Ching, T. (2014). Part of our world: Influences on caregiver decisions about communication choices for children with hearing loss. *Deafness and Education International, 16*(2), 61–85. doi:10.1179/1557069X13Y.0000000026

Crowe, K., McLeod, S., & Ching, T. (2012). The cultural and linguistic diversity of 3-year-old children with hearing loss. *Journal of Deaf Studies and Deaf Education, 17*(4), 421–438. doi:10.1093/deafed/enq034

Crowe, K., McLeod, S., McKinnon, D. H., & Ching, T. (2014). Speech, sign, or multilingualism for children with hearing loss: Quantitative insights into caregivers' decision making. *Language, Speech, and Hearing Services in Schools, 45*(3), 234–247.

Cummins, J. (1991). Interdependence of first-and second-language proficiency in bilingual children. In E. Bialystock (Ed.), *Language processing in bilingual children* (pp. 70–89). Cambridge: Cambridge University Press.

Cummins, J. (2006). *The relationship between American Sign Language and English academic development: A review of the research.* Toronto: Ontario Association of the Deaf.

Cummins, J. (2007). Rethinking monolingual instructional strategies in multilingual classrooms. *Canadian Journal of Applied Linguistics, 10*(2), 221–240.

Dahlberg, G., & Bagga-Gupta, S. (2013). Communication in the virtual classroom in higher education: Languaging beyond the boundaries of time and space. *Learning Culture and Social Interaction, 2*(3), 127–142. doi:10.1016/j.lcsi.2013.04.003

Dahlberg, G., & Bagga-Gupta, S. (2014). Understanding glocal learning spaces. An empirical study of languaging and transmigrant positions in the virtual classroom. *Learning, Media and Technology, 39*(4), 468–487. doi:10.1080/17439884.2014.931868

Daniel, M. F., Lafortune, L., Pallascio, R., Splitter, L., Slade, C., & De la Garza, T. (2005). Modelling the development process of dialogical critical thinking in pupils aged 10 to 12 years. *Communication Education, 54*(4), 334–354.

Davies, P. (1999). What is evidence-based education? *British Journal of Educational Studies, 47*(2), 108–121. doi:10.1111/1467-8527.00106

De Quadros, R., Lillo-Martin, D., & Chen Pichler, D. (2014). Sobreposição no desenvolvimento bilíngue bimodal [Code-blending in bimodal bilingual development]. *Revista Brasileira de Linguística Aplicada, 14*, 799–834.

DeLana, M., Gentry, M. A., & Andrews, J. (2007). The efficacy of ASL/English bilingual education: Considering public schools. *American Annals of the Deaf, 152*(1), 73–87.

Delgado, G. (1984). *The Hispanic deaf: Issues and challenges for bilingual special education.* Washington DC: Gallaudet University Press.

DeLuzio, J., & Girolametto, L. (2011). Peer interactions of preschool children with and without hearing loss. *Journal of Speech Language and Hearing Research, 54*(4), 1197–1210. doi:10.1044/1092-4388(2010/10-0099)

De Quadros, R., Lillo-Martin, D., & Pichler, D. C. (2016). Bimodal bilingualism: Sign and spoken language. In M. Marschark & P. Spencer (Eds.), *The Oxford handbook of deaf studies in language* (pp. 181–196). New York: Oxford University Press.

De Raeve, L. (2015). Classroom adaptations for effective learning by deaf students. In H. Knoors & M. Marschark (Eds.), *Educating deaf learners: Creating a global evidence base* (pp. 547–572). New York: Oxford University Press.

Dewaele, J. M., Petrides, K. V., & Furnham, A. (2008). Effects of trait emotional intelligence and sociobiographical variables on communicative anxiety and foreign language anxiety among adult multilinguals: A review and empirical investigation. *Language Learning, 58*(4), 911–960. doi:10.1111/j.1467-9922.2008.00482.x

Dickinson, J. (2010). Access all areas: Identity issues and researcher responsibilities in workplace settings. *Text & Talk, 30*(2), 105–124. doi:10.1515/text.2010.006

Dockreill, J. E., & Shield, B. M. (2006). Acoustical barriers in classrooms: The impact of noise on performance in the classroom. *British Educational Research Journal, 32*(3), 509–525. doi:10.1080/01411920600635494

Donati, C., & Branchini, C. (2013). Challenging linearization: Simultaneous mixing in early bimodals. In T. Biberauer & I. Roberts (Eds.), *Challenges to linearization* (pp. 93–128). Berlin: Mouton de Gruyter.

Dubuisson, C., Parisot, A. M., & Vercaingne-Ménard, A. (2008). Bilingualism and deafness: Correlations between deaf students' ability to use space in Quebec Sign Language and their reading comprehension in French. In

C. Plaza-Pust & E. Morales-Lopez (Eds.), *Sign bilingualism: Language development, interaction, and maintenance in sign language contact situations* (pp. 51–72). Amsterdam: John Benjamins.

Dunn, A. L., & Fox Tree, J. E. (2009). A quick, gradient Bilingual Dominance Scale. *Bilingualism: Language and Cognition, 12*(3), 273–289. doi:10.1017/S1366728909990113

Dye, M., & Hauser, P. (2014). Sustained attention, selective attention and cognitive control in deaf and hearing children. *Hearing Research, 309*, 94–102. doi:10.1016/j.heares.2013.12.001

Dye, M., Hauser, P., & Bavalier, D. (2008). Visual attention in deaf children and adults In M. Marschark & P. Hauser (Eds.), *Deaf cognition foundations and outcomes*. New York: Oxford: University Press.

Easterbrooks, S., & Beal-Alvarez, M. A. (2013). *Literacy instruction for students who are deaf and hard of hearing*. New York: Oxford University Press.

Emerson, R., R. I. Fretz, and L. L. Shaw. (2011). *Writing ethnographic fieldnotes* (2nd ed.). Chicago: Chicago University Press.

Emmorey, K. (2002). *Language, cognition, and the brain: Insights from sign language research*. Mahwah, NJ: Lawrence Erlbaum.

Emmorey, K., Borinstein, H. B., Thompson, R. & Gollan, T. (2008). Bimodal bilingualism. *Bilingualism: Language and Cognition, 11*(1), 43–61. doi:10.1017/S1366728907003203

Emmorey, K., & Petrich, J. (2012). Processing orthographic structure: Associations between print and fingerspelling. *Journal of Deaf Studies and Deaf Education, 17*(2), 194–204.

Engeström, Y. (2001). Expansive learning at work: Toward an activity theoretical reconceptualization. *Journal of Education and Work, 14*(1), 133–156. doi:10.1080/13639080020028747

Evans, C. (2004). Literacy development in deaf students: Case studies in bilingual teaching and learning. *American Annals of the Deaf, 149*(1), 17–27.

Feldman, H. M., Dollaghan, C. A., Campbell, T. F., Kurs-Lasky, M., Janosky, J. E., & Paradise, J. L. (2000). Measurement properties of the MacArthur communicative development inventories at ages one and two years. *Child Development, 71*(2), 310–322.

Fitzpatrick, E. M., & Olds, J. (2015). Practitioners' perspectives on the functioning of school-age children with cochlear implants. *Cochlear Implants International, 16*(1), 9–23. doi:10.1179/1754762814y.0000000080

Ford, H., & Kent, S. (2013). The experiences of bilingualism within the deaf and the hearing world: The views of d/Deaf young people. *Deafness and Education International, 15*(1), 29–51. doi:10.1179/1557069X12Y.0000000013

Friedner, M. (2014). The church of deaf sociality: Deaf churchgoing practices and "Sign Bread and Butter" in Bangalore, India. *Anthropology and Education Quarterly, 45*(1), 39–53. doi:10.1111/aeq.12046

Fung, C., Chow, B. W. Y., & McBride-Chang, C. (2005). The impact of a dialogic reading program on deaf and hard-of-hearing kindergarten and early primary school-aged students in Hong Kong. *Journal of Deaf Studies and Deaf Education, 10*(1), 82–95. doi:10.1093/deafed/eni005

Fung, C., & Tang, G. (2013). *Simultaneous acquisition of Hong Kong Sign Language and Cantonese: Violation of code-blending grammar*. Paper presented at the 1st Symposium on Sign Language Acquisition, Universidade Catolica, Lisbon, Portugal.

Gallaudet Research Institute. (2008). *Regional and national summary report of data from the 2007–2008 National survey of deaf and hard-of-hearing children*. Washington DC: Gaullaudet Research Institute.

Gann, C. J., Gaines, S. E., Antia, S., Umbreit, J., & Liaupsin, C. J. (2015). Evaluating the effects of function-based interventions with deaf or hard-of-hearing students. *Journal of Deaf Studies and Deaf Education, 20*(3), 252–265. doi:10.1093/deafed/envo11

Garberoglio, C. L., Cawthon, S. W., & Bond, M. (2014). Assessing English literacy as a predictor of postschool outcomes in the lives of deaf individuals. *Journal of Deaf Studies and Deaf Education, 19*(1), 50–67. doi:10.1093/deafed/ento38

García, O. (2009). *Bilingual education in the 21st century: A global perspective*. Malden, MA/Chichester: Wiley-Blackwell.

García, O., & Flores, N. (2012). Multilingual pedagogies In M. Martin-Jones, A. Blackledge, & A. Creese (Eds.), *The Routledge handbook of multilingualism* (pp. 232–246). London: Routledge.

García, O., & Li Wei. (2014). *Translanguaging: Language, bilingualism and education*. Hampshire: Palgrave Macmillan.

García, O., & Sylvan, C. (2011). Pedagogies and practices in multilingual classrooms: Singularities in pluralities. *Modern Language Journal, 95*(3), 385–400. doi:10.1111/j.1540-4781.2011.01208.x

Gaustad, M. G., & Kelly, R. R. (2004). The relationship between reading achievement and morphological word analysis in deaf and hearing students matched for reading level. *Journal of Deaf Studies and Deaf Education, 9*(3), 269–285.

Gayle, B. M., Preiss, R. W., & Allen, M. (2006). How effective are teacher-initiated classroom questions in enhancing student learning? In B. M. Gayle, R. W. Preiss, N. Burrell, & M. Allen (Eds.), *Classroom communication and instructional processes* (pp. 279–293). Mahwah: Lawrence Erlbaum

Gernier De García, B. (2000). Meeting the needs of Hispanic/Latino deaf students. InK. M. Christensen & G.L. Delgado (Eds). *Deaf plus: A Multicultural perspective* (pp. 148–198). San Diego: Dawn Sign Press.

Gesser, A. (2007). Learning about hearing people in the land of the deaf: An ethnographic account. *Sign Language Studies, 7*(3), 269–283.

Gort, M., & Sembiante, S. F. (2015). Navigating hybridized language learning spaces through translanguaging pedagogy: Dual language preschool teachers' languaging practices in support of emergent bilingual children's performance of academic discourse. *International Multilingual Research Journal, 9*(1), 7–25. doi:10.1080/19313152.2014.981775

Gregory, S., Smith, S., & Wells, A. (1997). Language and identity sign bilingual deaf children. *Deafness & Education International, 21*(3), 31–38.

Grimes, M., Thoutenhoofd, E. D., & Byrne, D. (2007). Language approaches used with deaf pupils in Scottish schools: 2001–2004. *Journal of Deaf Studies and Deaf Education, 12*(4), 530–551.

Groce, N. E. (1985). *Everyone here spoke sign language: Hereditary deafness on Martha's Vineyard*. Cambridge, MA/London: Harvard University Press.

Grosjean, F. (1992). Another view of bilingualism. In R. J. Harris (Ed.), *Cognitive processing in bilinguals. Advances in psychology* (pp. 51–62). Oxford: North-Holland.

Grosjean, F. (1996). Living with two languages and two cultures. Cultural and language diversity and the deaf experience. In I. Parasnis (Ed.), *Cultural and language diversity and the deaf experience* (pp. 20–37). Cambridge: Cambridge University Press.

Grosjean, F. (2001). The right of the deaf children to grow up bilingual. *Sign Language Studies, 1*(2), 110–114.

Grosjean, F. (2008). *Studying bilinguals*. Oxford: Oxford University Press

Grosjean, F. (2010). Bilingualism, biculturalism, and deafness. *International Journal of Bilingual Education and Bilingualism, 13*(2), 133–145.

Guiberson, M., & Atkins, J. (2012). Speech-language pathologists' preparation, practices, and perspectives on serving culturally and linguistically diverse children. *Communication Disorders Quarterly, 33*(3), 169–180.

Gumperz, J. (1964). Linguistic and social interaction in two communities. *American Anthropologist, 66*(6_PART 2), 137–153. doi:10.1525/aa.1964.66.suppl_3.02a00100

Gutiérrez, K., Baquedano-López, P., Alvarez, H., & Chiu, M. (1999). Building a culture of collaboration through hybrid language practices. *Theory into Practice, 38*(2), 87–93. doi:10.1080/00405849909543837

Gutierrez, K. D. (1993). How talk, context, and script shape contexts for learning: A cross-case comparison of journal sharing. *Linguistics and Education, 5*(3), 335–365. doi:10.1016/0898-5898(93)90005-U

Hall, J. K., Cheng, A., & Carlson, M. T. (2006). Reconceptualizing multicompetence as a theory of language knowledge. *Applied Linguistics, 27*(2), 220–240. doi:10.1093/applin/aml013

Halliday, M. A. K. (1993). Towards a language-based theory of learning. *Linguistics and Education, 5*(2), 93–116. doi:10.1016/0898-5898(93)90026-7

Haptonstall-Nykaza, T. S., & Schick, B. (2007). The transition from fingerspelling to English print: Facilitating English decoding. *Journal of Deaf Studies and Deaf Education, 12*(2), 172–183.

Harris, M., & Terlektsi, E. (2011). Reading and spelling abilities of deaf adolescents with cochlear implants and hearing aids. *Journal of Deaf Studies and Deaf Education, 16*(1), 24–34.

Hauser, P. C. (2000). Code switching: American Sign Language and cued English. In M. Metzger (Ed.), *Bilingualism and identity in deaf communities* (pp. 43–78). Washington DC: Gallaudet University Press.

Herdina, P., & Jessner, U. (2002). *A dynamic model of multilingualism: Perspectives of change in psycholinguistics* (Vol. 121). Clevedon: Multilingual Matters.

Herman, R. (2015). Language assessment of deaf learners. In H. Knoors & M. Marschark (Eds.), *Educating deaf learners: Creating a global evidence base* (pp. 197–212). New York: Oxford University Press.

Herman, R., & Roy, P. (2006). Evidence from the wider use of the BSL Receptive Skills Test. *Deafness and Education International, 8*(1), 33–47.

Hermans, D., De Klerk, A., Wauters, L., & Knoors, H. (2014). The twin-school: A co-enrollment program in the Netherlands. In M. Marschark, G. Tang, & H. Knoors (Eds.), *Bilingualism and bilingual deaf education* (pp. 396–423). New York/Oxford: Oxford University Press.

Hermans, D., Knoors, H., Ormel, E., & Verhoeven, L. (2008). The relationship between the reading and signing skills of deaf children in bilingual education programs. *Journal of Deaf Studies and Deaf Education, 13*(4), 518–530.

Hermans, D., Ormel, E., & Knoors, H. (2010). On the relation between the signing and reading skills of deaf bilinguals. *International Journal of Bilingual Education and Bilingualism, 13*(2), 187–199.

Hermans, D., Wauters, L., De Klerk, A., & Knoors, H. (2014). Quality of instruction in bilingual schools for deaf children: Through the children's eyes and the camera's lens. In M. Marschark, G. Tang, & H. Knoors (Eds.), *Bilingualism and bilingual deaf education* (pp. 272–291). New York/Oxford: Oxford University Press.

Hickok, G., Love-Geffen, T., & Klima, E. S. (2002). Role of the left hemisphere in sign language comprehension. *Brain and Language, 82*(2), 167–178.

Hicks, C. B., & Tharpe, A. M. (2002). Listening effort and fatigue in school-age children with and without hearing loss. *Journal of Speech, Language, and Hearing Research, 45*(3), 573–584.

Hiddinga, A., & Crasborn, O. (2011). Signed languages and globalization. *Language in Society, 40*(4), 483–505. doi:10.1017/s0047404511000480

Hintermair, M. (2015). Social relations of deaf learners: Important resources for socioemotional well-being and academic success. In H. Knoors & M. Marschark (Eds.), *Educating deaf learners: Creating a global evidence base* (pp. 283–310). New York: Oxford University Press.

Hoffmann-Dilloway, E. (2010). Many names for mother: The ethno-linguistic politics of deafness in Nepal. *South Asia: Journal of South Asia Studies, 33*(3), 421–441. doi:10.1080/00856401.2010.520652

Hoffmeister, R. (2000). A piece of the puzzle: ASL and reading comprehension in deaf children. In C. Chamberlain, J. P. Morford, & R. I. Mayberry (Eds.), *Language acquisition by eye* (pp. 143–163). Mahwah, NJ: Lawrence Erlbaum.

Holzinger, D., & Fellinger, J. (2014). Sign language and reading comprehension: No automatic transfer. In M. Marschark, G. Tang, & H. Knoors (Eds.), *Bilingualism and bilingual deaf education* (pp. 102–133). New York/ Oxford: Oxford University Press.

Hornberger, N. (1990). Creating successful learning contexts for bilingual literacy. *Teachers College Record, 92*(2), 212–229.

Hornberger, N., & Link, H. (2012). Translanguaging and transnational literacies in multilingual classrooms: A biliteracy lens. *International Journal of Bilingual Education and Bilingualism, 15*(3), 261–278.

Hornsby, B. W. Y., Werfel, K., Camarata, S., & Bess, F. H. (2014). Subjective fatigue in children with hearing loss: Some preliminary findings. *American Journal of Audiology, 23*(1), 129–134. doi:10.1044/1059-0889

Howe, C., & Littleton, K. (2010). *Educational dialogues: Understanding and promoting productive interaction.* London: Routledge.

Hrastinski, I., & Wilbur, R. B. (2016). Academic achievement of deaf and hard-of-hearing students in an ASL/English bilingual program. *Journal of Deaf Studies and Deaf Education, 21*(2), 1-15

Humphries, T., & MacDougall, F. (2000). "Chaining" and other links: Making connections between American Sign Language and English in two types of school settings. *Visual Anthropology Review, 15*(2), 84–94.

Hunsicker, D., & Goldin-Meadow, S. (2013). How handshape type can distinguish between nouns and verbs in homesign. *Gesture, 13*(3), 354–376. doi:10.1075/gest.13.3.05hun

Hymes, D., & Gumperz, J. (1986). *Directions in sociolinguistics: The ethnography of communication.* Oxford: Basil Blackwell.

Ishikawa, M. (2013a). Examining the effect of written languaging: The role of metanotes as a mediator of second language learning. *Language Awareness, 22*(3), 220–233. doi:10.1080/09658416.2012.683435

Ishikawa, M. (2013*b*). Metanotes (written languaging) in a translation task: Do L2 proficiency and task outcome matter? *Innovation in Language Learning and Teaching*, 1–15. doi:10.1080/17501229.2013.857342

Jackson-Maldonado, D., Marchman, V. A., & Fernald, L. C. H. (2013). Short-form versions of the Spanish MacArthur-Bates Communicative Development Inventories. *Applied Psycholinguistics*, *34*(4), 837–868. doi:10.1017/S0142716412000045

Jarvis, J., Iantaffi, A., & Sinka, I. (2003). Inclusion in mainstream classrooms: Experiences of deaf pupils. In M. Nind, J. Rix, K. Sheehy, & K. Simmons (Eds.), *Inclusive Education: Diverse Perspectives* (pp. 206–218). London: David Fulton.

Jensen, T. W. (2014). Emotion in languaging: Languaging as affective, adaptive, and flexible behavior in social interaction. *Frontiers in Psychology*, *5*(July). doi:10.3389/fpsyg.2014.00720

Jessner, U. (2008). A DST model of multilingualism and the role of metalinguistic awareness. *Modern Language Journal*, *92*(2), 270–283. doi:10.1111/j.1540-4781.2008.00718.x

Johnson, G., Pfister, A. E., & Vindrola-Padros, C. (2012). Drawings, photos, and performances: Using visual methods with children. *Visual Anthropology Review*, *28*(2), 164–178. doi:10.1111/j.1548-7458.2012.01122.x

Johnson, R. E., Liddell, S. K., & Erting, C. J. (1989). *Unlocking the curriculum: Principles for achieving access in deaf education*. Washington, DC: Gallaudet University.

Kanto, L., Huttunen, K., & Laakso, M. L. (2013). Relationship between the linguistic environments and early bilingual language development of hearing children in deaf-parented families. *Journal of Deaf Studies and Deaf Education*, *18*(2), 242–260.

Karchmer, M. A., & Mitchell, R. E. (2005). Parental hearing status and signing among deaf and hard of hearing students. *Sign Language Studies*, *5*(2), 231–244. doi:10.1353/sls.2005.0004

Keating, E., & Mirus, G. (2003). Examining interactions across language modalities: Deaf children and hearing peers at school. *Anthropology and Education Quarterly*, *34*(2), 115–135.

Kelly, G., & Brown, C. (2002). Communicative demands of learning science through technological design: Third grade students' construction of solar energy devices. *Linguistics and Education*, *13*(4), 483–532. doi:10.1016/S0898-5898(03)00005-6

Kelly, R., Lang, H. G., & Pagliaro, C. M. (2003). Mathematics word problem solving for deaf students: A survey of practices in grades 6–12. *Journal of Deaf Studies and Deaf Education*, *8*(2), 104–119. doi:10.1093/deafed/eng007

Kelman, C. A., & Branco, A. U. (2009). (Meta) communication strategies in inclusive classes for deaf students. *American Annals of the Deaf,* 154(4), 371–381.

Kharkhurin, A. V. (2008). The effect of linguistic proficiency, age of second language acquisition, and length of exposure to a new cultural environment on bilinguals' divergent thinking. *Bilingualism: Language and Cognition,* 11(2), 225–243. doi:10.1017/S1366728908003398

Klatter-Folmer, J., van Hout, R., Kolen, E., & Verhoeven, L. (2006). Language development in deaf children's interactions with deaf and hearing adults: A Dutch longitudinal study. *Journal of Deaf Studies and Deaf Education,* 11(2), 238–251. doi:10.1093/deafed/enj032

Knoors, H. (2007). Educational responses to varying objectives of parents of deaf children: A Dutch perspective. *Journal of Deaf Studies and Deaf Education,* 12(2), 243–253.

Knoors, H. (2016). Foundations for language development in deaf children and the consequences for communication choices. In M. Marschark & P. Spencer (Eds.), *The Oxford handbook of deaf studies in language* (pp. 19–31). New York: Oxford University Press.

Knoors, H., & Marschark, M. (2012). Language planning for the 21st century: Revisiting bilingual language policy for deaf children. *Journal of Deaf Studies and Deaf Education,* 17(3), 291–305. doi:10.1017/S027226310808073X;

Knoors, H., & Marschark, M. (2014). *Teaching deaf learners: Psychological and developmental foundations.* New York: Oxford University Press.

Knoors, H., & Marschark, M. (2015). Educating deaf students in a global context. In H. Knoors & M. Marschark (Eds.), *Educating deaf learners: Creating a global evidence base* (pp. 1–22). New York: Oxford University Press.

Knoors, H., & Renting, B. (2000). Measuring the quality of education: The involvement of bilingually educated deaf children. *American Annals of the Deaf,* 145(3), 268–274.

Knoors, H., Tang, G., & Marschark, M. (2014). Bilingualism and bilingual deaf education: Time to take stock. In M. Marschark, G. Tang, & H. Knoors (Eds.), *Bilingualism and bilingual deaf education* (pp. 1–2). New York: Oxford University Press.

Knoors, H., & Vervloed, M. (2011). Educational programming for deaf children with multiple disabilities: Accommodating special needs. In M. Marschark & P. Spencer (Eds.), *The Oxford handbook of deaf studies, language, and education* (2nd ed., Vol. 1, pp. 82–96). New York: Oxford University Press.

Kontra, E. H., & Csizér, K. (2013). An investigation into the relationship of foreign language learning motivation and sign language use among deaf and hard of hearing. *IRAL–International Review of Applied Linguistics in Language Teaching, 51*(1), 1–22. doi:10.1515/iral-2013-0001

Koutsoubou, M. (2010). The use of narrative analysis as a research and evaluation method of atypical language: The case of deaf writing. *International Journal of Bilingual Education and Bilingualism, 13*(2), 225–241.

Koutsoubou, M., Herman, R., & Woll, B. (2006). Bilingual language profiles of deaf students: An analysis of the written narratives of three deaf writers with different language proficiencies. *Deafness and Education International, 8*(3), 144–168.

Koutsoubou, M., Herman, R., & Woll, B. (2007). Does language input matter in bilingual writing? Translation versus direct composition in deaf school students' written stories. *International Journal of Bilingual Education and Bilingualism, 10*(2), 127–151.

Kramsch, C. (2011). Language and culture. In J. Simpson (Ed.), *The Routledge handbook of applied linguistics* (pp. 305–318). London: Routledge

Krausneker, V. (2008). Language use and awareness of deaf and hearing children in a bilingual setting. In C. Plaza-Pust & E. Morales-Lopez (Eds.), *Sign bilingualism: Language development, interaction and maintenance in sign language contact situations* (pp. 195–222). Amsterdam: John Benjamins.

Kress, G., & van Leeuwen, T. (2001). *Multimodal discourse.* London: Arnold.

Kritzer, K. L. (2009). Barely started and already left behind: A descriptive analysis of the mathematics ability demonstrated by young deaf children. *Journal of Deaf Studies and Deaf Education, 14*(4), 409–421. doi:10.1093/deafed/enp015

Kuhn, D., Cheney, R., & Weinstock, M. (2000). The development of epistemological understanding. *Cognitive Development, 15*(3), 309–328.

Kusters, A. (2009). Deaf on the lifeline of Mumbai. *Sign Language Studies, 10*(1), 36–68. doi:10.1353/sls.0.0035

Kusters, A. (2010). Deaf utopias? Reviewing the sociocultural literature on the world's "Martha's Vineyard situations." *Journal of Deaf Studies and Deaf Education, 15*(1), 3–16. doi:10.1093/deafed/enp026

Kusters, A. (2011). Deaf and disability studies: Interdisciplinary perspectives. *Journal of Deaf Studies and Deaf Education, 16*(4), 555–555. doi:10.1093/deafed/enr005

Kusters, A. (2014). Language ideologies in the shared signing community of Adamorobe. *Language in Society, 43*(2), 139–158. doi:10.1017/S0047404514000013

Kyle, F., & Harris, M. (2010). Predictors of reading development in deaf children: A 3-year longitudinal study. *Journal of Experimental Child Psychology, 107*, 229–243.

Kyle, F., & Harris, M. (2011). Longitudinal patterns of emerging literacy in beginning deaf and hearing readers. *Journal of Deaf Studies and Deaf Education*, *16*(3), 289–304.

Ladd, P. (2003). *Understanding deaf culture: In search of deafhood*. Clevedon/Buffalo, NY: Multilingual Matters.

Laevers, F. (1994). Innovative project experiential education and the definition of quality in education. In F. Laevers (Ed.), *Defining and assessing quality in early childhood education* (pp. 159–172). Leuven, Netherlands: Leuven University Press.

Lane, H. L. (1992). *The mask of benevolence: Disabling the deaf community*. New York: Knopf.

Langereis, M., & Vermeulen, A. (2015). School performance and wellbeing of children with CI in different communicative-educational environments. *International Journal of Pediatric Otorhinolaryngology*, *79*(6), 834–839. doi:10.1016/j.ijporl.2015.03.014

Lantolf, J., & Thorne, S. (2006). *Sociocultural theory and the genesis of second language development*. Oxford: Oxford University Press

Larsen-Freeman, D., & Cameron, L. (2008). *Complex systems and applied linguistics*. Oxford: Oxford University Press.

Lefstein, A. (2008). Changing classroom practice through the English National Literacy Strategy: A micro-interactional perspective. *American Educational Research Journal*, *45*(3), 701–737.

Lefstein, A., & Israeli, M. (2015). Applying linguistic ethnography to educational practice: Notes on the interaction of academic research and professional sensibilities. In J. Snell, S. Shaw & F. Copland (Eds.), *Theory and method in linguistic ethnography. inguistic ethnography: Interdisciplinary explorations* (pp. 187–206). Hampshire, UK: Palgrave Macmillan.

Leigh, G., & Crowe, K. (2015). Responding to cultural and linguistic diversity among deaf and hard-of-hearing learners. In H. Knoors & M. Marschark (Eds.), *Educating deaf learners: Creating a global evidence* (pp. 69–92). New York: Oxford University Press.

Leigh, G., Newall, J. P., & Newall, A. T. (2010). Newborn screening and earlier intervention with deaf children: Issues for the developing world. In M. Marschark & P. Spencer (Eds.), *The Oxford handbook of deaf studies, language and education* (Vol. 2, pp. 345–359). New York: Oxford University Press.

Leigh, I., Maxwell-McCaw, D., Bat-Chava, Y., & Christiansen, J. B. (2009). Correlates of psychosocial adjustment in deaf adolescents with and without cochlear implants: A preliminary investigation. *Journal of Deaf Studies and Deaf Education*, *14*(2), 244–259. doi:10.1093/deafed/enn038

Lemke, J. L. (2002). Language development and identity: Multiple times-cales in the social ecology of learning. In C. J. Kramsch (Ed.), *Language acquisition and language socialization: Ecological perspectives* (pp. 68–87). London: Continuum.

Levesque, E., Brown, P. M., & Wigglesworth, G. (2014). The impact of bimodal bilingual parental input on the communication and language development of a young deaf child. *Deafness & Education International, 16*(3), 161–181. doi:10.1179/1557069X13Y.0000000033

Lewis, G., Jones, B., & Baker, C. (2012). Translanguaging: Developing its conceptualisation and contextualisation. *Educational Research and Evaluation, 18*(7), 655–670.

Lichtig, I., Couto, M. I. V., Mecca, F. F. D. N., Hartley, S., Wirz, S., & Woll, B. (2011). Assessing deaf and hearing children's communication in Brazil. *Journal of Communication Disorders, 44*(2), 223–235.

Lillo-Martin, D., De Quadros, R., Pichler, D. C., & Fieldsteel, Z. (2014). Language choice in bimodal bilingual development. *Frontiers in Psychology, 5.* doi:10.3389/fpsyg.2014.01163

Lindahl, C. (2015). *Signs of significance: A study of dialogue in a multimodal, sign bilingual science classroom (English).* PhD dissertation. Stockholm University, Stockholm.

Linell, P. (2009). *Rethinking language, mind, and world dialogically: Interactional and contextual theories of human sense-making.* Charlotte, NC: Information Age.

Li Wei. (2011). Multilinguality, multimodality, and multicompetence: Code- and mode-switching by minority ethnic children in complementary schools. *Modern Language Journal, 95*(3), 370–384.

Li Wei, & Dewaele, J. M. (2012). Multilingualism, empathy and multicompetence. *International Journal of Multilingualism, 9*(4), 352. doi:10.1080/14790718.2012.714380

Lucas, C. (2001). *The sociolinguistics of sign languages.* Cambridge/New York: Cambridge University Press.

Lucas, C., & Valli, C. (1992). *Language contact in the American deaf community.* San Diego: Academic Press.

Luckner, J. L., & Cooke, C. (2010). A summary of the vocabulary research with students who are deaf or hard of hearing. *American Annals of the Deaf, 155*(1), 38–67. doi:10.1353/aad.0.0129

Mahon, M. (2009). Interactions between a deaf child for whom English is an additional language and his specialist teacher in the first year at school: Combining words and gestures. *Clinical Linguistics and Phonetics, 23*(8), 611–629. doi:10.1080/02699200802491140

Mahon, M., Vickers, D., McCarthy, K., Barker, R., Merritt, R., Szagun, G., & Rajput, K. (2011). Cochlear-implanted children from homes where English is an additional language: Findings from a recent audit in one London centre. *Cochlear Implants International, 12*(2), 105–113.

Makoni, S., & Pennycook, A. (2006). *Disinventing and reconstituting languages* (Vol. 62). Clevedon/Buffalo, NY: Multilingual Matters.

Maltby, M. (2007). *Principles of hearing aid audiology* (2nd ed.). London: Whurr.

Maltby, M., & Knight, P. (2000). *Audiology: An introduction for teachers and other professionals*. London: Fulton.

Marian, V., Blumenfeld, H. K., & Kaushanskaya, M. (2007). The Language Experience and Proficiency Questionnaire (LEAP-Q): Assessing language profiles in bilinguals and multilinguals. *Journal of Speech Language and Hearing Research, 50*(4), 940–967. doi:10.1044/1092-4388(2007/067)

Marian, V., & Schroeder, S. (2012). A bilingual advantage for episodic memory in older adults. *Journal of Cognitive Psychology, 24*(5), 591–601. doi:10.1080/20445911.2012.669367

Marschark, M., & Hauser, P. (2008). *Deaf cognition: Foundations and outcomes*. New York: Oxford University Press.

Marschark, M., & Hauser, P. (2012). *How deaf children learn*. New York: Oxford University Press.

Marschark, M., & Knoors, H. (2012). Educating deaf children: Language, cognition, and learning. *Deafness and Education International, 14*(3), 136–160. doi:10.1179/1557069X12Y.0000000010

Marschark, M., Knoors, H., & Tang, G. (2014). Perspectives on bilingualism and bilingual education for deaf learners. In M. Marschark, G. Tang, & H. Knoors (Eds.), *Bilingualism and bilingual deaf education* (pp. 445–476). New York/Oxford: Oxford University Press.

Marschark, M., Lang, H., & Albertini, J. (2002). *Educating deaf students: From research to practice*. New York: Oxford University Press.

Marschark, M., & Lee, C. (2014). Navigating two languages in the classroom: Goals, evidence and outcomes. In M. Marschark, G. Tang, & H. Knoors (Eds.), *Bilingualism and bilingual deaf education* (pp. 213–241). New York/Oxford: Oxford University Press.

Marschark, M., Machmer, E., & Convertino, C. (2016). Understanding language in the real world. In M. Marschark, & P. Spencer (Eds.), *The Oxford handbook of deaf studies in language* (pp. 431–451). New York: Oxford University Press.

Marschark, M., Pelz, J. B., Convertino, C., Sapere, P., Arndt, M. E., & Seewagen, R. (2005). Classroom interpreting and visual information processing in mainstream education for deaf students: Live or Memorex®? *American Educational Research Journal, 42*(4), 727–761.

Marschark, M., Sapere, P., Convertino, C., & Pelz, J. (2008). Learning via direct and mediated instruction by Deaf students. *Journal of Deaf Studies and Deaf Education, 13*(4), 546–561. doi:10.1093/deafed/enn014

Marschark, M., Sapere, P., Convertino, C., & Seewagen, R. (2009). Educational interpreting: Access and outcomes. In Marschark, M., Peterson, R., & Winston, E. A. (Eds.). (2005). *Sign language interpreting and interpreter education: Directions for research and practice.* Chicago: Oxford University Press:, pp. 57–83.

Marschark, M., Sapere, P., Convertino, C., Seewagen, R., & Maltzen, H. (2004). Comprehension of sign language interpreting: Deciphering a complex task situation. *Sign Language Studies, 4*(4), 345–366, 405–406.

Marschark, M., Sarchet, T., Convertino, C., Borgna, G., Morrison, C., & Remelt, S. (2012). Print exposure, reading habits, and reading achievement among deaf and hearing college students. *Journal of Deaf Studies and Deaf Education, 17*(1), 61–74. doi:10.1093/deafed/enr044

Marschark, M., Sarchet, T., Rhoten, C., & Zupan, M. (2010). Will cochlear implants close the gap in reading achievement for deaf students?. In M. Marschark & P. Spencer (Eds.), *The Oxford handbook of deaf studies, language, and education* (Vol. 2, pp. 127–143). New York: Oxford University Press.

Marschark, M., Spencer, P., Adams, J., & Sapere, P. (2011). Teaching to the strengths and needs of deaf and hard-of-hearing children. *European Journal of Special Needs Education, 26*(1), 17–23. doi:10.1080/08856257.2011.543542

Marschark, M., & Wauters, L. (2011). Cognitive functioning in deaf adults and children. In M. Marschark & P. Spencer (Eds.), *The Oxford handbook of deaf studies, language, and education* (2nd ed., Vol. 1, pp. 486–499). New York: Oxford University Press.

Martin, D., Bat-Chava, Y., Lalwani, A., & Waltzman, S. B. (2011). Peer relationships of deaf children with cochlear implants: Predictors of peer entry and peer interaction success. *Journal of Deaf Studies and Deaf Education, 16*(1), 108–120. doi:10.1093/deafed/enq037

Martin-Beltrán, M. (2014). "What do you want to say?" How adolescents use translanguaging to expand learning opportunities. *International Multilingual Research Journal, 8*(3), 208–230. doi:10.1080/19313152.2014.914372

Martínez-Roldán, C. M., & Sayer, P. (2006). Reading through linguistic borderlands: Latino students' transactions with narrative texts. *Journal of Early Childhood Literacy, 6*(3), 293–322.

Mason, L. (2001). Introducing talk and writing for conceptual change: A classroom study. *Learning and Instruction, 11*(4), 305–329. doi:10.1016/S0959-4752(00)00035-9

Matthews, T. J., & Reich, C. F. (1993). Constraints on communication in class-rooms for the deaf. *American Annals of the Deaf,* 138(1), 14–18.

Mayberry, R. (2007). When timing is everything: Age of first-language acquisition effects on second-language learning. *Applied Psycholinguistics,* 28(03), 537–549. doi:10.1017/S0142716407070294

Mayer, C. (2007). What really matters in the early literacy development of deaf children. *Journal of Deaf Studies and Deaf Education,* 12(4), 411–431.

Mayer, C. (2009). Issues in second language literacy education with learners who are deaf. *International Journal of Bilingual Education and Bilingualism,* 12(3), 325–334. doi:10.1080/13670050802153368

Mayer, C. (2016). Rethinking total communication: Looking back, moving forward. In M. Marschark & P. Spencer (Eds.), *The Oxford handbook of deaf studies in language* (pp. 32–44). New York: Oxford University Press.

Mayer, C., & Akamatsu, T. (2000). Deaf children creating written texts: Contributions of American Sign Language and signed forms of English. *American Annals of the Deaf,* 145(5), 394–401.

Mayer, C., Akamatsu, T., & Stewart, D. (2002). A model for effective practice: Dialogic inquiry with students who are deaf. *Exceptional Children,* 68(4), 485–502.

Mayer, C., & Leigh, G. (2010). The changing context for sign bilingual education programs: Issues in language and the development of literacy. *International Journal of Bilingual Education and Bilingualism,* 13(2), 175–186.

Mayer, C., & Wells, G. (1996). Can the linguistic interdependence theory support a bilingual-bicultural model of literacy education for deaf students? *Journal of Deaf Studies and Deaf Education,* 1 93–107

McConkey-Robbins, A. (2007). Clinical management of bilingual families and children with cochlear implants. *Loud and Clear,* 1, 1–12.

McConkey-Robbins, A., Waltzman, S. B., & Green, J. E. (2004). Bilingual oral language proficiency in children with cochlear implants. *Archives of Otolaryngology–Head & Neck Surgery,* 130(5), 644–647. doi:10.1001/archotol.130.5.644

McIlroy, G., & Storbeck, C. (2011). Development of deaf identity: An ethnographic study. *Journal of Deaf Studies and Deaf Education,* 16(4), 494–511. doi:10.1093/deafed/enr017

McLeod, S., Harrison, L. J., & McCormack, J. (2012). The intelligibility in context scale: Validity and reliability of a subjective rating measure. *Journal of Speech, Language, and Hearing Research,* 55(2), 648–655. doi:10.1044/1092-4388(2011/10-0130)

McQuarrie, L., & Abbott, M. (2013). Bilingual deaf students' phonological awareness in ASL and reading skills in English. *Sign Language Studies, 14*(1), 80–100. doi:10.1353/sls.2013.0028

Meier, R., Cormier, K., & Quintos-Pozos, D. (2003). *Modality and structure in signed and spoken languages.* Cambridge: Cambridge University Press.

Menéndez, B. (2010). Cross-modal bilingualism: Language contact as evidence of linguistic transfer in sign bilingual education. *International Journal of Bilingual Education and Bilingualism, 13*(2), 201–223.

Mercer, N. (1995). *The guided construction of knowledge: Talk amongst teachers and learners.* Clevedon: Multilingual Matters.

Mercer, N. (2000). *Words and minds: How we use language to think together.* London: Routledge.

Mercer, N. (2008). The seeds of time: Why classroom dialogue needs a temporal analysis. *Journal of the Learning Sciences, 17*(1), 33–59. doi:10.1080/10508400701793182

Mercer, N., & Dawes, L. (2008). The value of exploratory talk. In N. Mercer (Ed.), *Exploring talk in schools: Inspired by the work of Douglas Barnes* (pp. 55–72). London: Sage.

Mercer, N., & Howe, C. (2012). Explaining the dialogic processes of teaching and learning: The value and potential of sociocultural theory. *Learning Culture and Social Interaction, 1*(1), 12–21. doi:10.1016/j.lcsi.2012.03.001

Mercer, N., & Littleton, K. (2007). *Dialogue and the development of children's thinking: A sociocultural approach.* New York: Routledge.

Miller, E. M., Lederberg, A. R., & Easterbrooks, S. R. (2013). Phonological awareness: Explicit instruction for young deaf and hard-of-hearing children. *Journal of Deaf Studies and Deaf Education, 18*(2), 206–227. doi:10.1093/deafed/ens067

Millet, A., & Estève, I. (2010). Transcribing and annotating multimodality: How deaf children's productions call into the question the analytical tools. *Gesture, 10*(2–3), 297–320. doi:10.1075/gest.10.2-3.09mil

Minjeong, K. (2012). Intertextuality and narrative practices of young deaf students in classroom contexts: A microethnographic study. *Reading Research Quarterly, 47*(4), 404–426. doi:10.1002/rrq.029

Mirzaei, A., & Eslami, Z. R. (2015). ZPD-activated languaging and collaborative L2 writing. *Educational Psychology, 35*(1), 5–25. doi:10.1080/01443410.2013.814198

Mitchell, R. E., Young, T. A., Bachleda, B., & Karchmer, M. A. (2006). How many people use ASL in the United States?: Why estimates need updating. *Sign Language Studies, 6*(3), 306–335, 355–356.

Molander, B. O., Halldén, O., & Lindahl, C. (2010). Ambiguity–A tool or obstacle for joint productive dialogue activity in deaf and hearing students' reasoning about ecology. *International Journal of Educational Research, 49*(1), 33–47.

Monaghan, L., Schmaling, C., Nakamura, K., & Turner, G. T. E. (2003). *Many ways to be deaf: International variation in deaf communities.* Washington DC: Gallaudet University Press.

Moores, D. (2001). *Educating the deaf: Psychology, principles, and practices* (Vol. 5). Boston: Houghton Mifflin.

Moores, D. (2010). The history of language and communication issues in deaf education. In M. Marschark & P. Spencer (Eds.), *The Oxford handbook of deaf studies, language, and education* (Vol. 2, pp. 17–30). New York: Oxford University Press.

Morford, J. P., & Hänel-Faulhaber, B. (2011). Homesigners as late learners: Connecting the dots from delayed acquisition in childhood to sign language processing in adulthood. *Linguistics and Language Compass, 5*(8), 525–537. doi:10.1111/j.1749-818X.2011.00296.x

Morford, J. P., Wilkinson, E., Villwock, A., Piñar, P., & Kroll, J. F. (2011). When deaf signers read English: Do written words activate their sign translations? *Cognition, 118*(2), 286–292.

Morgan, G. (2015). Social-cognition for learning as a deaf student. In H. Knoors & M. Marschark (Eds.), *Educating deaf learners: Creating a global evidence base* (pp. 261–282). New York: Oxford University Press.

Morgan, G., & Woll, B. (Eds.). (2002). *Directions in sign language acquisition.* Amsterdam/Philadelphia: John Benjamins.

Mortimer, E., & Scott, P. (2003). *Meaning making in secondary science classrooms.* Buckingham: Open University Press.

Most, T. (2003). The use of repair strategies: Bilingual deaf children using sign language and spoken language. *American Annals of the Deaf, 148*(4), 308–314.

Most, T., & Aviner, C. (2009). Auditory, visual, and auditory-visual perception of emotions by individuals with cochlear implants, hearing aids, and normal hearing. *Journal of Deaf Studies and Deaf Education, 14*(4), 449–464. doi:10.1093/deafed/enp007

Mouvet, K., Hardonk, S., Matthijs, L., Van Puyvelde, M., Loots, G., & Van Herreweghe, M. (2013). Analyzing language practices in mother-child interaction against the background of maternal construction of deafness. *Language & Communication, 33*(3), 232–245. doi:10.1016/j.langcom.2013.07.003

Mudgett-DeCaro, P., & Hurwitz, T. A. (1997). Classroom dialogues and deaf identities. *American Annals of the Deaf, 142*(2), 96–99.

Mühlhäusler, P. (2000). Language planning and language ecology. *Current Issues in Language Planning, 1*(3), 306–367. doi:10.1080/14664200008668011

Najarian, C. G. (2006). *"Between worlds": Deaf women, work and intersections of gender and ability*. New York: Routledge

Napier, J. (2006). Comparing language contact phenomena between Auslan-English interpreters and deaf Australians. In C. Lucas (Ed.), *Mutilingualism and sign languages: From the Great Plains to Australia* (pp. 39–77). Washington DC: Gallaudet Universty Press.

Nicholas, J. G., & Geers, A. E. (2013). Spoken language benefits of extending cochlear implant candidacy below 12 months of age. *Otology and Neurotology, 34*(3), 532–538. doi:10.1097/MAO.0b013e318281e215

Niederberger, N. (2008). Does the knowledge of a natural sign language facilitate deaf children's learning to read and write? Insights from French Sign Language and written French data. In C. Plaza-Pust & E. Morales-Lopez (Eds.), *Sign bilingualism: Language development, interaction, and maintenance in sign language contact situations* (pp. 29–50). Amsterdam: John Benjamins.

Nielsen, D. C., Luetke, B., & Stryker, D. S. (2011). The importance of morphemic awareness to reading achievement and the potential of signing morphemes to supporting reading development. *Journal of Deaf Studies and Deaf Education, 16*(3), 275–288.

Nonaka, A. M. (2014). (Almost) everyone here spoke Ban Khor Sign Language-Until they started using TSL: Language shift and endangerment of a Thai village sign language. *Language and Communication, 38*(1), 54–72. doi:10.1016/j.langcom.2014.05.005

Nystrand, M., Wu, L. L., Gamoran, A., Zeiser, S., & Long, D. A. (2003). Questions in time: Investigating the structure and dynamics of unfolding classroom discourse. *Discourse Processes, 35*(2), 135–198. doi:10.1207/s15326950dp3502_3

O'Connell, N. P., & Deegan, J. (2014). 'Behind the teacher's back': An ethnographic study of deaf people's schooling experiences in the Republic of Ireland. *Irish Educational Studies, 33*(3), 229–247. doi:10.1080/03323315.2014.940683

Office of National Statistics. (2011). *Census: Aggregate data (England and Wales)*. Retrieved from http://infuse.ukdataservice.ac.uk.

Ormel, E., & Giezen, M. (2014). Bimodal bilingual cross-language interaction: Pieces of the puzzle. In M. Marschark, G. Tang, & H. Knoors (Eds.), *Bilingualism and bilingual deaf education* (pp. 74–101). New York/Oxford: Oxford University Press.

Ormel, E., Hermans, D., Knoors, H., & Verhoeven, L. (2012). Cross-language effects in written word recognition: The case of bilingual deaf children. *Bilingualism, 15*(2), 288–303.

Otheguy, R., García, O., & Reid, W. (2015). Clarifying translanguaging and deconstructing named languages: A perspective from linguistics. *Applied Linguistics Review, 6*(3), 281–307. doi:10.1515/applirev-2015-0014

Padden, C. (2006). Learning to fingerspell twice: Young signing children's acquisition of fingerspelling. In B. Schick, M. Marschark & P. E. Spencer (Eds.), *Advances in the sign language development of deaf children* (pp. 189–201). New York: Oxford University Pres

Padden, C. (2008). Forword In C. Plaza-Pust & E. Morales-López (Eds.), *Sign bilingualism: Language development, interaction, and maintenance in sign language contact situations.* pp. xi–xiv Amsterdam: John Benjamins.

Padden, C., & Humphries, T. (2005). *Inside deaf culture.* Cambridge, MA: Harvard University Press.

Pagliaro, C. M., & Ansell, E. (2012). Deaf and hard of hearing students' problem-solving strategies with signed arithmetic story problems. *American Annals of the Deaf, 156*(5), 438–458. doi:10.1353/aad.2012.1600

Paradis, J. (2010). The interface between bilingual development and specific language impairment. *Applied Psycholinguistics, 31*(2), 227–252. doi:10.1017/S0142716409990373

Parasnis, I. (1997). Cultural identity and diversity in deaf education. *American Annals of the Deaf, 142*(2), 72–79.

Peal, E., & Lambert, W. E. (1961). The relation of bilingualism to intelligence. *Psychological Monographs: General and Applied, 76*(27), 1–23.

Pennycook, A. (2010). *Language as a local practice.* London: Routledge.

Percy-Smith, L., Busch, G., Sandahl, M., Nissen, L., Josvassen, J. L., Lange, T., & Cayé-Thomasen, P. (2013). Language understanding and vocabulary of early cochlear implanted children. *International Journal of Pediatric Otorhinolaryngology, 77*(2), 184–188. doi:10.1016/j.ijporl.2012.10.014

Petitto, L. A., Katerelos, M., Levy, B. G., Gauna, K., Tétreault, K., & Ferraro, V. (2001). Bilingual signed and spoken language acquisition from birth: Implications for the mechanisms underlying early bilingual language acquisition. *Journal of Child Language, 28*(2), 453–496.

Pfau, R., Steinbach, M., & Woll, B. (Eds.). (2012). *Sign language: An international handbook.* Berlin: Walter de Gruyter.

Pirrie, A. (2001). Evidence-based practice in education: The best medicine? *British Journal of Educational Studies, 49*(2), 124–136. doi:10.1111/1467-8527.t01-1-00167

Plaza-Pust, C. (2014). Language development and language interaction in sign bilingual language acquisition. In M. Marschark, G. Tang, & H. Knoors (Eds.), *Bilingualism and bilingual deaf education* (pp. 23–54). New York: Oxford University Press.

Plaza-Pust, C., & Morales-Lopez, E. (Eds.). (2008b). *Sign bilingualism: Language development, interaction, and maintenance in sign language contact situations*. Amsterdam: John Benjamins.

Poveda, D., Morgade, M., & Pulido, L. (2010). Multimodality and deaf children's participation in informal literature socialization contexts. *AIBR Revista de Antropologia Iberoamericana, 5*(1), 126–151.

Poveda, D., Pulido, L., Morgade, M., Messina, C., & Hédlová, Z. (2008). Storytelling with sign language interpretation as a multimodal literacy event: Implications for deaf and hearing children. *Language and Education, 22*(4), 320–342. doi:10.1080/09500780802152580

Power, D., Hyde, M., & Leigh, G. (2008). Learning English from signed English: An impossible task? *American Annals of the Deaf, 153,* 37–47.

Prinz, P. M., & Strong, M. (1998). ASL Proficiency and English literacy within a bilingual deaf education model of instruction. *Topics in Language Disorders, 18*(4), 47–60.

Probyn, M. (2015). Pedagogical translanguaging: Bridging discourses in South African science classrooms. *Language and Education, 29*(3), 218–234. doi:10.1080/09500782.2014.994525

Punch, R., & Hyde, M. (2011). Social participation of children and adolescents with cochlear implants: A qualitative analysis of parent, teacher, and child interviews. *Journal of Deaf Studies and Deaf Education, 16*(4), 474–493. doi:10.1093/deafed/enr001

Qi, D. S., & Lapkin, S. (2001). Exploring the role of noticing in a three-stage second language writing task. *Journal of Second Language Writing, 10*(4), 277–303. doi:10.1016/S1060-3743(01)00046-7

Quinto-Pozos, D. (2008). Sign language contact and interference: ASL and LSM. *Language in Society, 37*(02), 161–189.

Quinto-Pozos, D. (2011). Teaching American Sign Language to hearing adult learners. *Annual Review of Applied Linguistics, 31*(Mar), 137–158. doi:10.1017/S0267190511000195

Rampton, B. (1991). Second language learners in a stratified multilingual setting. *Applied Linguistics, 12*(3), 229–248.

Rampton, B. (1995). *Crossing: Language and ethnicity among adolescents*. London: Longman.

Rampton, B., Maybin, J., & Roberts, C. (2015). Theory and method in linguistic ethnography. In J. Snell, S. Shaw & F. Copland (Eds.), *Linguistic ethnography: Interdisciplinary explorations* (pp. 14–50). Hampshire: Palgrave Macmillan.

Rathmann, C., Mann, W., & Morgan, G. (2007). Narrative structure and narrative development in deaf children. *Deafness and Education International, 9*(4), 187–196.

Rättyä, K. (2013). Languaging and visualisation method for grammar teaching: A conceptual change theory perspective. *English Teaching, 12*(3), 87–101.

Reznitskaya, A., & Gregory, M. (2013). Student thought and classroom language: Examining the mechanisms of change in dialogic teaching. *Educational Psychologist, 48*(2), 114–133. doi:10.1080/00461520.2013.775898

Reznitskaya, A., Kuo, L. J., Clark, A. -M., Miller, B., Jadallah, M., Anderson, R. C., & Nguyen-Jahiel, K. (2009). Collaborative reasoning: A dialogic approach to group discussions. *Cambridge Journal of Education, 39*(1), 29–48.

Richie, R., Yang, C., & Coppola, M. (2014). Modeling the emergence of lexicons in homesign systems. *Topics in Cognitive Science, 6*(1), 183–195. doi:10.1111/tops.12076

Rieffe, C. (2012). Awareness and regulation of emotions in deaf children. *British Journal of Developmental Psychology, 30*(4), 477–492. doi:10.1111/j.2044-835X.2011.02057.x

Rinaldi, P., & Caselli, C. (2009). Lexical and grammatical abilities in deaf Italian preschoolers: The role of duration of formal language experience. *Journal of Deaf Studies and Deaf Education, 14*(1), 63–75.

Rinaldi, P., Caselli, C., Onofrio, D., & Volterra, V. (2014). Language acquisition by bilingual deaf preschoolers: Theoretical and methodological issues and empirical data. In M. Marschark, G. Tang, & H. Knoors (Eds.), *Bilingualism and bilingual deaf education* (pp. 54–73). Oxford/New York: Oxford University Press.

Roberts, C. (2011). Institutional discourse. In J. Simpson (Ed.), *The Routledge handbook of applied linguistics* (pp. 81–95). London: Routledge.

Rojas-Drummond, S., & Mercer, N. (2003). Scaffolding the development of effective collaboration and learning. *International Journal of Educational Research, 39*(1), 99–111. doi:10.1016/S0883-0355(03)00075-2

Roos, C. (2013). Young deaf children's fingerspelling in learning to read and write: An ethnographic study in a signing setting. *Deafness and Education International, 15*(3), 149–178.

Roos, C. (2014). A sociocultural perspective on young deaf children's fingerspelling: An ethnographic study in a signing setting. *Deafness and Education International, 16*(2), 86–107. doi:10.1179/1557069X13Y.0000000029

Rosenberg, G. G. (2010). Classroom acoustics and personal FM technology in management of auditory processing disorder. *Seminars in Hearing, 23*(4), 309–318. doi:10.1055/s-0030-1262325

Roy, C., & Metzger, M. (2014). Researching signed language interpreting research through a sociolinguistic lens. *Translation and Interpreting, 6*(1), 158–176. doi:ti.106201.2014.a09

Rudner, M., Andin, J., Rönnberg, J., Heimann, M., Hermansson, & Tjus, T. (2015). Training literacy skills through sign languag Education International, 17(1), 8–18. doi:10.1179/1557069X14Y.

Salter, J. (2015). *Developing understandings of deaf students' learr stream secondary classrooms: Teaching assistants' perspective* sertation. University of Leeds. White Rose e-thesis on-line ht whiterose.ac.uk/10613/

Sams, C., & Mercer, N. (2006). Teaching children how to use langua maths problems. *Language and Education, 20*(6), 507–528. d le678.0

Saussure, F. (2006). *Writings in general linguistics*. Oxford: Oxford U Press.

Schick, B., Williams, K., & Kupermintz, H. (2006). Look who's being hind: Educational interpreters and access to education for deaf and of-hearing students. *Journal of Deaf Studies and Deaf Education, 11*(1), doi:10.1093/deafed/enj007

Schmaling, C. (2000). *Managa Hannu: Language of the hands: A descriptive ysis of Hausa Sign Language*. Hamburg: Signum.

Schmidt, M., & Čagran, B. (2008). Self-concept of students in inclusive settir *International Journal of Special Education, 23*(1), 8–17.

Scott, P. (2008). Talking a way to understanding in science. In N. Mercer (Ed *Exploring talk in schools: Inspired by the work of Douglas Barnes* (pp. 17–37 London: Sage.

Scott, P., Ametller, J., Mortimer, E., & Emberton, J. (2010). Teaching and learning disciplinary knowledge. In K. Littleton & C. Howe (Eds.), *Educational dia- logues: Understanding and promoting productive interaction* (pp. 289–303). London: Routledge.

Scott, P., Mortimer, E., & Aguiar, O. (2006). The tension between authoritative and dialogic discourse: A fundamental characteristic of meaning making interactions in high school science lessons. *Science Education, 90*(4), 605–631. doi:10.1002/sce.20131

Sedova, K., Salamounova, Z., & Svaricek, R. (2014). Troubles with dialogic teaching. *Learning Culture and Social Interaction, 3*(4), 274–285. doi:10.1016/ j.lcsi.2014.04.001

Senghas, R. J., & Monaghan, L. (2002). Signs of their times: Deaf communities and the culture of language. *Annual Review of Anthropology, 31,* 69–97.

Senghas, R. J., Senghas, A., & Pyers, J. E. (2014). The emergence of Nicaraguan sign language: Questions of development, acquisition, and evolution. In J. Langer, S. T. Parker, & C. Milbrath (Eds). *Biology and Knowledge*

Revisited: From Neurogenesis to Psychogenesis (pp. 287–306). Lawrence Erbaum Associates.

Sharpe, T. (2008). How can teacher talk support learning? *Linguistics and Education, 19*(2), 132–148. doi:10.1016/j.linged.2008.05.001

Singleton, J. L., & Newport, E. L. (2004). When learners surpass their models: The acquisition of American Sign Language from inconsistent input. *Cognitive Psychology, 49*(4), 370–407. doi:10.1016/j.cogpsych.2004.05.001

Spencer, P., & Marschark, M. (2010). *Evidence-based practice in educating deaf and hard-of-hearing students*. New York: Oxford University Press.

Steinberg, A., Bain, L., Li, Y., Delgado, G., & Ruperto, V. (2003). Decisions Hispanic families make after the identification of deafness. *Journal of Deaf Studies and Deaf Education, 8*(3), 291–314. doi:10.1093/deafed/eng016

Stokoe, W. C. (1960). Sign language structure: An outline of the visual communication system of the American deaf. Studies in Linguistics. *Occasional Papers 8.* (Vol. 10, pp. 3–37). Buffalo, NY: University of Buffalo Department of Anthropology and Linguistics,.

Stone, C., & West, D. (2012). Translation, representation and the Deaf 'voice'. *Qualitative Research, 12*(6), 645–665. doi:10.1177/1468794111433087

Strand, S., Malmberg, L., & Hall, J. (2015). *English as an Additional Language (EAL) and educational achievement in England: An analysis of the National Pupil Database*. Oxford: Oxford University Press.

Sutherland, H., & Young, A. (2007). 'Hate English! Why? ' Signs and English from deaf children's perception results from a preliminary study of deaf children's experiences of sign bilingual education. *Deafness and Education International, 9*(4), 197–213.

Sutton-Spence, R. (2010). The role of sign language narratives in developing identity for Deaf children. *Journal of Folklore Research, 47*(3), 265–305. doi:10.2979/jfolkrese.2010.47.3.265

Sutton-Spence, R., & Woll, B. (1999). *The linguistics of British Sign Language: An introduction*. Cambridge: Cambridge University Press.

Suzuki, W. (2012). Written languaging, direct correction, and second language writing revision. *Language Learning, 62*(4), 1110–1133. doi:10.1111/j.1467-9922.2012.00720.x

Suzuki, W., & Itagaki, N. (2009). Languaging in grammar exercises by Japanese EFL learners of differing proficiency. *System, 37*(2), 217–225. doi:10.1016/j.system.2008.10.001

Svartholm, K. (2010). Bilingual education for deaf children in Sweden. *International Journal of Bilingual Education and Bilingualism, 13*(2), 159–174.

Swaan, A. d. (2001). *Words of the world: The global language system.* Cambridge: Polity.

Swain, M. (2006). Languaging, agency and collaboration in advanced language proficiency. In H. Brynes (Ed.), *Advanced language learning: The contribution of Halliday and Vygotsky* (pp. 95–108). London: Continuum.

Swain, M., & Deters, P. (2007). "New" Mainstream SLA Theory: Expanded and enriched. *Modern Language Journal, 91*, 820–836. doi:10.1111/j.0026-7902.2007.00671.x

Swain, M., & Lapkin, S. (2000). Task-based second language learning: The uses of the first language. *Language Teaching Research, 4*(3), 251–274.

Swain, M., Lapkin, S., Knouzi, I., Suzuki, W., & Brooks, L. (2009). Languaging: University students learn the grammatical concept of voice in French. *Modern Language Journal, 93*(1), 5–29. doi:10.1111/j.1540-4781.2009.00825.x

Swanwick, R. (2001). The demands of a sign bilingual context for teachers and learners: An observation of language use and learning experiences. *Deafness and Education International, 3*(2), 62–79.

Swanwick, R. (2002). Sign bilingual deaf children's approaches to writing: Individual strategies for bridging the gap between BSL and written English. *Deafness and Education International, 4*(2), 65–83.

Swanwick, R. (2010). Policy and practice in sign bilingual education: Development, challenges and directions. *International Journal of Bilingual Education and Bilingualism, 13*(2), 147–158.

Swanwick, R. (2015). Re-envisioning learning and teaching in deaf education: Toward transactions between research and practice. In H. Knoors & M. Marschark (Eds.), *Educating deaf learners: Creating a global evidence base* (pp. 595–616). New York: Oxford University Press.

Swanwick, R. (2016). Deaf children's bimodal bilingualism and education. *Language Teaching, 49*(1), 1–34.

Swanwick, R., Dammeyer, J., Hendar, O., Kristoffersen, A., Salter, J., & Simonsen, E. (2014). Shifting contexts and practices in sign bilingual education in Northern Europe: Implications for professional development and training. In M. Marschark, G. Tang, & H. Knoors (Eds.), *Bilingualism and bilingual deaf education* (pp. 292–312). New York: Oxford University Press

Swanwick, R., Kitchen, R., & Clarke, P. (2012). Practitioner talk on deaf children's reading comprehension: Analysing multiple voices. *Deafness and Education International, 14*(2), 100–120. doi:10.1177/027112140831462;

Swanwick, R., & Marschark, M. (2010). Enhancing education for deaf children: Research into practice and back again. *Deafness and Education International, 12*(4), 217–235.

Swanwick, R., Simpson, K., & Salter, J. (2014). *Language planning in deaf education: Guidance for practitioners by practitioners.* London: The National Sensory Impairment Partnership.

Swanwick, R., & Watson, L. (2007). Parents sharing books with young deaf children in spoken English and in BSL: The common and diverse features of different language settings. *Journal of Deaf Studies and Deaf Education, 12*(3), 385–405.

Swanwick, R., Wright, S., & Salter, J. (2016). Investigating deaf children's plural and diverse use of sign and spoken languages in a super diverse context. *Applied Linguistics Review, 7*(2), 2–32.

Sutherland, H., & Young, A. (2014). Research with deaf children and not on them: A study of method and process. *Children & Society, 28*(5), 366–379.

Tang, G., Lam, S., & Yiu, K. (2014). Language development of deaf and hard-of-hearing students in a sign bilingual and co-enrollment environment In M. Marschark, G. Tang, & H. Knoors (Eds.), *Bilingualism and bilingual deaf education* (pp. 313–341). New York: Oxford University Press.

Tang, G., Yiu, C., & Lam, S. (2015). Awareness of Hong Kong Sign Language and manually coded Chinese by deaf students learning in a sign bilingual and co-enrollment setting. In H. Knoors & M. Marschark (Eds.), *Educating deaf learners: Creating a global evidence base* (pp. 117–148). New York: Oxford University Press.

Teschendorf, M., Janeschik, S., Bagus, H., Lang, S., & Arweiler-Harbeck, D. (2011). Speech development after cochlear implantation in children from bilingual homes. *Otology and Neurotology, 32*(2), 229–235.

Tevenal, S., & Villanueva, M. (2009). Are you getting the message? The effects of SimCom on the message received by deaf, hard of hearing, and hearing students. *Sign Language Studies, 9*(3), 266–286, 379–380.

Thibault, P. (2011). First-order languaging dynamics and second-order language: The distributed language view. *Ecological Psychology, 23*(3), 210–245. doi:10.1080/10407413.2011.591274

Thomas, E., El-Kashlan, H., & Zwolan, T. A. (2008). Children with cochlear implants who live in monolingual and bilingual homes. *Otology and Neurotology, 29*(2), 230–234.

Thumann-Prezioso, C. (2005). Deaf parents' perspectives on deaf education. *Sign Language Studies, 5*(4), 415–440.

Tizard, B., & Hughes, M. (1984). *Young children learning: Talking and thinking at home and at school.* London: Fontana.

Tomasuolo, E., Valeri, G., Di Renzo, A., Pasqualetti, P., & Volterra, V. (2013). Deaf children attending different school environments: Sign language abilities and theory of mind. *Journal of Deaf Studies and Deaf Education, 18*(1), 12–29. doi:10.1093/deafed/ens035

Torrance, N., & Olson, D. R. (1991). *Literacy and orality.* Cambridge: Cambridge University Press.

Toscano, R. M., McKee, B., & Lepoutre, D. (2002). Success with academic English: Reflections of deaf college students. *American Annals of the Deaf, 147*(1), 5–23.

Tough, J. (1977). *The development of meaning.* London: Allen and Unwin.

Tracy, R. (2000). Language mixing as a challenge for linguistics. In S. Döpke (Ed.), *Cross-linguistic structures in simultaneous bilingualism* (pp. 11–36). Amsterdam: John Benjamins.

Trezek, B. J., Paul, P. V., & Wang, W. (2011). Processes and components of reading. In M. Marschark & P. Spencer (Eds.), *The Oxford handbook of deaf studies, language anbd education* (2nd ed., Vol. 1, pp. 99–114). New York: Oxford University Press.

Trussell, J. W., & Easterbrooks, S. R. (2014). The effect of enhanced storybook interaction on signing deaf children's vocabulary. *Journal of Deaf Studies and Deaf Education, 19*(3), 319–332. doi:10.1093/deafed/ent055

Valentine, G., & Skelton, T. (2008). Changing spaces: The role of the internet in shaping deaf geographies. *Social & Cultural Geography, 9*(5), 469–485.

van Beijsterveldt, L. M., & van Hell, J. (2010). Lexical noun phrases in texts written by deaf children and adults with different proficiency levels in sign language. *International Journal of Bilingual Education and Bilingualism, 13*(4), 439–468.

van Beijsterveldt, L. M., & van Hell, J. G. (2009). Structural priming of adjective-noun structures in hearing and deaf children. *Journal of Experimental Child Psychology, 104*(2), 179–196.

van Beijsterveldt, L. M., & van Hell, J. G. (2012). Temporal reference marking in narrative and expository text written by deaf children and adults: A bimodal bilingual perspective. *Bilingualism, 15*(1), 128–144.

Van Deusen-Phillips, S. B., Goldin-Meadow, S., & Miller, P. J. (2001). Enacting stories, seeing worlds: Similarities and differences in the cross-cultural narrative development of linguistically isolated deaf children. *Human Development, 44*(6), 311–336. doi:10.1159/000046153

Van Herreweghe, M., & Vermeerbergen, M. (2010). Deaf perspectives on communicative practices in South Africa: Institutional language policies in educational settings. *Text & Talk, 30*(2), 125–144. doi:10.1515/text.2010.007

Velasco, P., & García, O. (2014). Translanguaging and the writing of bilingual learners. *Bilingual Research Journal, 37*(1), 6–23.

Vermeulen, A., De Raeve, L., Langereis, M., & Snik, A. (2012). Changing realities in the classroom for hearing-impaired children with cochlear implant. *Deafness and Education International, 14*(1), 36–47. doi:10.1179/1557069X12Y.0000000004

Vertovec, S. (2007). Super-diversity and its implications. *Ethnic and Racial Studies, 30*(6), 1024–1054. doi:10.1080/01419870701599465

Vygotsky, L. S. (1962). *Thought and language.* Cambridge, MA: MIT Press.

Vygotsky, L. S. (1978). *Mind in society: The development of higher psychological processes.* Cambridge, MA: Harvard University Press.

Vygotsky, L. S. (1986). *Thought and language.* Cambridge, MA: MIT Press.

Walford, G. (2008). *How to do educational ethnography.* London: Tufnell.

Walker, E., & Tomblin, J. B. (2014). The influence of communication mode on language development in children with cochlear implants. In M. Marschark, G. Tang, & H. Knoors (Eds.), *Bilingualism and bilingual deaf education* (pp. 134 -151). New York: Oxford University Press.

Waltzmann, S. B., Robbins, A. M., Green, J. E., & Cohen, N. L. (2003). Second oral language capabilities in children with cochlear implants. *Otology & Neurotology, 24*(5), 757–763. doi:10.1097/00129492-200309000-00012

Watson, L. M., Archbold, S. M., & Nikolopoulos, T. P. (2006). Children's communication mode five years after cochlear implantation: Changes over time according to age at implant. *Cochlear Implants International, 7*(2), 77–91.

Wauters, L. N., & Knoors, H. (2008). Social integration of deaf children in inclusive settings. *Journal of Deaf Studies and Deaf Education, 13*(1), 21–36. doi:10.1093/deafed/enm028

Wegerif, R. (2011). Towards a dialogic theory of how children learn to think. *Thinking Skills and Creativity, 6*(3), 179–190. doi:http://dx.doi.org/10.1016/j.tsc.2011.08.002

Weinreich, U. (1953). *Languages in contact.* The Hague: Mouton.

Wells, G. (1986). *The meaning makers: Children learning language and using language to learn.* Portsmouth: NH: Heinemann.

Wells, G. (1999). *Dialogic inquiry: Towards a sociocultural practice and theory of education.* Cambridge: Cambridge University Press.

Wenger, E. (1998). *Communities of practice: Learning, meaning and identity.* Cambridge: Cambridge University Press.

Wheeler, A., Archbold, S., Gregory, S., & Skipp, A. (2007). Cochlear implants: The young people's perspective. *Journal of Deaf Studies and Deaf Education, 12*(3), 303–316. doi:10.1093/deafed/enm018

Wheeler, A., Archbold, S. M., Hardie, T., & Watson, L. M. (2009). Children with cochlear implants: The communication journey. *Cochlear Implants International, 10*(1), 41–62.

Wheeler, A., Gregory, S., & Archbold, S. (2004). *Supporting young people with cochlear implants in secondary school*. London: RNID.

Wilbur, R. B. (2000). The use of ASL to support the development of English and literacy. *Journal of Deaf Studies and Deaf Education, 5*(1), 81–104. doi:10.1093/deafed/5.1.81

Williams, C. (2012). Promoting vocabulary learning in young children who are d/deaf and hard of hearing: Translating research into practice. *American Annals of the Deaf, 156*(5), 501–508. doi:10.1353/aad.2012.1597

Williams, C., & McLeod, S. (2012). Speech-language pathologists' assessment and intervention practices with multilingual children. *International Journal of Speech-Language Pathology, 14*(3), 292–305.

Willoughby, L. (2012). Language maintenance and the deaf child. *Journal of Multilingual and Multicultural Development, 33*(6), 605–618.

Wolbers, K. A., Bowers, L. M., Dostal, H. M., & Graham, S. C. (2014). Deaf writers' application of American Sign Language knowledge to English. *International Journal of Bilingual Education and Bilingualism, 17*(4), 410–428. doi:10.1080/13670050.2013.816262

Woll, B., & Adam, R. (2012). Sign language and the politics of deafness. In M. Martin-Jones, A. Blackledge, & A. Creese (Eds.), *The Routledge handbook of multilingualism* (pp. 100–115). London: Routledge

Woll, B., & Sutton-Spence, R. (2011). Sign languages. In J. Simpson (Ed.), *The Routledge handbook of applied linguistics* (pp. 359–372). London: Routledge.

Woll, B., Sutton-Spence, R., & Elton, F. (2001). Multilingualism: The global approach to sign languages. In C. Lucas (Ed.), *The sociolinguistics of sign languages* (pp. 8–32). Cambridge: Cambridge University Press.

Wolters, N., & Isarin, J. (2015). Reciprocity in school peer relationships of deaf and hard-of-hearing early adolescents: Promoting empowerment. In H. Knoors & M. Marschark (Eds.), *Educating deaf learners: Creating a global evidence base* (pp. 311–336). New York: Oxford University Press.

Wood, D., Wood, H., Griffiths, A., & Howarth, I. (1986). *Teaching and talking with deaf children*. Chichester: Wiley.

World Health Organization. (2015). Deafness and hearing loss: Fact sheet No. 300. Retrieved December 2015, from http://www.who.int/mediacentre/factsheets/fs300/en/

Yiu, C., & Tang, G. (2014). Social integration of deaf and hard-of-hearing students in a sign bilingual and co-enrollment environment. In M. Marschark, G. Tang, & H. Knoors (Eds.), *Bilingualism and bilingual deaf education* (pp. 342–367). New York/Oxford: Oxford University Press.

Young, A., & Temple, B. (2014). *Approaches to social research: The case of Deaf studies.* Oxford University Press (UK).

Zaidman-Zait, A. (2007). Parenting a child with a cochlear implant: A critical incident study. *Journal of Deaf Studies and Deaf Education, 12*(2), 221–241. doi:10.1093/deafed/en1032

Zeshan, U. (2011). Village sign languages. In G Mathur & D.J. Napoli (Eds). *Deaf Around the World: The Impact of Language.*(p. 221) Oxford University Press

INDEX

Adaptivity, 103
Affect, 68
Affiliation, 52
Agency, 98
Akamatsu, T., 132, 142
Albertorio, J. R., 169
Alexander, R. J., 129
Alexander, Robin, 145–148
American Sign Language (ASL)
    and sign language multilingualism, 50
    and terminology, 12
Arabic, 46, 168
Aragão, R., 67
Argumentation skills, 130
Arweiler-Harbeck, D., 47
ASL. *See* American Sign Language
Assessment
    of bimodal bilingualism, 31–32
    development of tools for, 59
    in dialogic approach to deaf
        education, 159
    and evidence base, 176

lack of tools for, 51
and languaging, 65
learning, 159
of newborn hearing, 25
summative, 159
Assets-based perspective, 6, 121, 188
Assistive listening devices, 157
Atkin, K., 118
ATLAS, 179
Attention, 8
"Auditory-oral," 78
Auditory-oral approach, 19
Australian Sign Language
        (AUSLAN), 48, 90
Authoritative talk, 149, 150, 158

Background noise, 74
Bagga-Gupta, S., 67, 178
Bagus, H., 47
Baker, C., 83
Bakhtin, M., 126, 191
Bangladeshi heritage children, 9, 42

BATOD. *See* British Association for
    Teachers of the Deaf
BDA. *See* British Deaf Association
Bilingual bicultural approach
    overview, 33
    and pedagogy, 20
Bilingual education, 20
Bilingualism
    conceptualizations of, 5–6
    integrative approaches to, 22
    and languaging, 69
    positive views of, 83
    terminology of, 13–15
    theoretical perspectives on, 183–184
    See also Multicompetency;
        Translanguaging
Bimodal bilingualism, 23–37
    and dialogic pedagogy, 156–157
    education for, 32–35
    evidence base for, 165
    language interaction in, 28–32
    language learning context of, 24–27
    language use with, 27–28
    and multicompetency, 113–115, 118
    and multilingualism, 37, 39
    overview, 13–15
    pedagogies for, 34–36
Blackledge, A., 84, 151–152
Boons, T., 47
Borrowing (translanguaging), 98
Branco, A. U., 144
British Academy, 9–10
British Association for Teachers of the
    Deaf (BATOD), 11
British Deaf Association (BDA), 11
British Sign Language (BSL)
    age-expected levels of, 26
    and multicompetency, 110, 115
    regional dialects in, 69
    and repertoire, 105
    and terminology, 12
    and translanguaging, 87–89, 92
    variants of, 70
Bronfenbrenner, U., 53
Brooks, L., 64
Bruner, J. S., 123
Bruno, M. M. G., 174
BSL. *See* British Sign Language
Busch, B., 105

Cantonese, 91, 112
Chinese, 91, 112, 168
Ching, T., 45, 48
CIs. *See* Cochlear implants
Classrooms. *See* Schools
Classroom talk, 142–145
Cochlear implants (CIs)
    audiological management with, 25
    and evidence base, 170, 177
    and multilingualism, 37, 42–43
    popularity of, 7–8
    and repertoire, 105
    and spoken language
        multilingualism, 45–47
    and translanguaging, 86, 91
Code blending
    and bimodal bilingualism, 31
    defined, 14
    in dialogic approach to deaf education,
        152, 155
    and multicompetency, 116
    and total communication, 19
    and translanguaging, 83, 87–88
Code switching
    with bimodal bilingualism, 31
    defined, 14
    in dialogic approach to deaf education,
        152, 154–156
    and multicompetency, 116
    and translanguaging, 83, 86–87
Co-enrolment, 72
Cognitive processes, 8. *See also specific
        processes, e.g.*: Working memory
Cohen, N. L., 46
Collaborative writing, 65
Communication
    language vs., 12
    and multicompetency, 103
Communicative sensitivity, 109, 115–117
Communities of practice, 138–139
Competency, 18, 183. *See also*
        Multicompetency
Comprehension, 14
Confidence, 137
Consortium for Research into Deaf
        Education (CRIDE) survey, 9, 54,
        167, 168
Contingency, 142–143, 146
Contrastive analysis, 115

Control (classroom talk), 143
Conversational analysis, 176
Cook, V., 102
Core beliefs, 67–68
Crasborn, O., 49–50
Creativity, 103
Creese, A., 84, 151–152
CRIDE survey. *See* Consortium for
    Research into Deaf Education survey
Crowe, K., 45, 48, 166, 169, 171, 172
Cultural awareness, 117–119
Cultural diversity
    and bimodal bilingualism, 33
    and dialogic approach to deaf
        education, 152
    and heritage language, 48
    and multicompetency, 104
    and pedagogy in deaf education,
        123–125
    and translanguaging, 16
    See also Language diversity
Cummins, J., 29

Deaf and hard-of-hearing (DHH), 11
Deaf children, 6–8. *See also specific
    headings*
Deaf education, 1–22
    developing evidence base for, 21–22
    discourses in, 58–59
    language and terminology in, 10–18
    from language to languaging in, 22
    languaging in, 77–79
    pedagogy in, 3, 19–21
    research context for, 9–10
    research questions in, 2–4
    theoretical perspectives in, 4–6
Deaf education research
    context for, 9–10
    questions in, 2–4
Deafened (term), 10
"Deafgain," 78
"Deafhood," 78
Deafness
    diversity within, 7–9
    early identification of, 70
Deaf populations, 10–12. *See also specific
    headings*
"Deaf space," 78
Decision making, 85

Deegan, J., 173
De Quadros, R., 31
DGS. *See* German Sign Language
DHH. *See* Deaf and hard-of-hearing
Diagnostic techniques, 25
Dialects, 69
Dialogic approach to deaf education, 141–162
    applications of, 139
    classroom talk in, 142–145
    and language diversity, 149–151
    overview, 20–21, 128–130, 184–185
    synergy in, 160–162
    teaching practices in, 145–150, 157–160
    and translanguaging, 151–157, 160
Dialogic mediation, 64–65
Dialogic teaching repertoires, 146–148
Dialogic theory of learning, 122, 125–128
Dickinson, J., 175
Discourse analysis, 176
Discourse practices, 85
Discussion, 148
Divergent thinking, 103
Diversity. *See* Cultural diversity; Language
    diversity
Dutch and Nederlandse Gebarentaal
    (NGT), 12
Dynamic systems approach to language,
    5, 106–107
Dynamism, 59, 63, 193

EAL. *See* English as an additional
    language
Eastern European children, 9
Ecological model, 53
Educational policy, 11, 27, 36, 40, 79
ELAN, 179
El-Kashlan, H., 46
Emerson, R. R., 175
Emotion, 68
Emotional maturity, 137
Emotional stability, 103
Empathy, 103
English as an additional language
    (EAL), 9, 44
Eslami, Z. R., 65
Ethnographic approaches, 173–179
Evidence base, 163–180
    for deaf education, 21–22
    and ethnographic approaches, 173–179

Evidence base (*Cont.*)
　future directions for building of, 180
　growing knowledge with, 179–180
　on individual language profiles,
　　166–167, 170–173
　for informing practice, 164–166
　and language landscapes, 167–170
　new methodologies in, 190–191
　for practice evaluation, 164
Executive function, 103

Families, 8, 26–27, 93, 171
Filipino, 168
Fingerspelling, 87, 96–97, 110
Flexibility, 103
Fluency
　of deaf children in group discussions, 74
　development of, 24–25
　and dialogic approach to deaf
　　education, 150
　multilingual, 46
　and repertoire, 59
　and sign bilingual approach, 33
Fluidity, 59
Fordham, L., 48
Foreign language learning model, 149
French, 46
French Sign Language (LSF), 12, 50
Friendships, 75, 159

Gallaudet University, 175, 183
García, O., 83
German, 46, 109
German Sign Language (DGS), 109
Gesser, A., 175
Global language system, 49–50
Grammatical concepts, 64
Green, J. E., 46
Group classroom work, 74, 144
Gumperz, J., 104, 106
Gynne, A., 67, 178

Hard-of-hearing
　and terminology, 10
　See also Deaf and hard-of-hearing
Hearing aids
　audiological management with, 25
　and multilingualism, 42–43
　See also Cochlear implants

Hearing children, 6–8
Hearing impaired (term), 10
Hearing loss
　categories of, 7–8
　and multilingualism, 43–45
　prevalence of, 45
　range of, 11
Hearing technologies
　accessibility of spoken English
　　with, 70
　and dialogic approach to deaf
　　education, 157
　and multilingualism, 42–43
　in school environments, 74, 135
　and translanguaging, 192
　types of, 7–8
　See also specific technologies,
　　e.g. Cochlear implants
Hebrew, 46
Heritage language
　and culture, 48
　gathering information on, 50
　and multilingualism, 52
　support for, 37, 46, 49
Heteroglossia, 150
Hiddinga, A., 49–50
Hispanic deaf children, 169
HKSL. See Hong Kong Sign Language
Holden-Pit, L., 169
Homesigns, 26, 71–72
Hong Kong Sign Language (HKSL),
　91, 112
Hornberger, N., 85
Hungary, 169

Identity
　in dialogic approach to deaf
　　education, 185
　and languaging, 59, 61, 67, 79
　social, 61, 67
　and translanguaging, 152
Individual language plans, 52–53
Individual language profiles, 54, 165–167,
　170–173
Institutional languaging, 19, 68, 79
Interference, 98, 102
Interlanguage, 102
Internal dialogue, 77
"Interthinking," 129

Janeschik, S., 47
Japanese, 65–66
Jones, B., 83

Keating, E., 75
Kelman, C. A., 144
Klatter-Folmer, J., 89
Knoors, H., 133, 143
Knouzi, I., 64
Korean, 168
Krausneker, V., 90

Laevers, F., 143
Lambert, W. E., 113
Lang, S., 47
Language
    communication vs., 12
    context of, 22
    in deaf education, 10–18
Language action, 188
Language balance, 108
Language blending. *See* Code blending
Language diversity
    asset-focused model of, 121
    and classroom talk, 142
    and deaf children's language
        experiences, 182
    and dialogic approach to deaf
        education, 122, 149–151
    and evidence base, 163, 165–166,
        171–173, 180
    and learning, 8
    and multilingualism, 58–59
    overview, 15
    and prevalence of English, 48
    and translanguaging, 85
Language dominance, 92, 108
Language equivalence, 108
Language Experience and Proficiency
    Questionnaire (LEAP-Q), 172
Language influence, 97
Language interaction
    in bimodal bilingualism, 28–32
    and multicompetency, 112–113
Language landscapes, 54, 167–170
Language learning, 24–27
Language mixing
    and bimodal bilingualism, 31
    defined, 14

Language planning
    ecological approach to, 53
    information needed for, 31
    tools for, 9–10
Language plurality
    and classroom talk, 142
    and deaf children's language
        experiences, 182
    and evidence base, 163, 165–166,
        171–173, 180
    and multilingualism, 58–59
    overview, 15
    and translanguaging, 85
Language policy, 3
Language processing, 28–29, 112, 165
Language proficiency, 171–172
Language Proficiency Profile, 51
Language profiles. *See* Individual language
    profiles
Language resources
    in bilingualism and
        multilingualism, 32, 59
    change in, 5
    defined, 104
    discrepancies between language
        demands and, 185
    and individual language profiles, 166
    and languaging, 62, 69, 73
    and multicompetency, 101–104, 108, 111,
        116, 119
    and pedagogy in deaf education, 133–135
    soft assembly of, 6, 106
    and teaching practices, 157
    and translanguaging, 83, 84, 92, 93, 98
Language switching. *See* Code switching
Language synthesis
    model of, 31
    overview, 14
Language transfer
    with bimodal bilingualism, 29–31
    evidence of, 97
    and linguistic competency, 183
    and multicompetency, 112
Languaging, 61–80
    and assets-based perspective, 188
    as being in the world, 66–68, 71–72
    and challenges for deaf learners, 73–77
    in the classroom, 72–73
    context of, 22

Languaging (*Cont.*)
  in deaf education, 77–79
  institutional, 19, 68, 79
  and learning, 63–66
  overview, 16–18, 62–63
  and pedagogy in deaf education, 79–80,
    121, 122, 131
  as social variation, 69–71
  and translanguaging, 82 (*See also*
    Translanguaging)
"Langue" (structuralism), 62
Langues de Sign Français. *See* French Sign
  Language
Lapkin, S., 64
LBG. *See* Sign-Supported German
LEAP-Q. *See* Language Experience and
  Proficiency Questionnaire
Learning, 58–59
  and languaging (*See* Languaging)
  and multilingualism, 58–59
  "unlocking," 182–183
  See also Pedagogy in deaf education
Learning assessment, 159
Learning skills, 136
Learning talk, 147
Leeds University, 52, 92
Leigh, G., 171
Lewis, G., 83
Lima, J. M., 174
Lindahl, C., 90
Linguistic ethnography, 173–179
Linguistic interdependence theory, 29
Linguist transfer. *See* Language transfer
Link, H., 85
Literacy
  and bimodal bilingual
    pedagogies, 34–35
  in dialogic approach to deaf education,
    160–161
  evidence base on, 165
  and pedagogy in deaf education,
    136–137
  and translanguaging, 93–98
Literature, 126
Littleton, K., 125, 129
Li Wei, 85
Loudness thresholds, 7
LSF. *See* French Sign Language

MacArthur-Bates Communicative
  Development Inventories, 51
Mahon, M., 170
Mainstream schools, 70, 72–73
Manner, 3–4
Manually coded systems, 111, 152. *See also*
  Sign-Supported English
Marschark, M., 133, 165
Maturity, social and emotional, 137
Mayer, C., 132, 142
McConkey Robbins, A., 45–46
McKinnon, D. H., 45
McLeod, S., 45, 48, 172
Meaning making
  importance of, 183
  and multicompetency, 106
  and pedagogy in deaf education, 133
  and translanguaging, 82, 98
Measurement. *See* Assessment
Mercer, N., 125, 129
Metacognitive processes
  of deaf children vs. hearing
    children, 8
  and dialogic teaching, 130
Meta-communication, 144
Metalinguistic awareness, 103, 109,
    113–115, 160
Metanotes, 66
Metatalk, 66
Migrant communities, 168
Minjeong, K., 174
Mirus, G., 75
Mirzaei, A., 65
Mode, 3–4
Monaghan, L., 118
Mouthing, 87, 96, 110
Mouvet, K., 178
Multicompetency, 101–120
  and communicative sensitivity, 109,
    115–117
  and cultural awareness, 117–119
  of deaf children, 107–119
  definitions of, 101–103
  and language interaction, 112–113
  and metalinguistic awareness, 103, 109,
    113–115
  and opportunities for pedagogy,
    119–120

and repertoire, 104–107
translanguaging as evidence of, 103, 104,
    109–112
Multilingualism, 39–59
    and bimodal bilingualism, 37, 39
    case study examples, 54–58
    conceptualizations of, 5–6, 40–42
    defined, 40
    and discourses in deaf education, 58–59
    gathering language information on, 52–55
    global context of, 45
    integrative approaches to, 22
    and languaging, 69
    methodological issues with research
        on, 50–52
    sign language, 49–50
    spoken language, 45–49
    UK context of, 42–44
    See also Plurilingualism;
        Translanguaging
Multimodal analysis, 176

Najarian, C. G., 175
National Deaf Children's Society
    (NDCS), 11
National Sensory Impairment Partnership
    (NatSIP), 52
NDCS. *See* National Deaf Children's
    Society
Newborn hearing screening programs, 25
NGT. *See* Dutch and Nederlandse
    Gebarentaal
Norway, 169
NVivo, 179

O'Connell, N. P., 173
OGS. *See* Australian Sign Language
Oral deaf children, 12
Oral language
    defined, 12
    and terminology, 13
Outcome evidence, 164

Pair work (classrooms), 74
Pakistani heritage children, 9, 42
Parents, 8, 171
"Parole," 62
Partially deaf (term), 10

Partially hearing (term), 10
Peal, E., 113
Pedagogy in deaf education, 121–139
    big questions in, 134–137
    for bimodal bilingualism, 34–36
    coherent approach to, 187–188
    and communities of practice, 138–139
    dialogic approach to (*See* Dialogic
        approach to deaf education)
    and dialogic theory of learning, 122,
        125–128
    and languaging, 79–80
    and learning context, 138
    opportunities for, 119–120
    overview, 3, 19–21, 121–123
    and pedagogical framework, 130–134
    research questions on, 182–183
    sociocultural perspective on, 123–125
    theoretical perspectives on, 183–184
    translanguaging in
        (*See* Translanguaging)
    See also specific headings
Peer groups, 75
Phonics, 160
Plurality. *See* Language plurality
Plurilingualism
    conceptualizations of, 40–42
    defined, 40–41
    overview, 15
    See also Multilingualism
Population-based studies, 169–170
Positioning, 67–68, 78–79
Poststructuralism, 62
Practice evaluation, 164
Problem-solving skills, 130, 136
Process-oriented approaches, 164–165
Professional development and training,
    189–190

Rawlings, B., 169
Reading development, 6–7, 160–161.
    See also Literacy
Reciprocity, 146
Refugee communities, 168
Renting, B., 143
Repertoire
    defined, 41, 183
    and languaging, 70

Repertoire (*Cont.*)
  and multicompetency, 104–107 (*See also*
    Multicompetency)
  and multilingualism, 59
  overview, 18
Research. *See* Evidence base
Reznitskaya, A., 130
Robbins, A. M., 46
Roma people, 9
Russian, 168

Scaffolded dialogue, 148
Scaffolding, 124, 128, 146, 147
"Scaffolding effect," 112
Schools
  acoustics of, 157
  data collection by, 167
  experiences of deafness in, 134–135
  language challenges in, 73–77
  learning context in, 138
  mainstream, 70, 72–73
Science education, 90, 130
Scott, P., 149
Screening techniques, 25. *See also*
    Assessment
SE. *See* Signed English
Second language instruction
    models, 149
SEE. *See* Signed Exact English
Self-esteem, 137
Self-perception, 66–67
Shared reading, 160–161
Sign and spoken language bilingualism,
    13. *See also* Bilingualism
Sign bilingual approach, 20, 33, 78.
    See also Bilingualism
Signed English (SE), 88
Signed Exact English (SEE) 88, 89
Sign language
  and bilingualism, 13
  development of, 6, 165
  exposure to, 70
  and homesigns, 71–72
  interplay between spoken language
    and, 2, 24
  prevalence of, 9
  spoken languages vs., 24, 79
  used by hearing parents, 8
  *See also specific headings; specific
    sign languages*
Sign language interpreters, 175

Sign language multilingualism, 49–50.
    See also Multilingualism
Sign-Supported English (SSE)
  and bimodal bilingualism, 35
  and comprehension, 14
  and multicompetency, 110, 111
  and translanguaging, 87–88, 185
Sign-Supported German (LBG), 90
Sign-Supported Speech (SSS), 14, 185
Simultaneous communication (SimCom),
    19–20, 35, 185
Social competences, 103, 159
Social identity, 61, 67
Social inclusion, 33
Social maturity, 137
Social variation, 69–71
Sociocultural theory of
    learning, 123–125, 184
Soft assembly of language, 6, 106
Student Oral Language Observation
    Matrix (SOLOM), 172–173
Spanish, 46, 168
Spencer, P., 165
Spoken language
  deaf children's experience of, 25
  development of, 6
  interplay between sign language
    and, 2, 24 (*See also* Bimodal
    bilingualism)
  sign language vs., 24, 79
  terminology of, 12–13
  See also Bimodal bilingualism
Spoken language
    multilingualism, 45–49
SSE. *See* Sign-Supported English
SSS. *See* Sign-Supported Speech
Stewart, D., 132, 142
Student Oral Language
    Observation, 51
Summative assessment, 159
Sutherland, H., 117
Suzuki, W., 65–66
Swaan, A. d., 49–50
Swain, M., 63, 64
Swanwick, R., 171, 177
Swedish Sign Language (STS), 50, 90

Talk
  authoritative vs. dialogic, 149, 150, 158
  classroom, 142–145
  in dialogic teaching, 145–150

Tang, G., 112
TC. *See* Total communication
Teachers, 76–77, 142–143
Teaching. *See* Pedagogy in deaf education
Technologies, hearing. *See* Hearing technologies
Teschendorf, M., 47
Textual analysis, 176
Thomas, E., 46
Total communication (TC), 19–20, 78, 185
Training, 189–190
Transfer, 98, 102
Translanguaging, 81–99
   and code blending, 87–88
   and code switching, 86–87
   contexts of, 88–93
   of deaf children, 85–93
   and dialogic approach to deaf education, 151–157, 160
   as evidence of multicompetency, 103, 104, 109–112
   existing work on, 191–192
   fluidity with, 184
   and language as resource, 98–99
   language components of, 95–97
   from languaging to, 82
   and literacy, 93–98
   overview, 16–18, 185–187
   and pedagogy in deaf education, 121, 122, 131, 133
   theory of, 82–85
   writing as, 97–98
   See also Multilingualism; Plurilingualism
Translation issues, 179
Twin school models, 73

United Kingdom, 42–44, 72, 73
University of Leeds, 177
"Unlocking learning," 182–183
US Annual Survey of Deaf and Hard-of-Hearing Children and Youth, 168, 169

Vietnamese, 168
Visual communication, 157
Visual perception, 8
Vocabulary, 160
Vygotsky, L. S., 63, 123, 124

Waltzmann, S. B., 46
Wells, G., 124, 128–129
Wheeler, A., 118
WHO. *See* World Health Organization
Willoughby, L., 48–49
Wood, David, 142–144, 149, 160
Working memory, 8, 103
World Health Organization (WHO), 45
Writing
   and bimodal bilingualism, 34–35
   collaborative, 65
   and languaging, 65–66
   research on development of, 6–7
   and translanguaging, 84
   as translanguaging, 97–98

Yiddish, 46
Young, A., 117

Zone of proximal development (ZPD), 65, 124, 128
Zwolan, T. A., 46